"This introductory text covers many topics of interest about behavior analytic services. The authors have prepared a reader-friendly text that will appeal to parents, caretakers, educators, behavior support staff, university students, and persons seeking professional credentials (e.g., BCBA, RBT). The text includes real-life examples, diagrams, graphs, and exercises to explain key points and enhance learning opportunities."

Kevin Murdock, *PhD, Board Certified Behavior Analyst—Doctoral; Consulting School Psychologist*

"Drs. Bailey and Burch have compiled answers for questions students don't even know they have. Questions are comprehensive and answers are concise. This book is a lifesaver for students and faculty alike."

Dawn Bailey, *PhD, Associate Professor, Oregon Institute of Technology*

"*How to Think Like a Behavior Analyst* provides the layperson with a wealth of information about the field of behavior analysis in terms that are easy to understand. It helps laypersons understand how behavior analysis can change people's lives."

Jeanne Brower, *M.S., BCBA, South Florida Area Director, Behavior Management Consultants*

D0781138

How to Think Like a...

Behavior Analyst

How to Think Like a Behavior Analyst is a revolutionary resource for understanding complex human behavior and making potentially significant quality-of-life improvements.

Practical and clearly written, this second edition addresses basic questions like how behavior analysts work, why specific methods and procedures are used, what alternative "fad" treatments are, and more. The updated text answers 70 frequently asked questions about behavior analysis using an accessible question-and-answer format. Most questions now include a Quick Take, which is a simple and easy-to-read answer to the question, and then a more in-depth Technically Speaking answer that is more challenging A brand-new chapter discusses ways of advancing one's career in the field and how to go to graduate school and become board certified.

This text is written for all professionals concerned with behavior, including undergraduate students in psychology and behavior analysis, parents, teachers, employers, and employees. The book can easily be used as a supplement to primary texts in introductory psychology courses, and the exercises that follow each question can be used to stimulate lively discussion in role-play and other active learning situations.

Jon S. Bailey, PhD, BCBA-D, Emeritus Professor of Psychology at Florida State University, teaches graduate courses for behavior analysts. Dr. Bailey is a founding director of the Behavior Analyst Certification Board, and he is past president of the Florida Association for Behavior Analysis (FABA).

Mary R. Burch, PhD, is a Board Certified Behavior Analyst®. Dr. Burch has more than 25 years' experience in developmental disabilities. She has been a behavior specialist, QMRP, unit director, and consulting behavior analyst in developmental disabilities, mental health, and preschool settings.

How to Think Like a...
Like a...
Behavior
Analyst

*Understanding the Science
That Can Change Your Life*

Jon S. Bailey and Mary R. Burch

SECOND EDITION

Routledge
Taylor & Francis Group

NEW YORK AND LONDON

Cover Design by CuneoCreative.com

Second edition published 2022
by Routledge
605 Third Avenue, New York, NY 10158

and by Routledge
4 Park Square, Milton Park, Abingdon, Oxon, OX14 4RN

Routledge is an imprint of the Taylor & Francis Group, an informa business

First edition published by Routledge 2006

Library of Congress Cataloging-in-Publication Data

A catalog record has been requested for this book

ISBN: 9780367750855 (hbk)
ISBN: 9780367750848 (pbk)
ISBN: 9781003160915 (ebk)

DOI: 10.4324/9781003160915

Typeset in Times New Roman
by Apex CoVantage, LLC

Dedication

To my mother, Noreen Bailey, who never understood
what I did, and to Jack Michael, who understood everything.
—*Jon S. Bailey*

And to my husband, who said, "You ought to write books."
—*Mary R. Burch*

Jack Michael

Contents

Figures

Preface to the Second Edition

A lot has happened in the field of applied behavior analysis (ABA) since the 1st edition of *How to Think Like a . . . Behavior Analyst* was published in 2006. Primarily this involves the creation in 2014 by the Behavior Analyst Certification Board (BACB) of a new hands-on position called the registered behavior technician (RBT). Since that time, the number of RBTs has become the single largest category of individuals certified by the BACB. At the time of this writing, there were nearly 90,000 RBTs. Creating this position was necessary to meet the demand created by the explosion of cases of autism spectrum disorder (ASD) among young children. ASD is estimated by the CDC to affect 1 in 54 children in the United States. Dr. Ivar Lovaas' research[1] in the 1980s showed that with intensive one-on-one behavioral treatment, it was possible to reverse many of the symptoms of ASD in roughly half of the children who received therapy from his treatment teams.

In 2006, there were less than 5,000 board certified behavior analysts (BCBAs). Today that number is nearly 45,000. Board Certified Assistant Behavior Analysts (BCaBAs) have grown to 4,750 from a little over 1,500 in 2006. This tiered workforce is clearly in great demand, since the CDC estimates that 17% of children in the 3–17-year age group have been diagnosed with a developmental disability[2] (this includes all disabilities, not just autism), and ABA is the first choice for evidence-based treatment for all of them. The latest data from the BACB indicate that nearly 75% of all behavior analysts work with clients diagnosed with autism spectrum disorder. The demand for services in ASD is driven by states requiring insurance companies to reimburse for ABA services. To date, 49 states require insurance companies to reimburse for ABA services.

Our experience has been that many different people have questions about behavior analysis, and this book was written to try to answer some of those questions. For parents who have recently received a diagnosis of ASD for their child whose physician said, "I know you will want the best treatment for your child, and the gold standard for that is applied behavior analysis" will want to learn more about this treatment, who provides it, and how they are trained and certified.

Teachers who have been told by their principal that, "We are pushing to have all our classroom aides become registered behavior technicians so we can more effectively implement behavior plans" will want to learn more about RBTs and how they can be useful in their classrooms. Some teachers who already have an acquaintance with ABA may decide to become board certified behavior analysts so that they can more effectively manage their classroom, implement successful behavior-change programs, and supervise their own RBTs.

Many college students are looking for a way to help others, and they may be interested in working with children with disabilities or disadvantaged children. These students may have been introduced to ABA by observing an RBT work with a younger brother or sister, and they have questions about how they could get involved in this profession.

Employers and employees will learn how behavior analysis is used in work settings in the questions pertaining to performance management. Everyone can learn how to make life better by being able to use positive reinforcement with people and situations encountered every day. For all these groups, we have written this book to provide a wide variety of questions and answers to common questions that come up in conversations, meetings, and on social media.

How to Think Like a . . . Behavior Analyst can be easily used as a supplement to primary texts for college classes. The exercises that follow each question can be used to stimulate lively discussions in role-play and other active learning situations. As you read *How to Think Like a . . . Behavior Analyst*, you will see the widespread applications of behavior analysis as a field and just how important it is for everyone to understand how behavior works. *How to Think Like a . . . Behavior Analyst* is not a theoretical or academic work. Our goal was to write an informative book that is practical, simple, clear, direct, and fun to read. But don't let the user-friendly nature fool you; underneath it all is the message that being trained in behavior analysis can improve your life and the lives of those around you.

HOW TO USE THIS BOOK

In this second edition, we have created two types of answers to some of the questions. The **Quick Take** answers give a brief overview of the information the reader needs to understand the topic at hand. For some questions, there are more in-depth answers where we delve into the research related to the question for the reader who wants to understand the science behind the concept; the header for these is **Technically Speaking.** For each answer, we have added endnotes that the curious reader can use to go to the original source, often an internet site, to read more about the issue, and we now have references at the end of each chapter for easy access to source material.

As in the first edition, we have at the end of each question **Key Concepts** to remind you of some of the important terms and core ideas in the answers provided, as well as **Exercises** for you to try if you want to delve further into the subject matter. We hope you enjoy learning about behavior analysis and are able to benefit in some way from the ideas presented here.

—*JSB*
—*MRB*

NOTES

1. Lovaas, O.I. (1987). Behavioral treatment and normal educational and intellectual functioning in young autistic children. *Journal of Consulting and Clinical Psychology*, 55, 3–9.
2. www.cdc.gov/ncbddd/autism/data.html

ACKNOWLEDGMENTS

We gratefully acknowledge the assistance of several individuals who provided expert advice and input and contributed new questions as well as answers to some questions.

Loren Eighme described a day in the life of an RBT, Hope McNally described her experience of being a BCBA, and Yamilex Molina prepared the answers to questions on training parents and foster parents in ABA as well as addressing the question related to social media. We have Devon Sundberg to thank for her consultation on dual relationships. Loren, Hope, and Yamilex reviewed the 50 questions from the first edition of *How to Think Like. . .* and recommended additional questions and a few deletions. Daniel Crafton provided a great anecdote from his experience as an RBT graduate student working in the classroom.

We also need to thank Clint Evans, the BehaviorChef; Morgan van Diepen, the creator of ABA Visualized, and Dr. Jessica Joseph, creator of Minority Behavior Analysts (MBAs), for giving permission to use the logos associated with their ABA-related social media platforms.

Dr. Mark Sundberg provided significant technical assistance in the section on Skinner's radical behaviorism. As one of the foremost experts on Skinner's writings, Dr. Sundberg's time and contribution are greatly appreciated. We would also like to thank Dr. Ken Wagner, a former PhD student and now a senior consultant at ALULA in the area of performance management, for his thoughtful input on the role of a behaviorally trained consultant in contemporary organizations.

TO OUR READERS

We strongly support section 1.08 (Nondiscrimination) in the 2022 Ethics Code for Behavior Analysts. This Code item states: "Behavior analysts do not discriminate against others. They behave toward others in an equitable and inclusive manner regardless of age, disability, ethnicity, gender expression/identity, immigration status, marital/relationship status, national origin, race, religion, sexual orientation, socioeconomic status, or any other basis proscribed by law."

In this book, questions are based on real-world cases. We have changed the names but maintained the gender identity of those involved (e.g., referring to the child's "mom" and "dad" because the parents were a heterosexual couple).

Introduction

Professional behavior analysts[1] are *problem solvers*. As effective problem solvers, behavior analysts must be skilled amateur *detectives* who search for clues as to why a behavior occurs or does not occur. Because they must be able to find effective evidence-based treatments, being a *scientist* at heart is an important trait as well. Sometimes behavior analysts must *advocate* for a client who is being abused or having her rights ignored. To do this effectively, they need to act like a *social worker* whose job involves protecting vulnerable individuals. Behavior analysts are required to be acquainted with the law and child protection agencies in their communities so they can respond effectively as *mandated reporters*. When problem behaviors are the result of a medical or biological condition, the behavior analyst must know enough about nursing to watch for medication side effects and common medical conditions. Once *behavior therapists* can determine what is triggering a problem behavior, they will develop and test an individualized behavior plan, *teach* caregivers the proper execution of the plan, and finally, oversee the plan's successful implementation. All of these roles come into play nearly every week in the life of a professional behavior analyst. They have an exciting job that comes with tremendous responsibilities, but the payoff is huge. Behavior

> *"Professional behavior analysts are problem solvers."*

analysts can usually see the fruits of their labor in a matter of weeks or a few months, depending on the particular circumstances of the case.

As *amateur detectives*, behavior analysts are always looking for the environmental variables that might produce a problem behavior. As an example, Jake was a fourth grader who was constantly off task and wandered around the classroom. Jake's constant bothering of his peers presented a significant problem for Jake's teacher, who exclaimed that she had "tried everything." Dan, a behavior analyst assigned to Jake's case, sat in the back of the class and quietly observed. He noticed that when given math problems or art assignments, Jake was well behaved. However, with anything that involved reading, Jake would drop his head and let his pencil roll down his desk onto the floor. He didn't bother to pick it up. This was a clue to the behavior analyst, who saw a connection and asked the teacher if he could sit with Jake for a few minutes. Dan quickly realized that Jake could not read. It was no wonder he was wandering around the classroom; it was a lot more interesting (even if the teacher got after him) than staring at a page full of letters and words he could not understand. Dan concluded that Jake didn't need a poorly conceived motivation system or a "self-monitoring" requirement; he needed a tutor. In this case, Dan had to put on his advocate hat, making the case to the teacher and then to the principal that Jake needed in-school or after-school tutoring, preferably both. Dan had to pull some strings to make this happen because he was convinced that Jake was bright enough to learn to read if he was just given the chance. In this role, Dan acted like a *social worker*, watching out for this vulnerable child who did not need to be sent to the principal's office every single day during reading period. Finally, Dan understood that Jake needed to be highly motivated if he was going to catch up on reading skills, so Dan quickly dove into the behavior analysis journals to find the most effective classroom token system to recommend to the teacher. On behalf of his client, to be successful, this behavior analyst had to wear four additional hats: detective, scientist, advocate, and social worker.

Mae, a behavior analyst working in home settings, arrived at the home of a new client to do one-on-one training for language skills. As soon as she arrived, Mae noticed the child was scratching at his legs.

She could see welts on his small bare arms. Mae brought these wounds to the attention of the parents, who responded, "They'll go away in a few days; they always do." By the time she got to her car, Mae found herself scratching her ankles and realized the problem was fleas, and she now had them, too. Mae knew from a health class that scratching the bites could cause an infection, and she decided she had to do something. Operating as a *mandated reporter*, she contacted the county health department, alerted them to this situation, and expressed her concern for this child's welfare.

Sandy, another behavior analyst, was assigned to work with a young male client after he arrived home from school each afternoon. After a long day, Carl was not too thrilled with learning to play table games and was distracted by the swimming pool that his parents recently had installed in the back yard. Sandy was specifically told not to take Carl anywhere near the pool since he could not swim. Sandy had a friend who had been a certified swim instructor before she came to graduate school. With her friend Lee in tow, Sandy set up a meeting with the parents and asked if they would allow Sandy and Lee to provide swimming lessons for their son. As it turned out, Carl wasn't quite ready for swimming lessons. Instead, he needed some desensitization[2] to putting his face in the water and then submerging himself in the shallow end of the pool. Sandy and Lee developed a five-step task analysis[3] for this maneuver and over the rest of the summer practiced with Carl twice a week. After six weeks, Carl was able to fully submerge himself an average of eight times per session and was deemed ready for beginning swim lessons. In this case, Sandy *advocated* for her client and determined he was not actually ready for swim lessons because of his pool phobia. She developed a desensitization

> *"Behavior analysis has often been described as 'the best kept secret in psychology.'"*

therapy program and implemented it successfully. Sandy followed the steps that a good *behavior therapist* would follow, which are to determine the needs of the client, find a way to meet those needs, and then create a behavior plan much like a *teacher* does for her classes. As with Carl's swimming program, the plan should be perfectly adapted to the client's current level of functioning.

All of these special abilities constitute the full repertoire of the behavior analyst. The need for all of these competencies became apparent in the evolution of the profession over the past 50 years. It all began back in the mid-1960s with one child called "Dicky." We will get to his story later, but let's start with some basics about this "new" field.

Behavior analysis has often been described as "the best kept secret in psychology." As a well-established, evidence-based treatment approach based on learning theory, behavior analysis has been making a significant difference in the lives of many thousands of developmentally disabled individuals for 50+ years. Behavior analysis procedures have been developed to teach basic self-help skills, functional language, and community competences to individuals with disabilities to allow them to live and enjoy rich and varied lives.

The very same procedures have been used in special education classrooms and standard elementary school settings, where teachers are now able to take control of their rowdy, out-of-control students and produce model students who complete their homework on time, are respectful of others, and enjoy learning.

Still other applications of behavioral procedures include training parents and foster parents to use the power of positive reinforcement to lovingly raise children who listen, take responsibility, and actively participate in family life. This field, applied behavior analysis, caught fire in 1993 with the publication of the best-selling, true-life story of Catherine Maurice and her two autistic children. Frustrated by pediatricians, psychologists, and psychiatrists who essentially told her that her autistic child would need to be institutionalized, Maurice sought help on her own and discovered the groundbreaking work of Ivar Lovaas. Lovaas showed that with intensive behavioral treatment, up to 50% of autistic children could recover. Ms. Maurice found a behavior analyst therapist, and, as we say, the rest is history. *Let Me Hear Your Voice: A Family's Triumph Over Autism*[4] was an overnight sensation with parents all over the United States. Suddenly, the best-kept secret was out in the open, and a huge demand for qualified behavior analysts was created. Within ten years, over 50 graduate programs emerged that were approved to teach behavior analysis, and a certification program, the Behavior Analyst Certification Board, began testing and certifying behavior analysts to meet the sudden need. Now undergraduate students everywhere are taking courses on operant conditioning, learning theory, functional analysis, behavioral theory, research methods, and ethics, and graduate students are learning the professional skills necessary to bring this technology to families, schools, rehabilitation settings, and more. With this boom in popularity, there seemed to be a need for a book that would help the beginning student as well as consumers and the everyday citizen understand what this fascinating field was all about.

This is a book for everyone who is concerned with behavior. *How to Think Like a . . . Behavior Analyst* answers questions that are often posed by college students, parents, employers, employees, and professionals who work with humans or animals. Ideas, trends, techniques, and practical information pertaining to the exciting field of behavior analysis are presented in a concise, user-friendly format.

The question-and-answer format of *How to Think Like a . . . Behavior Analyst* answers 70 frequently asked questions about behavior analysis. Each of the informative answers is presented in an educational and entertaining manner.

In Part One, The Big Picture, beginners in psychology and behavior analysis can learn about the basic principles of the field, how behavior analysts work, why specific methods and procedures are used, and alternative "fad" treatments that are floating around the internet.

For parents and teachers, *How to Think Like a . . . Behavior Analyst* provides basic background information and detailed examples of how behavior analysis can be used to help children. Employers and employees will learn how behavior analysis is used in work settings in the questions pertaining to performance management. Everyone can learn how to make life better by being able to use positive reinforcement with people and situations encountered every day.

Additional topics covered by *How to Think Like a . . . Behavior Analyst* include frequently asked questions: Is behavior really all that predictable? What exactly is evidence-based treatment? In Chapter 2, "General Issues", we discuss: What is a history of reinforcement? and Can you change someone's personality? Chapter 3 addresses questions involving behavioral research methods and the question, 'Is it possible to find the "cause" of a behavior?' Chapter 4 on the philosophy of behavior analysis raises questions about the behavioral position on "free will" and the skepticism behavior analysts have about other approaches. Chapter 5 on applications of behavior analysis includes information on who provides these behavior-analytic services, whether parents can be a client, and how dog obedience classes work and what to expect from them. Chapter 6 covers the behavioral take on other fields of psychology, including counseling and cognitive psychology, as well as brushing therapy and alternative treatments such as camel's milk and hyperbaric oxygen "therapy." Chapter 7 addresses common myths and the media and includes a very entertaining commentary on Dr. Phil and behavior analysis representations on TV.

Part Two, Becoming a Professional includes Chapter 8, "Starting Your Career in Behavior Analysis," and addresses common questions about becoming a RBT and what it means to be supervised in this position. Chapter Nine, "Advancing Your Career in ABA," provides information on going on to graduate school to become a BCBA and what it takes to become board certified. The last chapter, Chapter 10 answers important questions about the ethics of being a behavior analyst, the problem of dual relationships, and how to report unethical conduct.

How to Think Like a . . . Behavior Analyst, 2nd edition is not a theoretical or academic work. Our goal was to write an informative book that is practical, simple, clear, direct, and fun to read. But don't let the user-friendly nature fool you; underneath it all is the message that being trained in behavior analysis can improve your life and the lives of those around you.

NOTES

1. We use the term behavior analyst to include both Registered Behavior Technician® and Board Certified Behavior Analyst®.

2. A method of treating fear responses by gradual, repeated exposure to a feared stimulus.
3. A method of breaking any complex task into small sequential steps so the task can readily be learned.
4. Maurice, C. (1994). *Let Me Hear Your Voice: A Family's Triumph Over Autism*. New York: Random House.

Part

One

The Big Picture

One

Basic Concepts and Principles

DOI: 10.4324/9781003160915-2

QUESTION #1.
What *Is* Behavior Analysis?

Quick Take

Behavior analysis is an approach to understanding human behavior that looks at the powerful influence of the physical and social environment on behavior. A primary goal of behavior analysis is to seek ways of modifying the environment in order to produce significant behavior change. Applied

> *"Behavior analysts think like scientists part of the time and caring clinicians the rest of the time."*

behavior analysis, often referred to simply as "behavior analysis," is an evidence-based approach to treatment. Behavior analysts think like scientists part of the time and caring clinicians the rest of the time. Existing for more than half a century, behavior analysis is still *new* to many consumers around the world. Those who are aware of the behavior analysis approach often think it is a treatment for children with autism, since so much work has been done focusing on this population over the past 25 years. Behavior analysis has a reach far beyond autism, and in numerous areas, behavior analysts work directly with clients or supervise staff. These behavior analysts are hands-on professionals who are passionate about helping others, and they are thrilled to see positive behavior changes—this is their primary reward for being in this field.

As behavior analysts, we believe that environment plays such an important role because humans (and non-human animals) have evolved to adapt to the environment. When the environment changes, humans change their behavior to thrive or to simply survive. Humans do what they can to maximize the rewards that are available in the immediate environment. If those rewards become scarce, a person moves to another location where there are more rewards, or they attempt to modify the environment to make it richer in rewards. The aspects of the environment that are most valued are referred to as rewards or reinforcers because they strengthen behavior.

Perhaps the most significant aspect of the environment that behavior analysts look at is the immediate *social* environment. This includes parents, of course, and grandparents if they are nearby. When a child is older, other children in the neighborhood can be a significant source of reinforcement, and after that, teenagers seek out the company of other teens almost exclusively. The *analysis* part of *behavior analysis* is a key part of this relatively new field because by determining the triggers or *causes* (we call them functional variables), we know which parts of the environment need to be changed.

An example of a case related to the environment was a teacher who was frustrated by Noah, an elementary school student. Noah was constantly off task and bothering other children in the classroom. The teacher tried putting Noah at a table by himself and reprimanded him when she had a break, but nothing seemed to work. The teacher was considering the use of time-out with Noah. She had learned about this in a workshop held on a planning day. First, she called in a behavior analyst[1] who observed from the back of the room.[2] The behavior analyst noted that Noah was not off task all the time but primarily during math period and especially when the teacher handed out the daily worksheets. The behavior analyst obtained copies of worksheets from the teacher and asked for permission to sit with Noah while he completed his work. Over the course of the next 30 minutes, the behavior analyst switched the work sheets, alternating them from easy to hard. She discovered that Noah did not have the necessary skills to solve the worksheets the teacher was giving him each day. The work was above his level, and because Noah was frustrated, he quickly gave up. On the rare occasions when Noah could solve the problems, he did so and seemed to really enjoy the work. Through careful analysis, the behavior analyst discovered that the micro-environment was aversive to Noah and he was engaging in escape behavior (off-task, bothering other students). What he needed was not a reprimand but more appropriate materials and possibly a short-term math tutor to get him up to speed with the other children.

In another similar case, a behavior analyst was working in-home with parents who complained that their child, Emma, would not listen to them or complete chores or her homework. The parents reported that Emma also picked on her little sister "all the time." The behavior analyst began with direct observations of the child to determine the environmental variables that may have been contributing to Emma's inappropriate behavior. After observing carefully for a few hours, the behavior analyst noticed a pattern. Emma came home from school, ran straight to her room without so much as a "Hi, Dad," and started playing *My Little Pony*, a popular video game. Emma didn't interact with her little sister at all. Dad said that Emma "knows" she is supposed to do her homework first, followed by her chores, and then she could play the video game. His method of handling Emma's behavior was to charge up to her room and start scolding her. Emma would cry and say, "I hate you," and attempt to push Dad out of her bedroom. It seemed to the behavior analyst that Emma was sending a message to the parents that said loud and clear, "I prefer my video game to doing chores or homework." Dad had come to the correct conclusion about the sequence but did not have an effective method for handling the problem.

The behavior analyst suggested to Dad that the next day when Emma got home that he would be waiting for her, stop her when she came in the door, and say, "Let's talk, Emma. How was your day?" After inquiring about Emma's day, the behavior analyst guided Dad to say, "Emma, we're going to try something new today. Here is your list of chores. As soon as they are done, come see me about your video game." Emma pouted and started to cry, but Dad held the line just as the behavior analyst had advised him. A little while later, Emma approached her dad and said, "I'm having trouble with this chore. Can you help me?" Dad explained the chore, and when it was completed, he handed over the video game. After a few days, Dad changed the routine a little, so that when Emma came in from school, he said, "Let's take a look at your homework for today." He escorted her to the kitchen table and helped her get started. When the homework was complete, Dad checked it, praised

Emma's good work, and gave her the short list of chores. "When you are finished with these chores, Emma, come see me and you can play your video game until dinner." Before long, Emma began to respond to the praise and contingent access to her game with a big smile.

The previous cases describe two simple cases of a behavior analysis approach to solving a behavior problem. These children did not need counseling or scolding or time-out; they just needed a change in their routines and micro-environments. The teacher in the first case could not figure this out because she had too many children to manage and instruct. The dad in the second case had no idea about using a video game as a reinforcer for chore completion. It was not surprising that he didn't know any better. As with many parents his age, he was raised with a punishment model.

"These children did not need counseling or scolding or time-out—they just needed a change in their routines and micro-environments."

Analyzing behavior in clinical settings is not always as simple as these two cases. Cases seen by behavior analysts are often very complicated and require a great deal of time and the use of sophisticated methods such as functional behavior analysis, which we will discuss later in the book. However, the process is basically the same: Observe the behavior directly (don't rely on interviews or second-hand information),

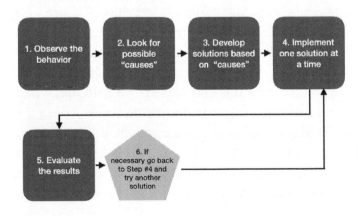

FIGURE 1.1 A six-step behavior analysis model for solving behavior problems.

look for possible triggers or "causes" of the problem behavior, develop tests to determine the actual factors, implement a possible solution, and evaluate the results (if necessary, go back to step #1 and try another approach).

Technically Speaking

One of the earliest cases in our field (Wolf et al., 1964) provides us with an outstanding example of how behavior analysts think about human behavior. "Dicky" was a 3-year-old child with multiple severe behavior problems. In the early 1960s, he was referred to pioneering behavior analysts Mont Wolf, Todd Risley, and Hayden Mees at the University of Washington. As a result of cataract surgery, when he was a little over 2 years old, Dicky was required to wear special corrective lenses or lose his vision entirely. For more than a year, Dicky's parents struggled with futile attempts to get him to wear the glasses. Dicky not only would not wear his glasses, but he would throw such severe tantrums that he became unmanageable and had to be institutionalized. At the time he was referred to the behavioral team in Washington, Dicky had been diagnosed at different times as mentally retarded, autistic, psychotic, brain damaged, and schizophrenic. These varying diagnoses were the result of multiple behavior problems that included lack of normal social and verbal repertoires, poor eating habits, head-banging, face-slapping, hair-pulling, and face-scratching. At the advice of their family physician, Dicky's parents tried restraints, sedatives, and tranquilizers, all to no avail. Finally, Dicky was admitted to a children's mental hospital where more precise treatment could be offered. Enter our groundbreaking behavior analysts. Wolf et al. (1964) took one look at the interaction between Dicky and his mother and instantly identified the problem. Dicky's mother was reinforcing the behavior (not intentionally, mind you) with her "ineffectual fussing." Dicky's problem was in large part the result of out-of-whack social contingencies, not retardation or supposed childhood schizophrenia. The solution: the behavioral team decided to use "time-out," which had never been documented before in a case like this. Time-out involves separating the child from all sources of reinforcement for a short time, contingent on inappropriate behavior—in this case the severe tantrums. Dicky was returned to the hospital ward environment as soon as the tantrum stopped. Result: Within two and a half months, the severe head-banging, hair-pulling, and face-scratching were reduced to zero. Zero.

While this is only part of the story, it exemplifies many key features of the way that behavior analysts think and act. First, this was a *single case*, involving one child in desperate need of therapy. In addition, Drs. Wolf, Risley, and Mees were interested in taking the case because it represented a complex set of *socially significant behaviors* of near life-threatening proportions. They quickly concluded that these were *learned behaviors*, and they proceeded to analyze the environment to identify the *maintaining variable*. The process of analyzing a behavior involved carefully observing the interaction of the child with the caregivers to see how the child responded. In Dicky's case, they determined that it was the mother's attention (certainly not intentional) that appeared to be the key. Wolf and his colleagues understood that to get control over the attention, the child would need to be treated in their treatment facility where they could train and supervise the staff.

> *"The process of analyzing a behavior involves carefully observing the interaction of the child with the caregivers to see how the child responds."*

After demonstrating clear and dramatic control over this most serious behavior, the behavior analysts then proceeded to attack the remaining problems by *shaping* glasses-wearing; treating the glasses-throwing which developed soon after; implementing successful interventions for teaching verbal behavior; and finally, tackling the messy problem of food throwing, food stealing, and eating with his fingers. In each case, Wolf et al. (1964) observed the target behavior, conducted an analysis by looking for controlling variables, and then instituted a change in procedures to reduce and then eliminate the inappropriate behavior (food throwing, food stealing, eating with fingers) or teach new behaviors (eating with a spoon and learning to name pictures, name objects in his environment, and then to answer simple questions such as, "Where are you going tonight?")

The next step was to generalize these amazing changes to Dicky's home environment. He improved enough within three months to make his first foray to his home, where his parents, with the training they had received from the behavior analysts, were able to put him to bed without his having a severe tantrum. In three more months, he was gradually faded back into the home, and the parents were given full training for all of Dicky's significant behaviors.

This is a perfect example of some fundamental ways that behavior analysts think. We think that it is important to treat *socially significant behaviors* not just to study them but to actually analyze and provide treatment, *effective* treatment. Behavior analysts focus on treatment that works to produce a socially significant change in behavior, not just a tiny statistically significant change, but a real-life, dramatic change that everyone can see. Analyzing the behavior in this case involved direct observation of the caregivers' reaction to Dicky's glasses-wearing and tantrum behaviors. In other cases that we'll discuss later in the book, it was necessary to actually change environmental variables to determine the effect they had on a target behavior. To Wolf et al. (1964), Dicky was not a "participant" in an experiment. He was a troubled little boy with a family that loved him and wanted him to be at home and live a normal life. Although unstated, it was clear that this was the goal of our pioneering behavior analysts when they took on this original landmark case more than 50 years ago. Finally, Wolf et al. (1964) were not satisfied to simply change the behavior; they wanted to *generalize the results* to Dicky's home setting. It was important to this team of behavior analysts that the parents learn how to manage their son's behavior.

This study is a classic in the field not just because it represents one of the earliest demonstrations of how behavior analysts think and treat behavior but because of the final comment from Dicky's mother after he

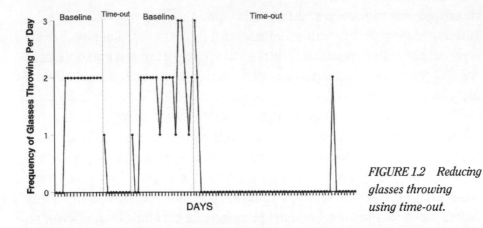

FIGURE 1.2   Reducing glasses throwing using time-out.

had been at home for six months: "Dicky continues to wear his glasses, does not have tantrums, has no sleeping problems, is becoming increasingly verbal, and is a new source of joy to the members of his family."

• •

Key Concepts:

Applied behavior analysis, environment, socially significant behaviors, learned behaviors, maintaining variables, reinforcement, analyze behaviors, effective treatments, shaping, the generalization of behavior

EXERCISES:

1. Make note during the next couple of days of the behavior of people around you. Do you see any behaviors that are socially significant problems that could benefit from some sort of behavioral intervention?
2. Now, using the internet, go to the webpage for the *Journal of Applied Behavior Analysis* (https://onlinelibrary.wiley.com/journal/19383703) and, using key words, find articles describing treatments for a behavior that you have observed.

QUESTION #2.

What Does *Analysis* Mean in ABA, and How Exactly Do You Analyze Someone's Behavior?

Quick Take

The "analysis" in *behavior analysis* refers to the behavior analyst attempting to determine what exactly produces or "causes" the target behavior to occur. This can be done with precision in a laboratory situation and less so in a classroom or home setting. Most of the time, a skilled and experienced behavior analyst can figure out the "controlling variables" by interviewing key people and by direct observation. The behavior analyst will ask questions such as, "What happened just before the behavior occurred?" and also, "What happened right after the behavior occurred?" We refer to these as *antecedents* and *consequences*. Antecedents may often trigger a response, and consequences often reward responses. This is often referred to as an A B C analysis:

> *"The 'analysis' in behavior analysis refers to the behavior analyst's attempting to determine what exactly produces or 'causes' the target behavior to occur."*

Antecedent >> Behavior >> Consequence

When a second-grade teacher says, "It seems as though Liam is very likely to say he has a stomachache when I hand out math worksheets," it gives the behavior analyst working in the classroom a strong clue as to the cause of Liam's asking to go see the nurse. This can be tested to determine if the theory is correct by observing to see if Liam acts sick when science projects are scheduled or when the teacher says, "Okay, it's time to clear your desk for our geography test." Another question would be if Liam has stomach problems when it is time to go outside to play or when it is time to eat lunch. This informal trial-and-error method does not always work, of course, but this is where the behavior analyst, using her detective skills, would start.

In a home situation, the behavior analyst would ask the parents to describe the behavior of concern, again asking for some indication of what happened before and after the incident. "Hmm, it seems like whenever his sister is getting attention, Jeremy is more likely to throw something at her, bump into her, or even pinch her to make her cry. He gets this mean little smile on his face when his sister cries. She's only two and doesn't understand. Jeremy is five, smart and strong. We have tried sending him to his room, but that doesn't seem to do any good." This situation is more complicated than the one in the classroom. In this case, there is also a victim whose response may serve as a reward for the throwing/bumping/pinching behavior. One way to test if this is correct is to have the parents change their interaction with the 2-year-old a few times. Rather than providing a big positive attention moment for her, they could play it down to a "Thank you, Sally," response instead of a big smile and hug, saying, "I'm so proud of you; you're my favorite little girl, Sally!" If the toned-down response to Sally does not set off the aggression, then it would seem that *big attention* is the "cause" of the problem.

In both examples, the next step is to implement a treatment or intervention plan to see if the target behavior can be modified.

Technically Speaking

A more precise, and as it turns out more complex, way to find the controlling variables for any given behavior is to conduct a functional analysis or FA. This is done by setting up a controlled setting where certain conditions can be created one at a time to see what effect each one has on a specific problem behavior. This work was initially done at Johns Hopkins University School of Medicine by Dr. Brian Iwata and his colleagues (Iwata et al., 1982, 1994). They were working with severely challenging self-injurious behaviors (SIBs) such as head banging, self-biting and eye gouging in nine participants ranging in age from 3½ to 13½ years old. It was impossible to understand what was causing these critical behaviors, although the researchers had clues gained from informal observations. They set up a multielement research design where each of four conditions could be established independently based on: social disapproval, academic demand, unstructured play, and alone. These conditions were presented for eight 15-minute sessions per day for an average of eight days per participant. Results showed that the unstructured play condition produced the least amount of SIBs overall. For five of the participants, self-injury was highest during the alone condition, indicating that the behavior was producing some sort of stimulation, even though it must have been painful. Two participants[3] showed the highest level of SIB during the academic demand condition, suggesting that the responses were maintained by escape. In this condition, the researchers removed the demand if the participants engaged in the SIB. One participant showed the most SIBs during the social disapproval condition in which, when he banged his head or slapped his face, the experimenter said, "Don't do that; you're going to hurt yourself." This showed that, for this participant, the behavior was maintained by attention. For two of the participants, the data were so mixed that it was not possible to see any controlling variable.

Since the Iwata et al. (1982, 1994) study was first published, functional analysis has become a required prerequisite to interventions. This model of determining controlling variables for behavior has been used in thousands of experiments. Before a treatment is put in place, experimenters and therapists alike need to know whether their client is engaging in

"Knowing the controlling variables tells the experimenter or therapist what changes to make in the environment in order to make the behavior less likely to occur and to produce humane, effective treatments."

the behavior to get attention or to escape some sort of task requirement or demand, or that possibly the behavior is just a source of stimulation. Knowing the controlling variables tells the experimenter or therapist what changes to make in the environment in order to make the behavior less likely to occur and to produce humane, effective treatments.

● ●

Key Concepts:
Analysis, controlling variables, antecedents, consequences, multi-element research design

EXERCISES:

1. If you are in a position to observe some problematic behavior, take some A-B-C data by looking for antecedents (what comes before) or consequences (what comes after). What do your data show?

2. Now, using the internet, go to the webpage for the *Journal of Applied Behavior Analysis* (https://onlinelibrary.wiley.com/journal/19383703). Using key words, find any articles describing treatments for the behavior that you have observed.

QUESTION #3.

What Exactly Is Evidence-Based Treatment? Isn't There Evidence for All Treatments?

In the summer of 2003, it was a hot, muggy Saturday evening in Milwaukee when an 8-year-old boy with "violent tendencies" met his death at the hands of church leaders.[4] These trusted religious authorities were trying to rid this innocent child of the demons they believed to be the cause of his strange and unpredictable behaviors. And while these well-intended, god-fearing souls certainly did not intend to murder this little boy, by using a "treatment" with no basis whatsoever in any clinical or behavioral research literature, they essentially sentenced him to death.

While it may seem bizarre, this was not the first or only time that children have been innocent victims of misguided, uninformed adults who have no knowledge or comprehension of the concept of evidence-based treatment. This concept, which is also known as "empirically validated therapies," refers to a fairly recent awareness (mid-1990s) by therapeutic professionals that the time has come to pass judgment on those treatments that cannot stand up to scientific scrutiny. It is simply no longer tolerable for pseudo-professionals who offer miracle cures to be allowed to practice their craft at the expense of naïve and trusting citizens.

One such therapy is "water-intoxication," which supposedly will promote bonding in children with "attachment disorder." On the advice of counselors at a treatment center in Utah, the parents of a 4-year-old girl forced her to drink so much water that it lowered the concentration of sodium in her blood, causing fatal brain swelling.[5] Needless to say, water-intoxication

> *"Behavior analysts are relieved and proud to point out that our procedures have been evidence-based since the beginning of the field in the mid-1960s."*

is *not* an evidence-based treatment. It is based entirely on a counter-intuitive, theoretical notion called "paradoxical interventions" that will supposedly discourage unwanted behavior and cause children to draw closer to their adoptive parents.

Behavior analysts are relieved and proud to point out that our procedures have been evidence-based since the beginning of the field in the mid-1960s. Behavior analysts always work with specific, defined behaviors, as opposed to "symptoms" or interpretations of behavior. In the behavior analytic approach, data are taken before the treatment to provide a baseline that is used for comparison with later conditions. Another key component of behavior analysis is that *experimental control* is clearly demonstrated to show that it was the treatment that was the cause of the subsequent behavior change. Behavior analysis is unique in this respect, and as a result of 50 years of evidence-based, applied research, we can point to the development of highly effective treatments that are safe and dependable.

Behavior analysts believe that all therapies should adopt a similar sort of accountability system so that consumers can be informed of the effectiveness of the treatment. In our field, we actually have two levels of empirical validation. The first is internal, where the behavior analyst, as indicated earlier, designs the treatment in such a way that effects can be seen directly by examining the graphs of the data. The second method, called *social validation*, involves including the consumer in the process to make a judgment about the treatment effect. We basically employ the consumer as the ultimate judge of effectiveness. If clients (or their guardians) can't see the effect, we would conclude our intervention was not sufficient, and it would be back to the drawing boards to devise a better treatment.

Many methods or interventions that are used in everyday therapeutic or educational settings are devised on the spot by direct-care staff, teachers, therapists, or caregivers. Many of these interventions have never been tested to even see if they work; that is, they are *not* evidence based. Evidence-based treatment involves applying well-established research findings in the development of behavioral treatments and interventions. Made-up, half-baked procedures are not only *not* proven effective, but they may also be unethical as well as unsafe. Sometimes this can have tragic consequences. In an institution in Florida in the 1970s, children and young adults had their mouths washed out with soap or had to wear a sign around their necks that read, "I am a thief," as a form of punishment for cursing or taking another client's belongings. This make-it-up-as-you-go-along method resulted in bizarre, inhumane punishments (Bailey & Burch, 2016, pp. 5–13) for which several staff and the psychologist in charge were fired.

Evidence-based treatments are those that have been demonstrated to be effective in scientific journals. In applied behavior analysis, research is primarily published in the *Journal of Applied Behavior Analysis*, which is considered the flagship journal of our field.[6] What behavior analysts do, as an important part of developing an individualized treatment plan, is search for interventions and treatments that have proven effectiveness in top-rated behavioral journals. In their graduate programs, students are carefully trained in how to search for these proven treatments and how to adapt and apply them to any given case. To be safe and transparent, treatments should be approved by the parents or surrogates if the intention is to reduce a behavior.

There are dozens if not hundreds of unproven procedures being used today to treat human behavior in clinical and educational settings across the country. Many of these unproven procedures are recommended by professionals from other fields. These professionals might have no training in research methods and no appreciation for the need to only use those procedures that have been proven effective and are verified by the scientific community. Problems can occur when procedures are developed based on articles that are theoretically based rather than fact or science based. Behavioral interventions published in the *Journal of Applied Behavior Analysis* are both theoretically sound *and* data based.

• •

Key Concepts:
Evidence-based treatment, empirically validated therapies, experimental control, social validation

EXERCISES:

1. Find an article in the *Journal of Applied Behavior Analysis* that addresses social validation and examine the methods used to involve consumers in the determination of treatment effectiveness.
2. Find an article that does not employ social validation and describe a way to apply this procedure.

QUESTION #4.
Is Behavior Analysis Just Another Fad Treatment?

Unfortunately, there are many fad treatments in our culture. A fad treatment is one that becomes popular almost overnight, is often promoted by a celebrity, is widely touted in the media, quickly gains acceptance by average citizens, becomes commercially successful, and finally, is evaluated by behavioral scientists who determine that it is ineffective and possibly a dangerous fraud. Fads have been common since biblical times for the treatment of illnesses and proliferate as short-term interests in styles of music, dance, fashion, diets, and exercise programs, as well as "challenges" such as ice bucket dunking and planking or games like Pokémon Go.

> *"A fad treatment is one that becomes popular almost overnight, is often promoted by a celebrity, gains acceptance by average citizens, and finally, is evaluated by behavioral scientists who determine that it is ineffective and possibly a dangerous fraud."*

While fads in the culture are usually mere distractions or diversions, when it comes to the treatment of something as serious as autism, fads may actually be pseudoscientific, costly, and ineffective and cause harm. In autism, fads have been rampant since the mid-1980s. One of the earliest and most pervasive fads was facilitated communication (FC) (Zane et al., 2016).[7] Facilitated communication assumed that autistic children just had a communication disorder and that giving them a facilitator who could hold their hand and help them type would reveal their true selves. Sadly, this fad is still popular in some parts of the country despite hundreds of studies showing it is basically a fraud—the "facilitator" has been shown to be the one typing out the answers!

Behavior analysis has been around since the mid-1960s when the first experimentally controlled studies demonstrated that the behavior of autistic children could be improved in areas such as social skills and language. Research showing that problematic behaviors such as tantrums, aggression, and self-injurious behaviors could be dramatically reduced was being published in the *Journal of Applied Behavior Analysis* starting in 1968. This work, however, was "under the radar" of most citizens until the publication of Catherine Maurice's blockbuster book *Let Me Hear Your Voice: A Family's Triumph Over Autism* (Maurice, 1993). This very readable and compelling first-person account of a mother who *discovered* behavior analysis, found a therapist, and proceeded to support this evidence-based treatment with her two autistic children set off a wave of interest of tsunami proportions. For a while, behavior analysis may have looked like a fad because of the immediate increased demand for behavior analysis services. However, since there was a scientific basis for the treatment that has been replicated over and over, rather than a fad, this was a treatment that had staying power. In many ways, behavior analysis is like the invention of ice cream, the automobile, or air conditioning because it proved to be an actual break-through treatment that has a permanent place in our society.

"Currently, applied behavior analysis has the status as the gold standard for autism treatment around the world."

Currently, applied behavior analysis has the status as *the* gold standard for autism treatment around the world,[8] and far from being a fad, it has become the standard by which all other treatments are compared. It is funded by major insurance companies and the federal government and has been endorsed by the US surgeon general.

• •

Key Concepts:
Fad treatment, facilitated communication, gold standard, *Journal of Applied Behavior Analysis*

EXERCISES:

1. Go to the internet and search for facilitated communication research and look for articles that debunk this fad treatment.
2. If you are interested in autism treatment, get a copy of Catherine Maurice's book *Let Me Hear Your Voice*. This first-person account of behavior analysis treatment is very compelling.

QUESTION #5.
So, Is It Correct That Behavior Analysts Don't Have Theories, They Just Have Data?

You may recall from Question 3 the story of the 4-year-old girl who died from water-intoxication therapy. The excessive water was administered by her parents at the advice of counselors who had their own theory for "attachment disordered" children. This *theory* suggested that paradoxical interventions such as this would discourage inappropriate behavior and would somehow cause the little girl to draw closer to her parents. It is this sort of reckless theorizing that behavior analysts find totally abhorrent and often reinforces their conviction that we are simply better off without this sort of theory.

> *"These are 'theories' about observable behavior tied to the observable environment."*

This is not to say that behavior analysts don't have guesses, hunches, or ideas about how the environment affects human behavior. We do, but these are "theories" about observable behavior tied to the observable environment. Our speculations are tightly bound to the experiments being conducted, and it is rare that you will hear of any grand theory coming from a behavior analyst. While behavior analysts might be interested in understanding "attachment" (the enduring social emotional relationship between a child and a parent or other regular caregiver) (Zimbardo et al., 2005), simply having a theory about how it is formed is unlikely to help us improve the relationship between a specific child that we are treating and her parents who are desperately seeking answers. We are not saying that other researchers shouldn't pursue such lines of inquiry but rather that this is not the tradition of applied behavior analysis, where we have more immediate and pressing objectives.

For a child who is not "bonding" with her parents, we would first want to know what types of behaviors are of concern to the parents. These might include failure to make eye contact; a propensity for lying and stealing; and possibly even animal cruelty, starting fires, or other antisocial behaviors. Using a behavior-analytic *theory of behavior* (Skinner, 1953, 1969), we would analyze each behavior to determine the controlling variables. We would then set out a course of treatment for the parents whereby each behavior would be increased or decreased as desired. Nowadays, the treatment would probably not take place in a treatment center but rather in the setting where the controlling variables were operating. The behavior analyst would most likely spend many hours working with the parents in their home, teaching them the skills they would need, demonstrating special procedures and reinforcing them for behavior improvements shown by their child. Hundreds of studies have been conducted on behaviors such as these over the past 50 years, and an effective, reliable technology of parent training is well understood at this time (Wahler et al., 2004).

One early study illustrates this strategy quite nicely.[9] Dr. Robert Wahler, a professor at the University of Tennessee, and his assistants worked with two families who both had elementary school-aged boys who were described as "stubborn," "negativistic," and "headstrong." Observations were made in the homes of the children. As shown in Figure 1.3, Billy engaged in 100 to nearly 200 oppositional "units" of behavior in the 40-minute periods set aside for observational purposes. Wahler

> *"It is possible to determine procedures that can be used for individual participants to quickly change behavior, and those changes can be maintained over a considerable period of time."*

then analyzed the troubling behavior and concluded that the parents offered little in the way of negative consequences for not following requests. In addition, he found that their attention might not be all that

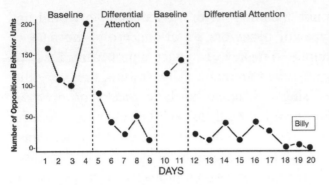

FIGURE 1.3 This graph shows the effects of time-out and differential attention on Billy's oppositional behavior in weekly observational sessions over a 20-week period.

reinforcing. The parents were trained to use time-out and differential reinforcement.[10] As Figure 1.3 also shows, when the differential attention condition was in place, the oppositional behavior dropped to near zero in only five weeks. This is quite dramatic, since Billy had demonstrated oppositional behavior for many months prior to treatment. As is common in this type of single-case-design research, Dr. Wahler returned to the baseline conditions (the parent quit using time-out and differential reinforcement) to determine if the behavior would reverse. You can see that the behavior did reverse very quickly over the next two weeks. When the parents again instituted the time-out and differential reinforcement, the troublesome oppositional behavior dropped quickly to zero and remained there for over two months. It is interesting to note that time-out only needed to be applied during week 12 (five times) and then not at all after that. This study exemplifies how our behavior theory works in practice. It is possible to determine procedures that can be used for individual participants to quickly change behavior, and those changes can be maintained over a considerable period of time.

Not having a separate theory for each and every type of behavior has not been a limitation to the field of behavior analysis. Our basic and applied researchers have been quite productive over the past 50 years developing effective interventions based on B.F. Skinner's original *theory of behavior*. This includes not only behavior therapy for deviant child behavior and parent training but also effective treatments for classrooms, residential facilities, sheltered workshops, business and industrial sites, and most recently executive coaching for CEOs of major corporations. Behavior analysis is a thriving, innovative field of productive basic and applied researchers and therapists who all derive their inspiration from one basic theory. Behavior analysts are motivated to expand and apply their knowledge primarily by the creative application of *data-based* approaches rather than theory testing.

* *

Key Concepts:
Theory of behavior, attachment disorder, paradoxical interventions, time-out, differential reinforcement

EXERCISES:

1. Think of a behavior-related topic that you find of interest and explore the search engine of the *Journal of Applied Behavior Analysis* to find studies that are relevant.
2. Look at the JABA studies (in #1) to determine if the authors engaged in the research because they were motivated by any particular theories.

QUESTION #6.

"Behavior Is a Function of the Environment." What Does This Mean?

Quick Take

"Behavior is learned in a specific setting, it is reinforced in that setting, and it is maintained over time with consequences in that setting."

Behavior analysts believe that *most* human behavior we see is learned over many years of family upbringing, incidental learning from peers, and deliberate training by their parents, relatives, teachers, mentors, supervisors, and others. From the time we are young children, we learn to not talk with our mouths full of food at the dinner table, to be respectful of our grandparents, and not to be loud and disruptive in a library. As adults, we should have been taught to look our supervisor in the eye and say, "Thank you," when receiving corrective feedback on the job. In all these cases, the behavior is learned in a specific setting, it is reinforced in that setting, and it is maintained over time with consequences in that setting. When there is a state trooper parked in the woods next to the interstate, many drivers will immediately hit the brakes to slow down and then speed up again once the highway patrol vehicle is out of sight. Over time, the ability to turn specific behaviors off and on as we enter and leave these settings becomes automatic. A conversation reduces to a whisper when we enter a church, synagogue, mosque, or library; that same conversation elevates to yelling at a football game when a completed pass is made in the last five seconds near the goal line.

Behavior analysts say that behavior is a *function* of the environment when they see that the behavior comes and goes in some settings and not others. While some people might say that the environment *causes* the behavior, this is incorrect. The behavior is actually caused by the *training* that took place in those settings. That training consists of the prompting of appropriate behavior, the quick delivery of reinforcers by a significant person *following* the behavior, and either

> *"The process of learning to engage in the proper behavior in the correct environment usually takes a few trials."*

the ignoring or disapproval of inappropriate behavior. The process of learning to engage in the proper behavior in the correct environment usually takes a few trials. For example, a fifth-grader might require a few instances of hearing, "Shhhh," from a librarian or rabbi before the library or synagogue becomes a stimulus for whispering.

The consistent application of consequences is critical to development of a pattern of behavior that occurs in one environment and not another. Children do not learn to engage in the appropriate behavior for a particular setting through "telling" alone. It is only when they experience consistent social and other consequences that the discrimination occurs. During this process, some "errors" along the way are expected. To maintain order in the classroom, if a teacher presents the rule, "If you want to speak, you need to hold up your hand and wait to be called on," she will then need to *always* ignore those who speak and only call on children with a raised hand. If the teacher makes a mistake and responds to someone who excitedly says, "I know the answer, I know!" this will cause a setback. The teacher will have to start over, remind the students of the rule, and start again only calling on those who have their hands up.

> *"Behavior can only be a function of the environment if someone in that environment has taken the time to apply consequences in a consistent manner to make it so."*

Behavior can only be a *function of the environment* if someone in that environment has taken the time to apply consequences in a consistent manner to make it so.

Technically Speaking

When Skinner (1953) used the expression *Behavior is a function of the environment*, he was speaking specifically about the response of a person to an interior stimulus such as a toothache, as opposed to the obviously complex external stimuli described previously. He went on to say:

> Events which take place during emotional excitement or in states of deprivation are often uniquely accessible for the same reason; in this sense our joys, sorrows, loves, and hates are peculiarly our own. With respect to each individual, in other words, a small part of the universe is private.[11]

This is often expressed as a formula shown below where B = behavior, f = function, and E = Environment.

$$B = f(E)^{12}$$

When a person's behavior turns on and off in the presence/absence of certain stimuli, we describe this as *stimulus control*. So, we might say that a person who tries to flatter his supervisor to gain advantage by saying, "I love your tie, Mr. Webb. You have great taste," is under the control of the supervisor as a stimulus. We presume that the person has been reinforced for such verbal behavior at some point in time. Mr. Webb would be considered an S^D (a *discriminative stimulus* for approach behavior), and his absence would be considered an S^Δ (S-delta, a stimulus that does not cue an approach response). After a discrimination is established, other similar stimuli may set the occasion for the same response. We refer to this as generalization, specifically *stimulus generalization*.

In behavior analysis, we believe the physical and social environment in which we live influences our behavior in many ways. This can be seen in a whole host of circumstances. Every day at Disney World Resort, thousands of people line up in an orderly fashion to have an adventure on their favorite rides, guided by stanchions and belt barriers. Their choice of places to dine is predetermined by themes that are present throughout the park: tacos, guacamole, and chips are available at the Epcot's Mexico pavilion, and several styles of crepes are offered at the pavilion representing France. The environmental engineers at Disney World are masters of crowd management. These engineers know how, in subtle ways, to affect the rides people choose, how they line up, and what they consume. It is to Disney's advantage to keep people coming to the parks and the revenue flowing. In schools, the teacher is the engineer by designing the curriculum to encourage engagement and learning, and the cafeteria staff selects menus that are intended to encourage healthy dining.

Behavior can be made to be a function of a specific environment by the consistent application of S^D and S^Δ conditioning. We contact different environments multiple times per day, and we are better off when we respond appropriately. As parents and teachers, we can teach children to make the behavioral discriminations through the consistent application of reinforcement that is contingent on appropriate behaviors in the presence of specific stimuli.

• •

Key Concepts:
Function of behavior, stimulus control, discriminative stimulus, crowd management, S^D and S^Δ conditioning

EXERCISES:

1. As you go about your day, attend to the way in which businesses such as bookstores, grocery stores, and department stores manage

customer movement and encourage certain purchasing behaviors. Take note also of the use of signage, the arrangement of counters, and displays of products designed to nudge you to buy specific merchandise.

2. If there is a particular setting that you enjoy and return to frequently, when you are there the next time, see if you can determine what makes the setting such an enjoyable, pleasant experience.

QUESTION #7.
Is Behavior Really All That Predictable?

This is really a good question and one that we hear frequently from people outside the field of behavior analysis. The brief answer is that it depends. The longer answer involves an examination of what *prediction* involves and expectations regarding the accuracy of the prediction. A few general observations regarding the prediction of behavior follow. First, *the best predictor of future behavior is past behavior*.[13] Second, the more information we have about a person, the behavior we are trying to predict, and the circumstances under which the behavior occurs, the better our prediction will be. In behavior analysis, we use special techniques to assist us with the prediction of future behavior.

We begin by having a fairly precise definition of the behavior we are studying. We initially look at behavior *topographically*, that is, the form of the behavior. For example, if we were studying self-injurious behavior of a little boy, we would look at whether the behavior was head banging, face-scratching, or some other specific behavior. We would define the behavior in terms of the position of the child's hand, whether he made a fist, how fast the movement occurred, and whether it appeared to be forceful. The second way we look at behavior is functionally; that is, regardless of the form of the behavior, what effect did it have? What seemed to be produced by the behavior? What effect did it have on the physical or social environment? See an example in Figure 1.4.

If a child who is severely developmentally disabled hits his head, what do the staff or house parents do? Does he get his way? Does he get out of doing something? Do people come running and feel sorry for him? The more we know about the result of the behavior, the better we are at predicting when he will do it next. As a matter of fact, one of the principal tools that behavior analysts use is a functional assessment. This is where various consequences are tested to determine which appear to be maintaining the behavior. By identifying the right consequence, we can get to the point that behavior can be predicted with good accuracy.

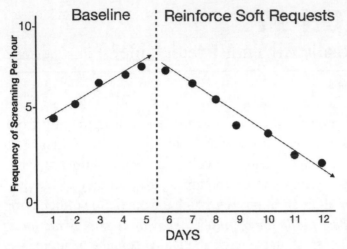

FIGURE 1.4   In this graph, the screaming is increasing in a predictable manner during baseline; then a reinforcer for "soft" requests is put in place, and the behavior also rapidly decreases in a predictable fashion.

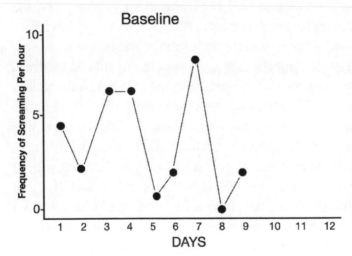

FIGURE 1.5   During baseline, the screaming is so variable that it is not possible to determine whether without treatment, it would increase or decrease in rate. It is essentially unpredictable.

Before we can do anything about changing a behavior, we have to be able to predict whether it is stable or increasing or decreasing. If, during Baseline, the behavior was variable, as shown in Figure 1.5, it would be impossible to determine whether the intervention had any effect.

So, the answer to the question, "Is behavior really all that predictable?" is yes. If we have enough of the right kind of data, behavior is very predictable. Behavior analysts use prediction as part of our analysis of behavior and attempt as much as possible to use scientific means to predict what people are going to do. Then, we try to predict the effects of certain treatments so that we can help people change their behaviors and improve their lives.

• •

Key Concepts:
Predictability, topography, function, variability, trending

EXERCISES:

1. If you have access to a setting where you can make some unobtrusive observations of behavior, observe and try to predict what the person is going to do next.
2. Graph the frequency of the behavior over time and try to predict the behavior from day to day.

SUMMARY OF BASIC CONCEPTS AND PRINCIPLES

Behavior analysts think about human behavior differently than most other human service professionals. We focus on the actual behavior as it is presented rather than looking at the behavior as a symptom of some deeper, underlying problem. We assume that these observed behaviors are learned and are maintained in the individual's natural environment. Although we are often presented with complex behavioral issues of unknown origin, our strategy is always to use data and proceed systematically.

TASK ANALYSIS FOR EFFECTIVE BEHAVIOR CHANGE

1. Define the behavior objectively.
2. Set up a data collection system (assessment) and gain consent from caregivers to collect data.
3. Gather enough data to determine the seriousness of the problem.
4. Graph the data (determine pattern of the behavior over time/stability of the behavior) and explain the results of the assessment in plain language to caregivers.
5. Conduct a functional analysis (i.e., determine the controlling variables for the behavior).
6. Use the results of the functional analysis (along with other information from interviews and informal observations. If needed, do a search of the research literature to determine what previous treatments have proven successful) to determine the controlling variables.
7. Develop a treatment plan based on #6 and gain consent from caregivers.
8. Implement the plan to make sure it works.

---

9. Demonstrate the treatment plan and train others such as the parents, teacher, stakeholders, or registered behavior technician (RBT) to implement the behavior plan.
10. Collect data throughout this process so that the effects of the treatment can be evaluated; revise as necessary.

The behavior analyst is looking for socially significant behavior changes that are sizeable enough to make an important difference in a person's life as well as improving the quality of their life to a significant degree. When possible, the behavior analyst employs a research design that demonstrates it was indeed the treatment that produced the effect and not some outside variable.

The typical behavior analyst is part clinician, part detective, and part scientist. Behavior analysts are client advocates who will try to obtain services for clients in order to improve their quality of life. A behavior analyst thinks of normal and abnormal behavior as being at two ends of a continuum where both are learned by the same principles of behavior. Abnormal behavior may be maladaptive or self-injurious, destructive, or dangerous. The behavior analytic view is that all abnormal behavior is learned and can be reduced: a replacement behavior can be found, taught to the individual, and maintained by new contingencies of reinforcement. A child or adult who is oppositional is a person who doesn't respond to requests. Such responses can be taught, and oppositional behaviors can be put on extinction so that they are no longer reinforced. The antisocial person is one who engages in behaviors that are inappropriate. These behaviors can likely be replaced with more socially appropriate behaviors by a careful rearrangement of the contingencies of reinforcement that surround the behaviors.

"A behavior analyst thinks of normal and abnormal behavior as being at two ends of a continuum where both are learned by the same principles of behavior."

All of this is routinely accomplished without the need for elaborate theories of personality, memory, motivation, or development. Behavior analysts have one core set of behavior principles (Michael, 1993) that can be applied in a wide variety of settings to help people of all ages and functioning levels.

NOTES

1. Most likely a Board Certified Behavior Analyst.
2. Permission from the parents would be necessary for this "assessment" of his behavior.
3. In the previous description of the Iwata et al. (1982, 1994) research, we have referred to "participants." In the original research, the participants were referred to as "subjects." This change in language came when our field became more sensitive and readily recognized that in research settings, we are dealing with people.
4. Associated Press, August 24, 2003, "Leaders were trying to heal boy who died during prayer, pastor says."
5. https://archive.sltrib.com/article.php?id=53270884&itype=CMSID
6. There are numerous other journals as well, including: *Analysis of Verbal Behavior, Behavior Analysis in Practice, Behavior Modification, Behavior Research and Therapy, Behavioral Interventions, Journal of Organizational Behavior Management.*
7. T. Zane, M.J. Weiss, S. Blanco, L. Otte, & J. Southwick (2016). Fads in special education. In R.M. Foxx & J.A. Mulick (Eds.), *Controversial Therapies for Autism and Intellectual Disabilities: Fad, Fashion, and Science in Professional Practice*, 2nd Edition. New York: Routledge, pp. 123–135.
8. https://autismtherapies.com/aba-gold-standard/
9. R.G. Wahler (1969). Oppositional children: A quest for parental reinforcement control. *Journal of Applied Behavior Analysis*, 2, 159–170.
10. Differential reinforcement involves following only some selected behaviors with a pre-selected reinforcer; this is also called shaping or behavior shaping.

11. It should be noted that Dr. Kurt Lewin preceded Skinner with his formula $B = f(P,E)$ where P = the person (Lewin, 1936). Skinner put a greater emphasis on the environment and left the P out of the formula.

12. Shull, R. L. (1991). Mathematical description of operant behavior: an introduction. In I. H. Iversen & K. A. Lattal (Eds.), Experimental Analysis of Behavior (Vol. 2, pp. 243-282). New York: Elsevier. (Call#: BF 319.5.O6 E97 1991)

13. This expression does not have an original author who can be cited at this time, although Guthrie (1944, p. 62) comes the closest to expressing this idea.

REFERENCES

Bailey, J.S., & Burch, M.R. (2016). *Ethics for Behavior Analysts*, 3rd Edition. New York: Routledge, Inc.

Guthrie, E.R. (1944). Personality in terms of associative learning. In J.M.V. Hunt (Ed.), *Personality and the Behavior Disorders*. New York: The Ronald Press.

Iwata, B.A., Dorsey, M.F., Slifer, K.J., Bauman, K.E., & Richman, G.S. (1994). Toward a functional analysis of self-injury. *Journal of Applied Behavior Analysis*, 27, 197–209. https://doi.org/10.1901/jaba.1994.27-197 (Reprinted from Analysis and Intervention in developmental Disabilities, 2, 3–20, 1982).

Lewin, K. (1936). *Principles of Topological Psychology*. New York: McGraw Hill, p. 216.

Maurice, C. (1993). *Let Me Hear Your Voice: A Family's Triumph Over Autism*. New York: Fawcett Columbine.

Michael, J. (1993). Concepts and principles of behavior analysis. Kalamazoo, MI: Association for Behavior Analysis.

Skinner, B.F. (1953). *Science and Human Behavior*. New York: Macmillan.

Skinner, B.F. (1969). *Contingencies of Reinforcement: A Theoretical Analysis*. New York: Appleton-Century-Crofts.

Wahler, R.G. (1969). Oppositional children: A quest for parental reinforcement control. *Journal of Applied Behavior Analysis*, 2, 159–170.

Wahler, R.G., Vigilante, V.A., & Strand, P.S. (2004). Behavioral contrast in a child's generalized oppositional behavior across home and school settings: Mother and teacher as one? *Journal of Applied Behavior Analysis*, 37, 43–51.

Wolf, M., Risley, T., & Mees, H. (1964). Application of operant conditioning procedures to the behaviour problems of an autistic child. *Behavior Research and Therapy*, 1, 305–312.

Zane, T., Weiss, M.J., Blanco, S., Otte, L., & Southwick, J. (2016). Fads in special education. In R.M. Foxx & J.A. Mulick (Eds.), *Controversial Therapies for Autism and Intellectual Disabilities: Fad, Fashion, and Science in Professional Practice*, 2nd Edition. New York: Routledge, pp. 123–135.

Zimbardo, P., Johnson, R., & Weber, A. (2005). *Psychology Core Concepts*. New York: Allyn & Bacon.

General Issues of Behavior Analysis

DOI: 10.4324/9781003160915-3

Chapter

Two

General Issues of
Behavior Analysis

QUESTION #8.

What Is a History of Reinforcement? Do People Have Their Own Unique Histories of Reinforcement?

Quick Take

History of reinforcement is a concept that describes what happens as you interact with your social and physical environment over time, learn new skills, and adapt to your environment. As an example, imagine this scenario. An adorable toddler with an angelic face is sitting in her highchair waiting for her lunch. She accidentally drops her favorite musical toy, and when her dad does not immediately pick it up, she begins to whine. Dad comes to the rescue, delivers the toy, and feels like a hero because the whining instantly stops. While it may seem as though everything is fine, this is the beginning of a history of reinforcement for whining. A few years later, the toddler, who is now 5 years old, doesn't hesitate before throwing a tantrum to get a Super Studio Disney Princess game. By the time she is 10 years old, there will be a conniption when she wants an iPad, and later, multiple outbursts will be related to demanding and receiving a Miata convertible for high-school graduation.

When whining results in children getting what they want as toddlers, this *intermittent reinforcement* of whining can last well into adulthood. This is when people start referring to the formerly cute little girl with the angelic face as a drama queen who pouts and whines when she doesn't get what she wants. The same sequence for her brother may also have started with whining and evolved with intermittent reinforcement into tantrums. The brother's demand for a Mustang that is promptly reinforced could eventually lead to a reputation in the office as a "difficult person."

Sometimes the history of reinforcement is not related to behavior that evolves over time. The "history" could involve a one-time incident. Sometimes, people have a one-time exposure to a situation such as a loose dog in their neighborhood that chases them and tries to bite, or they might get stuck in an elevator in an office building for a few hours, terrified that they are going to die. These *one-offs*, as they are called, can make a person fearful of dogs or make them search for the stairs rather than an elevator when they enter a tall building (if at some point, this person sees a therapist, they may even acquire the diagnosis of claustrophobic). If a person who is afraid of dogs sees a pup, even at a distance, it might not be a problem, but anything closer than 50 feet could cause the person to sweat, tremble, or have trouble breathing. The fear of dogs, known as cynophobia, can stay with a person for a very long time unless it is treated. When meeting a person with cynophobia, a behavior analyst would most likely consider the person's history of reinforcement (in this case, it would be a *punishment history*) as the likely explanation.

Each one of us grows up under different circumstances with a totally different history of reinforcement. Some young children are raised to wait patiently for adults to assist them. Later, they learn to do things for themselves, and this leads to becoming independent adults. Some children are surrounded by books and adults who love reading to them. Others have parents who are fascinated by the great outdoors, fast cars, contact sports, or space science. Important in all this is how the child was reinforced (constantly or intermittently) by the parents and whether the child comes into contact with reinforcers directly from the activity. If the latter, that is, the activity itself became reinforcing, the child could have a hobby, avocation, or career for life.

The behaviors that were reinforced, how they were reinforced, and the *schedule of reinforcement* that just happened to occur make up who we are. While some people refer to personality traits, behavior analysts are more likely to think of these persistent behaviors as shaped by early experiences. Even though a family creates a history of reinforcement in their child without realizing it or planning to do so, this history of reinforcement will largely determine if the child grows up to be a person who gives up easily or stays with a task even though it is difficult. It is the history of reinforcement that will determine if someone is curious, studious, athletic, or lazy. A child's socialization with peers could also determine if the child will grow up to be an adult who is easy to get along with or stubborn, and one who is outgoing or prefers more solitary activities. Specific behaviors related to the socialization of young children include learning to take turns, being cooperative, sharing, and showing an interest in others by asking questions and being a good listener. The goal of socialization is to essentially create a history of reinforcement for these behaviors in order to raise a child to be empathetic rather than selfish, caring rather than mean, and someone who strives to be a good person and good citizen.

Technically Speaking

A person's history of reinforcement is invisible to the rest of the world. It doesn't leave any scars, but you can see some clues if you study a person's behavior carefully for a period of time. You can deduce a history of reinforcement from how people respond to certain situations. What people order in restaurants, how they eat, and what they talk about over dinner provide plenty of clues about a person's history of reinforcement. Some people have food aversions that are no doubt a result of a bad experience such as force feeding or food poisoning, or they have strong preferences for certain drinks, preferring only bottled water or a specific craft beer.

The first author of *How to Think Like a . . . Behavior Analyst* has a personal history of reinforcement story that comes in the form of overdosing on strawberries when he was a child. On a fine summer day in northwestern Pennsylvania, he went to pick strawberries with his grandmother. It was one of those perfect days with big puffy clouds and a temperature of about 80°. The farmer gave them baskets and said, "I charge by the basket. Have fun." Jon started down the rows, looking for juicy ripe berries to take home. He was already thinking of the strawberry jam his grandmother would make that weekend. They would also have strawberry shortcake with delicious biscuits that only she could make, and there would be fresh homemade whipped cream on top. But it was 80°, he was working hard, and he was parched. "I could have one of those juicy strawberries right now just to see how they taste," he said to himself, and so he did. It was delicious and for a moment quenched his thirst, and so did the next one and the one after that. You can guess what happened. Soon, Jon was eating one strawberry for every one dropped in the basket. On the long drive home, he began to feel a little nauseous, and he crawled into the back seat of the 1954 Dodge sedan as it tossed and turned down the winding country road. Fortunately, his grandmother had quick reflexes and was able to pull over to the side of the road just in time for Jon to lunge out of back seat onto the side of the road, where he spewed a torrent of bright red, semi-digested liquid into the bushes.

Some people never recover from an experience like this, and they swear off the offending food item forever (this was a clear case of *respondent conditioning*; more on this in the next question). In Jon's case, he has reported, it was nearly 10 years before he was able to eat strawberries again. Nonetheless, this is just exactly how a history of reinforcement works. Other experiences produce different effects and also contribute to lifelong preferences. A 5-year-old rides out to the private airport with his dad to watch the small aircraft take off. They are able to get close enough to a friend's plane that they can feel the wind coming off the prop of the Cessna as it leaves the hangar, and the noise of the engine revving is palpable. It seems like magic to watch the plane glide down the runway and dip its wings just before it disappears into the clear blue sky. This sort of intensive, one-time experience can make that little boy want to fly and might control his choices for many years. Or a

"Understanding a person's history of reinforcement is critical in order to understand the person's behavior."

mother saves her money for weeks working at a part-time job and at Christmas takes her 6-year-old daughter to see the *Nutcracker* ballet. Somewhere between the Waltz of the Flowers and the appearance of the Sugar Plum Fairy, the little girl decides she wants to be a dancer. A lot of other things have to happen for this to occur, but the initial pairing history of reinforcement has a good foundation. Incidental events like this can shape a person's "personality."

One final example is a little frightening in its implications. A teenager stops at the Quick Stop convenience store on the way home from school, drops some change in the Coke machine, and gets . . . nothing. He has no more change and feels like he's been ripped off. He gives the machine a flat-handed, stiff-armed shove and suddenly, that familiar clunk-clunk comes from the flap in the machine. Out comes his Coke, and then another one, and he gets his change back! Knowing what we know about history of reinforcement, the behavior analyst would observe that hitting, shoving, and punching have just been reinforced, and quite immediately at that. We would predict that under similar circumstances, this behavior might occur again. If over the next few months and years, the adolescent, who has now developed a tendency to respond in an aggressive manner, learns that when he ramps up and gets physical in other situations, we say that a *class of behaviors* has been reinforced; there is the possibility of generalization from vending machines to people. A few instances where he pushes someone and gets his way could set in motion a chain of events that leads to a whole repertoire of threatening and aggressive behaviors that have now been reinforced on an intermittent basis. Fast forward to college. The young man discovers that when dealing with other people, if he raises his voice and threatens, they are often afraid and give in to his requests. Once again, he has been reinforced for the same behavior that started so long ago with a malfunctioning vending machine.[1] This is how a history of reinforcement is developed and how it can play out over time. It pays to be aware of contingencies of reinforcement and to understand the powerful effect they can have on behavior once they become part of a person's history of reinforcement.

It may seem like a stretch to go from a young man kicking a soft-drink machine to abusing another person several years later. The class of behavior involved here is an inability to control one's anger or a desire to have control. Abusers get angry if they don't get what they feel they are entitled to, and that reaction can start at an early age. As hard to believe as it may seem, reinforcement can work like this. Serial killers don't go from being model citizens one day to murdering people the next. Most documented cases related to abusers show a history that begins with animal abuse, then bullying other children, then progressing to actually hurting them.

Understanding a person's history of reinforcement is critical in order to understand the person's behavior.

• •

Key Concepts:
History of reinforcement, contingencies of reinforcement, intermittent reinforcement, punishment history, schedule of reinforcement, respondent conditioning, class of behaviors

EXERCISES:

1. Explain what we mean by history of reinforcement.
2. A college student who had poor judgment had something big to celebrate, so he went out with his friends and drank an excessive amount of alcohol. He woke up violently ill and spent the better part of the night hugging the toilet bowl. When he was able to call his friends a few days later, said he would never touch tequila again. How do you explain in behavioral terms what happened here?
3. How can you explain the behavior of young gang members who steal and will commit murder to protect the gang?
4. Cathy likes to visit her friend who lives in a big city. The friend has a roommate who wants to be a part of all the activities. The problem is, every single time they are somewhere having fun, the roommate says she does not feel well. She wants everyone to stop what they are doing, catch a cab, and take her home, even though she really doesn't appear to be sick. Explain how the roommate's behavior ("I'm sick; let's all go home") might have developed.

QUESTION #9.
Is All Behavior Learned?

Quick Take

Holding hands as they walked out of a darkened movie theatre one bright summer afternoon, an older couple seemed to be enjoying themselves until the man jerked his hand away, held it to his face and started sneezing. They were ultra-loud, super-sonic sneezes, the kind that made people who were nearby turn and stare. "Why do you have

> *"Sneezing is in a category called respondent behavior; respondent behavior is one form of behavior that is not learned."*

to be so darn loud?" said the embarrassed wife. Between sneezes, the man snapped, "I can't help it! I'm not doing it on purpose."

So, what do you think about Sneezy? Is he guilty? Maybe. Maybe not. Some people sneeze and use their voices to scream a loud, "AH-CHOO!" The yelling along with the sneeze is *operant or learned behavior*. But the actual sneeze can't be helped. Bright sunlight can actually *elicit* sneezing. Sneezing is in a category called respondent behavior; *respondent behavior* is one form of behavior that is not learned. In our daily lives, we engage in respondent behaviors and operant behaviors. The ratio of the first to the second is probably 1:20. Almost everything we do every day that is most important to us is learned or operant behavior. The remainder of behaviors are respondent, and they are so unusual that they really do stand out when they occur. As behavior analysts, we are almost entirely interested in learned or *operant behaviors*; we have some interest in respondent behaviors, especially if they are contributing some misery to a person's life. Some very important emotions and troublesome behaviors fit into the category of conditioned respondent behavior. A child is bitten by a dog and develops a fear or phobia of dogs. This is *respondent conditioning* at work, and the treatment for such behaviors requires a thorough understanding of respondent conditioning and the therapies associated with them. The field of behavior therapy is largely devoted to the treatment of anxieties, fears, phobias, and related traumatic behaviors that were most likely caused by some sort of respondent conditioning.

So, the short answer is that not all behavior is learned; respondent behaviors are automatic, such as an eye blink in the presence of a sudden puff of air near the eye or sneezes that are the result of exposure to sunshine. But, for the most part, the important behaviors in people's lives *are* learned verbal and motor behaviors that are both large and small, simple and complex. You learn how to drive a car, memorize a PIN, or give a speech. These are all learned behaviors.

Technically Speaking

A well-known example of *respondent conditioning* was shown in the work of Ivan Pavlov. Pavlov demonstrated that dogs salivate when meat powder is put in their mouths. Then he presented a neutral stimulus (the sound of a metronome) just before he put the powder in the dog's mouth. After presenting the meat and powder together several times, Pavlov presented the sound by itself. The dog now salivated when the sound was presented without meat powder.

In respondent conditioning, a neutral stimulus can become a conditioned stimulus if it is paired a number of times with an unconditioned stimulus.

Operant conditioning relates to learning by way of the behavioral principles of reinforcement, extinction, punishment, and stimulus control. As we saw in the case of Jon's conditioned aversion to strawberries in Question #8, some of our reactions to the environment in which we live are due to pairings with some aversive event. Much of this is accidental, of course. A child raised in a household with an alcoholic parent who can go into a rage over a single minor infraction may suffer the after-effects for years, and it may even affect their own child-rearing style.

This is a respondent-conditioning learned behavior. As we discussed previously, most learned behavior is learning-through-consequences or operant conditioning. We call this operant[2] learning, and the behaviors learned in this way are called operants. Driving is an operant behavior. Shooting pool and shooting baskets are operant behaviors. Following requests, instructions, and directions are all operants. Respecting your elders is an operant, and disrespecting them is also a learned behavior. Many parents complain about how their children "won't listen to me," or they describe them as defiant. Both of these are operant behaviors. Someone taught the child (we presume accidentally) not to pay attention to the parents when they speak, or they possibly even reinforced defiant behavior by allowing it to occur.

Complex behaviors are learned over time from the physical or social environment. There is a special technique to chopping wood, for example. A camper can figure out this useful skill on their own through trial and error and a process called *shaping*. This involves the natural consequences of each "chop" and starting with a small-diameter log and a hatchet. Beginning at this level, you have a fair chance of success and minimal odds of serious injury. The reinforcer in this case is a nice clean splitting of the log. During this learning process, there will be many odd splits that are not so reinforcing, but the natural consequences will shape up a good, strong swing in no time. Having mastered the hatchet technique, you are ready to split a log with a heavy ax or maul. After reading up on proper technique, you will learn the proper grip and stance and swing away, probably hitting off center several times before achieving the satisfying strike right in the middle (starting with dry wood is a good tip). Mother Nature will allow the shaping to take place, and soon you will have all the confidence you need to go camping and chop your own firewood!

Shaping is also done in the home, at school, and in ABA therapy. Parents, teachers, and behavior techs

"Behavior analysts think shaping is one of the most powerful techniques ever discovered, and they use it every day."

know how to start with a simple behavior, prompt and reinforce *successive approximations* to a more complex response, and eventually fade out the social reinforcer so that the behavior can be maintained by its natural consequences. By gradually raising the requirement for reinforcement, that is, shaping, very complex repertoires can be produced. A child can be taught to ride a bike, play a violin, or win at chess, all through *shaping*. A child with ASD and no language can first learn simple sounds, then short words, followed by short sentences and then to make functional requests and participate in short conversations. Behavior analysts think shaping is one of the most powerful techniques ever discovered, and they use this powerful procedure every day.

• •

Key Concepts:
Elicit, aversive event, respondent behaviors, respondent conditioning, operant behaviors, learned behavior, shaping, successive approximations

EXERCISES:

1. What is a respondent behavior? Give an example from your personal experience.
2. Is all behavior learned? Why or why not?
3. What is an operant behavior? Give an example from your personal experience.

QUESTION #10.
Can You Really Replace a Behavior? Can Bad Habits Actually Be Broken?

Quick Take

One of the tasks that behavior analysts are confronted with most often is dealing with unwanted behaviors, challenging behaviors, or even dangerous behaviors. Rather than using punishment to reduce these behaviors, behavior analysts think in terms of *replacing* these behaviors with those that are more acceptable or prosocial, or at least replacing problem behaviors with an alternative behavior. To begin, the behavior analyst must analyze the situation. This starts by asking the "Why?" question. Why does this behavior occur? If I tell Jeremy to stop doing this, why doesn't he stop? Why can't Chloe do something else instead of tantruming when I tell her to turn off her iPad and come to dinner?

> *"Rather than using punishment . . . behavior analysts think in terms of replacing these behaviors with those that are more acceptable or prosocial."*

All behaviors have functions, and it is primarily the immediate consequences that maintain them. These consequences can be in the form of obvious reinforcers such as attention or a tangible reward. The consequences can also be an escape from an aversive situation like a school assignment a child doesn't like or a demand that a parent made. Some behaviors have built-in or automatic consequences, such as spinning around or popping one's knuckles. When Chloe is having a tantrum, if mom says, "Okay, Chloe you can have five more minutes, but then you really need to come to the table," she has just reinforced the tantrum.

This probably was not on purpose, but those immediate consequences can really strengthen a behavior.

To understand the concept of *replacement behavior*, you have to: 1) pinpoint the behavior you want to replace (e.g., the tantrum), 2) identify the consequence (e.g., more screen time), 3) select a replacement behavior that has the same or an even more effective consequence (mom didn't specify this, but we assume it would be, "Okay, mommy, here I come"), and finally, 4) teach the person the replacement behavior.

Behavior analysts working with children with ASD are routinely faced with behaviors that need to be replaced. Flapping hands or fingers in front of the eyes, repeating words and phrases, throwing objects, or even biting another child or the therapist are all examples of behaviors that should be replaced. If the behavior and consequence are obvious, then selecting an appropriate replacement behavior to teach is the next task. For this, the behavior analyst must ask, "What would I like Savannah to do rather than shriek loudly when someone touches her toy?" If the child has some language, the therapist might teach her to say, "Please don't touch my toy; it bothers me." If there is no language, the therapist might try teaching Savannah to share her toys. Teaching sharing could take numerous sessions.

> *"If you are trying to break a bad habit, there are ways to do this that are evidence based and have been proven to work for nervous habits, tics, and stuttering."*

If you are trying to break a bad habit (behavior analysts call this "habit reversal"), there are ways to do this that are evidence based and have been proven to work for nervous habits, tics, and stuttering.[3] The steps for replacing a bad habit with some other acceptable behavior include 1) sharpening your awareness of the behavior, 2) developing a competing/replacement behavior, 3) arranging a reinforcer for the replacement behavior, and 4) using the new skill in a variety of settings to strengthen the behavior. If you are serious about breaking a bad habit, you may need to seek the assistance of a behavior analyst in your area (See BACB.com for a register of BCBAs).

Technically Speaking

A recent study[4] used the concept of reinforcing alternative behaviors to reduce stereotypy (a repetitive movement) that can stigmatize a child who engages in this unusual behavior. Three participant youths with ASD (ages 14–16) engaged in behaviors including body rocking, hand flapping, jumping, and so on at moderate to high levels (ranging from 20–80% of the time in controlled observational sessions). The researchers ran a test to see if the behaviors were socially maintained and found that they were not, which suggests that the behaviors were probably *automatically reinforced*. Next, they compared differential reinforcement of alternative behaviors (DRAs) with differential reinforcement of other behaviors (DROs) to see if they could reduce the stereotypic behaviors by delivering edible reinforcers contingent on completion of a small vocational task, such as folding shirts, stuffing envelopes, and sorting silverware, that would essentially compete with the stereotypy. Their results showed that when the participants were rewarded with edibles for engaging in a task that competed with body rocking, hand flapping, and so on, those behaviors reduced considerably to at or near zero levels.

* *

Key Concepts:
Replacement behavior, functions of behavior, automatically reinforced, habit reversal, DRA, DRO

EXERCISES:

1. What is a replacement behavior? Give an example.
2. Go to Google and type in "habit reversal," and see how this is applied for a wide variety of behaviors.
3. In settings for individuals with developmental disabilities, behavior analysts are often called upon to work on building "replacement behaviors." Is this a good idea? Are there ethical issues with this strategy?

QUESTION #11.
Can You Change Someone's Personality? Should You Even Try?

Quick Take

The American Psychological Association defines *personality* as, "Individual differences in characteristic patterns of thinking, feeling and behaving,"[5] but a behavior analyst would offer a different perspective. Behavior analysts know that since the behavior a person exhibits, their repertoire, is largely under control of the *contingencies* in each environment, the behavior will very likely match those contingencies. As B.F. Skinner said, "one's personality in the bosom of one's family may be quite different from that in the presence of intimate friends."[6] The bottom line for behavior analytic thinking on personality is that we would question the premise that there are "characteristic patterns of thinking, feeling and behaving" and rather look at the environments a person moves through and analyze the behavior in each environment.

Now to the question of *changing* a person's personality. As behavior analysts, we would want to know if an individual's behavior matches the contingencies of a given environment, and if not, would it be appropriate to try to modify the behavior? This comes up regularly with young children when they enter kindergarten. Many children who are 5 years old have not been well socialized at home so interacting with new peers can be quite a challenge. There is the small matter of working and playing cooperatively with the other children, treating them with respect, and respecting their property. The typical pre-kindergarten child cannot do any of these things at the beginning of the year, and it is the teacher's job to change the child's behavior to match the educational environment. It could be argued that this is an example of changing a child's personality. About the same time, this kindergartner may start taking soccer lessons and a year or two later sign up for a team. Once on a team, the coach will size up each child and begin teaching ball-holding, ball-stealing, and attacking skills, which are the total opposite of what the kindergarten teacher was emphasizing with playing cooperatively and respecting other's property! The well-rounded child by age 6 will have learned to sit quietly and listen to a story in one setting and to run like crazy and steal the ball in another. This could also be considered changing the personality of the child.

Similar sorts of multiple environments are encountered throughout life, and we are expected to adapt to each of them. We have one repertoire when interacting with irate customers, another when dealing with a demanding boss, and still a third when handling conflicts at home. You might say we all have multiple personalities, although hopefully, they are not as extreme as that depicted in The *Three Faces of Eve*.[7]

> *"Behavior analysts do not believe that it is possible to change a person's 'personality,' and they are not in the business of trying to do so."*

Technically Speaking

Behavior analysts do not believe that it is possible to change a person's "personality," and they are not in the business of trying to do so. However, we do believe that it is possible to help people more effectively adapt to their personal circumstances and working life. This is usually done by working with those who have some sort of known behavior deficit and then developing training methods to correct the deficit. The participants in these studies are either volunteers or under-age children whose parents have given consent for them to participate, and the applied research is always done in settings where the behavior occurs. The following list describes just some of the participants in behavior analysis studies that involve changing a person's behavior:

- socially withdrawn preschoolers,
- adults with autism,

- autistic youths,
- adults with developmental disabilities,
- children with hearing impairments,
- unassertive children,
- chronic schizophrenics,
- socially rejected boys
- adults with severe mental retardation,
- college students with autism,
- students with Asperger's syndrome.

In each of these studies (reviewed by the first author), the behavior analyst researchers work with the participants in the environment where the problem behavior occurs, find a way to measure the behavior(s), and establish a *baseline* in the appropriate setting; that is, children are observed in their classrooms and older students in natural work environments. Target behaviors include inappropriate or totally missing social interactions, absent social initiations, deficit social skills, or extreme anxiety. This latter individual and the study in which he participated will be described in a little more detail to give you some sense of how these studies are conducted.

A 30-year-old recent college graduate exhibiting extreme anxiety and deficient verbal skills in job interviews was treated with a social-skills training procedure that included instructions, modelling, behavior rehearsal, and videotape feedback. Three target behaviors—focused responses, overt coping statements, and subject-generated questions— were presented using a multiple-baseline design.

His social-communicative behaviors were rated by independent judges during *in vivo* job interviews, and in addition, the judges unobtrusively rated the subject's social-communicative behaviors in his temporary work setting before and after training. Here are the results:

Training resulted in expected changes for all three target behaviors and a decrease in the rate of speech disturbances. Training was found to generalize to novel interview questions and different interviewers. Furthermore, unobtrusive measures of eye contact, fluency of speech, appropriateness of verbal content, and composure supported the subject's report that training generalized to his daily social interactions on the job.

Perhaps most impressive was that this training helped him significantly improve his job situation.

During the last week of training the subject went for three serious job interviews. These three interviews resulted in three definite job offers, one of which he accepted. At present, he is an Administrative Assistant in a hospital with a salary that represents a 253% pay increase over the wage that he was receiving when the training began.[8]

So, our original point for this question was that behavior analysts do not believe in trying to change a person's "personality," but they do believe in helping people change their behavior to match the requirements of any given setting that they may encounter. In the previous case, the 30-year-old man was so nervous in job interviews and had such poor verbal skills that no one would hire him. As a result of the social-skills training program that reduced his anxiety and improved his verbal skills, he was able to impress the interviewers enough that they offered him a job. As behavior analysts, we feel that this powerful method of analyzing behavior and producing significant changes (so much so that they are noticed and appreciated by others) is a much better approach than categorizing personality types and trying to predict how people will do in certain types of jobs.

* *

Key Concepts:
Personality, contingencies in an environment, multiple environments, baseline, social skills training, changing behavior

EXERCISES:

1. Go to the webpage for the *Journal of Applied Behavior Analysis* (https://onlinelibrary.wiley.com/journal/19383703) and, using key words, see if you can find any categories of persons or clients with whom you might be interested in working. Read through the articles and see if you can determine the types of behavior the authors were studying and ask if they appear to be socially significant to you.
2. In your daily activities, observe your surroundings to see if there are certain requirements for a person to be successful in that environment, such as barista at a coffee shop, clerk at a retail store, manager at your gym. Make a list of these "success" behaviors and then think how you might go about improving them.

SUMMARY

Chapter 2 addresses general issues related to behavior analysis. This chapter describes what is meant by the term *history of reinforcement*, and it explains how a learning history develops. The differences between operant and respondent conditioning are delineated, and the topic of replacing behaviors with those that are more acceptable or prosocial is discussed. Finally, this chapter answers the frequently asked question pertaining to how behavior analysts view the concept of changing someone's personality.

NOTES

1. We are in no way excusing this totally inappropriate behavior, just trying to explain it behaviorally.
2. B.F. Skinner invented the word "operant" as a way of suggesting that the behavior operates on the environment to produce consequences that either increase it or decrease it. B.F. Skinner (1953). *Science and Human Behavior*. New York: Macmillan.

3. R.G. Miltenberger, R.W. Fuqua, & D.W. Woods (1998). Applying behavior analysis to clinical problems: Review and analysis of habit reversal. *Journal of Applied Behavior Analysis*, 31, 447–469.
4. C.B. Hedquist & E.M. Roscoe (2019). A comparison of differential reinforcement procedures for treating automatically-reinforced behavior. *Journal of Applied Behavior Analysis*, 53, 284–295. https://doi.org/10.1002/jaba.561.
5. www.apa.org/topics/personality
6. B.F. Skinner (1953). *Science and Human Behavior*. New York: Macmillan, p. 285.
7. 1957 movie starring Joanne Woodward about a woman with multiple personalities.
8. J.G. Hollandsworth, R.C. Glazeki, & M.E. Dressel (1978). Use of social-skills training in the treatment of extreme anxiety and deficient verbal skills in the job-interview setting. *Journal of Applied Behavior Analysis*, 11, 259–269. https://doi.org/10.1901/jaba.1978.11-259.

REFERENCES

Hedquist, C.B., & Roscoe, E.M. (2019). A comparison of differential reinforcement procedures for treating automatically-reinforced behavior. *Journal of Applied Behavior Analysis*, 53, 284–295. https://doi.org/10.1002/jaba.561

Hollandsworth, J.G., Glazeki, R.C., & Dressel, M.E. (1978). Use of social-skills training in the treatment of extreme anxiety and deficient verbal skills in the job-interview setting. *Journal of Applied Behavior Analysis*, 11, 259–269. https://doi.org/10.1901/jaba.1978.11-259

Miltenberger, R.G., Fuqua, R.W., & Woods, D.W. (1998). Applying behavior analysis to clinical problems: Review and analysis of habit reversal. *Journal of Applied Behavior Analysis*, 31, 447–469.

Skinner, B.F. (1953). *Science and Human Behavior*. New York: Macmillan, p. 285.

Chapter

Three

The Science and Technology of Behavior Analysis

DOI: 10.4324/9781003160915-4

QUESTION #12.

Behavioral Research Methods Seem to Be Quite Different From Those Used in Psychology. Is That Right?

Quick Take

Behavior analyst researchers are primarily interested in studying individual human behavior over time. Their purpose is to understand what variables affect a person's behavior and to find ways to change the behavior if that becomes necessary. This method is ideally suited to the practice of behavior analysis in which we work with

"Psychological research . . . is most often conducted with college students taking a general psychology course."

individuals in clinical or educational settings where behavior change is the name of the game. Psychological research, on the other hand, is most often conducted with college students taking a general psychology course. This very unrepresentative sample of young people is referred to as a "convenience" sample. These researchers use descriptive or inferential statistics to make generalizations about "human nature." In contrast, behavior analysts are not particularly interested in statistical analysis of group data, since it does not help us understand the behavior of the individual with whom we are working.

The type of statistical research used in psychology began in the 1940s when the US Department of Agriculture became interested in knowing how farmers felt about the New Deal agricultural programs.[1] Unable to sample all of the country's 6 million farmers for practical reasons, knowing the least number that could be interviewed to generalize to the whole population was important. The answer to this was 300,000.

In behavior analysis research, we rely on the methodology begun by Skinner to help us look carefully at individual performance. Using statistics for what we do yields results comparable to mixing many colors of paint and ending up with a color that looks like none of the originals. For example, if you are going to observe children in a classroom who are disruptive, you could take data on the number of times the children are acting out. Using a statistical research model, you would most likely average those numbers. This could create a false impression because the child you need to target is the one who is getting out of his seat 34 times, not all of the children, whose disruptions average 4 per day. For this reason, we use the research methodology of behavior analysis called "single-case design."[2] Behavior analysts who studied this classroom of disruptive children would evaluate each child's data independently of the other children.

Technically Speaking

The methods that behavior analysts use in their research are very common to scientists in biology, medicine, chemistry, and other related fields. When we are looking at humans and trying to change behavior, it is important that we have a clear picture of how each individual is performing. As Skinner developed his science of individual behavior, he had to first learn how to quantify individual performance over time, and for this he needed an apparatus. He discovered that if he created a small working environment where his pigeons and rats could operate a mechanism and receive food reinforcers, he could determine a great deal about their behavior. This apparatus was an "operant chamber" and became known as a "Skinner box."[3] Skinner found he could shape animals to press a lever or peck a key under some conditions and not others (green key vs red key) and to work at a fast and furious rate or very slowly, and he could teach a very complex skill that involved a chain of behaviors that were shaped independently and then linked together. His findings were replicated by other behavioral researchers at other universities and ultimately were extended to many species, including, of course, humans.

In Skinner's system, each individual subject or participant essentially serves as their own control, thus eliminating the need for a *control group*. The science of behavior that Skinner espoused consists of thousands and thousands of studies performed over half a century that clearly show that certain important variables consistently affect human performance.

We can use behavior analysis research methods to study the behavior of individual people in one setting or across settings, we can look at performance during both treatment and no-treatment conditions, and we can look at groups such as one classroom compared to another using single-case research design.

In short, the research methods used in applied behavior analysis have evolved to the point that applied behavioral researchers can study everyday human behavior in almost any setting.[4]

Note: Laboratory research in operant conditioning still continues and is published primarily in *The Journal of the Experimental Analysis of Behavior*; applied work with humans is published in *The Journal of Applied Behavior Analysis* and about a dozen other applied journals (for listing, please see Appendix).

• •

Key Concepts:
Behavior analytic research, single-case design, operant chamber, "Skinner Box", control group

EXERCISES:

1. If we were working with 25 adults in a sheltered workshop, why would we not want to use statistics to evaluate increases in the length of time they were on task? Basically, how would you evaluate improvements in performance (on-task behavior) in this setting?

2. Read a study where statistics is used to quantify the results. What can you determine about the performance of individual participants from these results?

QUESTION #13.

Can You Explain the Relationship Between Behavioral *Research* and Behavioral *Treatment*?

Quick Take

Behavior analysts think about behavioral treatment in much the same way that a behavioral researcher does. In many respects, behavior *treatment* looks a lot like the behavioral *research* from which it is derived. Both clinicians and researchers take baseline data, implement interventions, and provide ongoing evaluations of the interventions. Figure 3.1 shows the similarities.

As an example of one requirement of good methodology, behavioral researchers must perform inter-observer agreement (IOA) checks, whereas clinicians usually do not carry out such checks. So, if a behavior analyst were providing behavioral treatment for a child, she might observe that child, take daily data, and report the results to the habilitation team. If this were research, she would have to adhere to research standards. Most likely, the behavior analyst would not be taking the data on the treatment that she provided because she might be accused of being biased. She would have to have more than one observer watching the child and taking data. These two people would not talk to each

Behavior Analysis Research	Behavior Analysis Treatment
Take Baseline Before Intervention	Take Baseline Before Treatment
Determine the Controlling Variables	Find the Function of the Behavior
Implement First Intervention	Implement Treatment
Evaluate Intervention	Evaluate Treatment
Demonstrate Experimental Control	If It Works, Continue Treatment
Is Effect Socially Valid?	Is Client Satisfied With Results?

FIGURE 3.1   Similarities of ABA research and treatment.

other as they observed and recorded the data. At the end of the session, the researcher would calculate IOA, which is a measure of agreement between the two observers. If needed, our researcher would give additional training to observers.

While this level of experimental rigor is not required during behavioral treatment, you should adhere to as many of the standards for research as possible.

Researchers must also strive to test for *social validation* of their methods. Social validation answers questions about whether consumers or the public would find this research useful. Behavioral therapists rarely have to test for social validation. The fact that consumers want behavioral services—it is the gold standard, after all—provides the endorsement for initiating treatment; clients' families often push for continued treatment, which is the social validation for the outcomes.

Many behavioral consultants working in large organizations routinely use research protocols in their practices to demonstrate to corporate customers that the results they are achieving are valid and reliable. To clearly show systematic changes in behavior, they will employ sophisticated research designs that demonstrate that intervention effects were due to certain specific inputs and precise measurement of outcomes.

Technically Speaking

One of the purposes of applied behavioral research is to evaluate ABA procedures and compare them with other approaches to the same problem. A great example of this is a study published in 2016 on food selectivity.[5] In this study, the authors compared a popular occupational therapy technique to the problem of pediatric feeding disorder, a "modified sequential oral sensory treatment" (M-SOS), to an ABA approach. The M-SOS had not previously been subjected to rigorous evaluation and was deemed to have "limited empirical support" (p. 486), and an evaluation of clinical data suggested that "68% of children showed no advancement" (p. 487) even after 1–3 years of treatment. Peterson and colleagues in this study developed an experimental design which

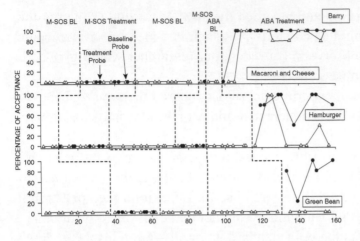

FIGURE 3.2 An example of a combination of multiple baseline with multielement and reversal designs showing that the ABA treatment gives 100% food acceptance in a few short sessions.

allowed them to directly test the M-SOS procedure with their ABA methodology; the design was a combination of a multiple baseline with multielement and reversal designs. As shown in Figure 3.2, the data are quite clear that food acceptance has zero impact on food acceptance, whereas the ABA treatment produces 100% response within just a few short sessions.

With this research completed, behavior analysts who are dealing with food selectivity can use the ABA methods described in this journal article with confidence that it will help their clients enjoy a wider range of foods at mealtimes and lead more healthful lives.

● ●

Key Concepts:
Behavioral research, behavioral treatment, research protocol, social validation

EXERCISES:

1. What are some of the extra requirements of behavioral research?

2. Go to the Wiley Online Library (https://onlinelibrary.wiley.com/journal/19383703) and search the key words for a behavior you are interested in and see if there are any published studies on it.
3. Observe a client-training program in a facility or school. Assuming that the necessary approvals could be obtained, would it be possible to make this training program into a research project?

QUESTION #14.
Is It Possible to Find the "Cause" of a Behavior?

Quick Take

> *"Behavior analysts are practical, reasonable people who are fascinated by human behavior."*

Behavior analysts are practical, reasonable people who are fascinated by human behavior. They are nearly obsessed with two questions: First, *Why did this behavior occur*—what "caused" it? And second, *What can I do to improve this behavior* for this person? How can I help them have a higher-quality life, with less pain and frustration and more enjoyment? Before we can begin to approach the second question, we must first answer the *"Why?"* question.

When behavior analysts ask the why question, we are not talking about the *original cause* of the behavior, since this may be impossible to determine. While some may believe that behavior cannot be changed

> *"When behavior analysts ask the why question, we are not talking about the original cause of the behavior, since this may be impossible to determine."*

unless the cause is known, this is not the case with behavior analysis. We look for stimuli in the immediate environment that appear to set the occasion for a behavior and also look for consequences that might be maintaining it; if we can isolate those variables, we can develop a treatment plan. The approach behavior analysts often use is a procedure developed in 1982 by Dr. Brian Iwata and his colleagues[6] called experimental functional analysis, or *functional analysis* for short. Simply put, we believe that a behavior that is occurring with some regularity probably has some "trigger" that produces it and some effect in the environment that is maintaining it. In the nearly 40 years since that original study was done, there have been hundreds and hundreds of studies published showing that the "causes" of a behavior can be discovered and useful treatments developed. A child who wanders around a classroom disturbing other children may not be showing signs of depression over the divorce of his parents but rather is avoiding schoolwork that is too difficult for him, and the other students occasionally reinforce the behavior with their remarks to him. The behavior analyst, working with the teacher, can determine if this is the case by changing the work sheets assigned to see if that makes a difference. If it does, and he stays in his seat and turns them in to the teacher, we can say that we have discovered at least one "cause" of the wandering around. All behavior problems are not this simple, of course, but they are approached in the same way by systematically changing the environment to see if there is a change in the behavior.

Technically Speaking

An example of this strategy can be seen in Figure 3.3. Jason, a 9-year-old boy with attention deficit hyperactivity disorder (ADHD) and an IQ of 77 engaged in extensive skin picking on several parts of his body, including his scalp.[7] It was reported by school officials that he had done this several times per day for several years and was on medication at the time of the referral, although the effect was limited, perhaps since it was administered inconsistently. As can be seen in the graph, the skin picking occurred approximately 70% of the time. The teacher noticed that Jason was less likely to engage in the behavior when the classroom task involved the use of something manipulative, and this gave the researchers an idea for an intervention. They proceeded to apply a series of interventions using an ABCBAB[8] single-case design that allowed the behavior analysts to determine that when they gave Jason something to manipulate with his hands, the skin picking nearly

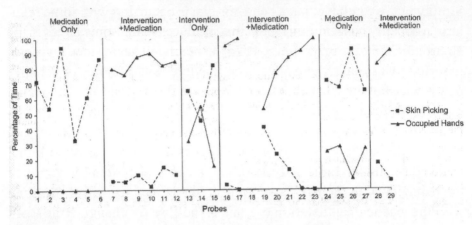

FIGURE 3.3   Reducing skin picking using an A B C B D B design.

disappeared. A layperson might say, "Oh, I see: he was just fidgeting and didn't realize he was scratching himself. Maybe he was bored, so when they gave him some plastic balls to play with, that occupied his hands and he didn't need to scratch himself anymore." The behavior analysts did not need to know the original cause of Jason's skin picking to be able to observe and measure the behavior and develop some ideas of what might be tested to reduce it.

● ●

Key Concepts:
Cause of behavior, functional analysis, functional assessment, trigger, behavior program

EXERCISES:

1. Louis is a 12-year-old boy with severe mental retardation. When he is sitting in his wheelchair, he will rub his eyes with the palm of his hand. His eyes get very red and irritated from this. Why is it important to know the cause of this behavior before treating it?

2. If you were asked to conduct a functional analysis on the eye-rubbing behavior, what are some questions you might ask?
3. Suppose the functional assessment showed that Louis engaged in eye rubbing for attention. What are some procedures you might use in a behavior program to treat eye rubbing?

QUESTION #15.

What Is the Connection of B.F. Skinner to Behavior Analysis?

Quick Take

"In Skinner's early work, he showed that fundamental principles of behavior could be found by studying a small number of 'subjects' over a long period of time."

We owe our origins primarily to Skinner (1938, 1953), who established the framework for the field with his early laboratory work and subsequently inspired several generations of applied researchers to work with populations who could benefit from a technology of human behavior. Skinner essentially taught us to think like behavior analysts when we look at what a person does or says, and he is widely considered to be the father of behavior analysis.

In Skinner's early work, he showed that fundamental principles of behavior could be found by studying a small number of "subjects" over a long period of time. While Skinner worked primarily with rats and pigeons, researchers who came after him found that this same general approach also worked well with human participants. In fact, as it turns out, most of the important variables that are relevant for individuals must be studied in this way to determine effective treatments; findings from group statistical research often have very little relevance for individuals in need of long-term treatment, whereas within-subject research is ideally suited to individual cases such as those involving autism and managed care (Morgan & Morgan, 2001). Skinner's primary contribution is his observation that most behavior is learned by individuals interacting with their environment. Skinner called this operant behavior, to be contrasted with Pavlov's respondent behavior (which was reflexive in nature).

Technically Speaking

Professor Skinner was an amazing, prolific genius who envisioned a science of psychology—the experimental analysis of behavior (EAB)—that could help us understand how behavior is acquired and how it is maintained over time. This led to the field of operant conditioning and the concept of operant behavior. Once a foundation of experimental work was established, the next step was to promote the application of the findings from EAB to people of all ages and conditions and in diverse settings, from preschools to assisted living centers, from classrooms to boardrooms, and in many more settings. This became the field of applied behavior analysis as we know it today. Skinner believed that a wide variety of average citizens, from parents to small business owners, as well as professionals, from social workers to physicians, and teachers to therapists, could use the basic principles of behavior to make the world a better place. Skinner's vision extended to cultural design. His fictional behavioral utopia, *Walden Two* (1948),[9] described in great detail how a community of 1,000 individuals could live off the land in peace and harmony with its own innovative school system, choice-of-work job assignments, and a method of self-governance that was totally transparent and based on equality of men and women.

Without a doubt, Skinner's greatest impact was through the large number of disciples who heard his lectures and read his many articles and books. They had their own vision of how the basic principles could be applied to improve the human condition and spread the word through their students. Drs. Jack Michael and Ted Ayllon applied this work to produce the first controlled study of the behavior of patients in a mental hospital (Ayllon & Michael, 1959),[10] and Baer et al. (1968)[11] laid out the blueprint for the field in the first issue of the *Journal of Applied Behavior Analysis*.

FIGURE 3.4   Professor B.F. Skinner.

● ●

Key Concepts:
Experimental analysis of behavior, operant behavior, *Walden Two*, *Journal of Applied Behavior Analysis*

EXERCISES:

1. Find a copy of *Walden Two*, and after reading it, think of ways that your community could be improved by some of the behavioral techniques described.
2. Look in the Wiley Online Library (internet) for articles in JABA on a topic in which you are interested. Explain how studying that behavior over a long period of time helps to understand it more thoroughly.

SUMMARY

This chapter starts explaining the difference in behavioral research methods and psychology research. Behavioral research consists primarily of single-case designs where each participant is used as their own "control." This method is in contrast to psychological research, which involves group statistical designs. Behavioral research also puts a premium on studying everyday human behavior in applied settings. The methods used in ABA research often can translate directly into practice. Since the similarities of behavioral research and behavioral practice are comparable by design, there is great interest in applying results found in experimental labs to common, routine environments. Behavioral research can be planned in such a way that two or more alternative treatments can be directly compared. When behavior analysts say that they are looking for the *cause* of a behavior, they are talking about some event or variable in the environment that consistently produces the behavior, not some event in the distant past. The father of ABA is B.F. Skinner, a professor from Harvard who discovered the importance of environment variables in producing and changing behavior.

NOTES

1. www.psychologicalscience.org/observer/when-behavior-met-statistics
2. J.S. Bailey & M.R. Burch (2018). *Research Methods in Applied Behavior Analysis*, 2nd Edition. New York: Routledge, Inc.
3. Skinner never called it this; he always referred to it as an operant chamber.
4. J.S. Bailey & M.R. Burch (2018). *Research Methods in Applied Behavior Analysis*, 2nd Edition. New York: Routledge, Inc.
5. K.M. Peterson, C.C. Piazza, & V.M. Volkert (2016). A comparison of a modified sequential oral sensory approach to an applied behavior-analytic approach in the treatment of food selectivity in children with autism spectrum disorder. *Journal of Applied Behavior Analysis*, 49, 485–511. https://doi.org/10.1002/jaba.332. Figure 4 p. 505.
6. This work was done at The John F. Kennedy Institute and Johns Hopkins University School of Medicine in Baltimore.
7. K.L. Lane, A. Thompson, C.L. Reske, L.M. Gable, & S. Barton-Arwood (2006). Reducing skin picking via competing activities. *Journal of Applied Behavior Analysis*, 39, 463–467.

8. Technically, this is a reversal design that starts with medication, then medication + intervention, then intervention only, then medication + intervention, then medication only, and finally medication + intervention.
9. B.F. Skinner (1948). *Walden Two*. Indianapolis, IN: Hackett Publishing Company, Inc.
10. T. Ayllon & J. Michael (1959). The psychiatric nurse as a behavioral engineer. *Journal of the Experimental Analysis of Behavior*, 2, 323–334.
11. D.M. Baer, M.M. Wolf, & T.R. Risley (1968). Some current dimensions of applied behavior analysis. *Journal of Applied Behavior Analysis*, 1, 91–97.

REFERENCES

Ayllon, T., & Michael, J. (1959). The psychiatric nurse as a behavioral engineer. *Journal of the Experimental Analysis of Behavior*, 2, 323–334.

Baer, D.M., Wolf, M.M., & Risley, T.R. (1968). Some current dimensions of applied behavior analysis. *Journal of Applied Behavior Analysis*, 1, 91–97.

Bailey, J.S., & Burch, M.R. (2018). *Research Methods in Applied Behavior Analysis*, 2nd Edition. New York: Routledge, Inc.

Lane, K.L., Thompson, A., Reske, C.L., Gable, L.M., & Barton-Arwood, S. (2006). Reducing skin picking via competing activities. *Journal of Applied Behavior Analysis*, 39, 463–467.

Morgan, D. L. and Morgan, R. K. (2001). Single-participant research design: Bringing science to managed care. *American Psychologist*, 56, 119–127.

Peterson, K.M., Piazza, C.C., & Volkert, V.M. (2016). A comparison of a modified sequential oral sensory approach to an applied behavior-analytic approach in the treatment of food selectivity in children with autism spectrum disorder. *Journal of Applied Behavior Analysis*, 49, 485–511. Figure 4 p. 505. https://doi.org/10.1002/jaba.332.

Skinner, B.F. (1938). The behavior of organisms. New York: Appleton-Century-Crofts.

Skinner, B.F. (1948). *Walden Two*. Indianapolis, IN: Hackett Publishing Company, Inc.

Skinner, B.F. (1953). *Science and human behavior*. New York: Macmillan Co.

Chapter Four

The Philosophy Behind Behavior Analysis

DOI: 10.4324/9781003160915-5

QUESTION #16.
What Is the Philosophy Behind Behavior Analysis?

Quick Take

Broadly speaking, behavior analysts are the applied specialists in the larger science of human behavior. They think like scientists and use the scientific method but are primarily concerned with applying the basic principles of behavior that were discussed in Chapter 1. The philosophy behind that science is *behaviorism*, and B.F. Skinner was

> *"Skinner was not willing to 'deny the existence of feelings, sensations, ideas, and other features of mental life.'"*

its major proponent.[1] Consisting of many components, this philosophy adheres to the acceptance of certain premises, including:[2]

Determinism—Determinism assumes that everything we observe has causes that can be investigated.

Empiricism—Behavior analysts rely on evidence gathered via observation and experimentation.

Rationalism—We believe that reason and logic are useful tools to help explain human behavior.

Operationalism—Operationalism is the notion that it is important to measure all interventions and behaviors that result from them.

Scientific skepticism—We assert that all explanations should be doubted until they are proven by valid and reliable scientific data.

Skinner's version is somewhat different from other scholars who preceded him (e.g., J.B. Watson) in that he was not willing to exclude from consideration those phenomena that were difficult to analyze. Skinner was not willing to "deny the existence of feelings, sensations, ideas, and other features of mental life."[3] To distinguish his philosophy from others, he called it *radical behaviorism*. This does not mean "radical" in the sense of someone who is an extremist or a fanatic but rather to capture the sense that this philosophy was thorough and fundamental. It would eventually, using scientific principles, be able to explain private events using the same basic principles as observable behavior. To roll this into one sentence, behavior analysts are skeptical of any explanation of behavior unless it is based on empirical data derived from reliable, valid methods that demonstrate experimental control. We would add to this that the experimental demonstration of cause-effect needs to produce socially significant changes in the behavior. Applying these strict standards of behaviorism should prevent practitioners and consumers from accepting as truth any "treatments" that are not valid.

As an example of the strict standards of behaviorism not being applied, the internet is rife with unproven, pseudoscientific, and even dangerous "cures" for autism, and the Food and Drug Administration has now stepped in to try to educate the public.[4] Their list of unscientific treatments includes chelation therapies, hyperbaric oxygen therapy, detoxifying clay baths, raw camel's milk, chlorine dioxide (Miracle Mineral Solution), and essential oils. Behavior analysts guided by the precepts of radical behaviorism are able to sort out these clearly unscientific "treatments" and recommend to their clients only treatments that meet our high standards.

Technically Speaking

Skinner's *radical* behaviorism proposes to explain experiences that make up what is called "mental life" that *methodological* behaviorism[5] wanted to exclude. Using the same principles that he developed to explain observable verbal and motor behavior, Skinner[6] includes thinking, reasoning, problem solving, "deciding," recalling information, and having an idea[7] as reasonable private events to include in his analysis. In his accounting of communications between two individuals (i.e., the verbal behavior of a speaker and a listener), he says that the speaker's verbal behavior is maintained by the response of the listener and that the two of them working together can solve problems that one person would not be able to solve alone. Skinner also points out that a person can be both a speaker and listener[8] and that in this way, it is possible to explain what is generally called "thinking."

An example of thinking: Wanda has earned five paid vacation days at her job and must use them by June 30 or lose them. She has friends who have offered her the use of their beach house at no charge, but she needs to fly there and back, so she would lose some vacation time traveling. Wanda has always wanted to visit New York City, which is only a 3-hour drive away, so she could maximize her five days but would have to pay for her hotel room. In trying to make a decision between these two choices, Wanda draws up a list of the pros and cons on a piece of paper. For each item, she puts a number of checkmarks depending on how important each one is to her. The factors include additional expenses, entertainment value, travel time, previous vacation experiences, and so on. If you were the proverbial fly on the wall, you could actually *see* her engaging in this decision-making process. Her "thinking" would be observable in terms of items listed and checkmarks made. This process would probably help Wanda understand how she arrived at her final decision. This is what Skinner means when he says that his philosophy and form of behaviorism are inclusive of processes that are not accounted for in other approaches such as methodological behaviorism.

* *

Key Concepts:
Behaviorism, radical behaviorism, methodological behaviorism, determinism, skepticism

EXERCISES:

1. What is the relationship between the philosophy of behavior analysis and the science of behavior?

2. What would radical behaviorism include in its scope of interest besides observable behavior? Make a list and explain why these items are included.
3. How would you go about teaching a child the problem-solving (*thinking*) process of finding a lost toy?

QUESTION #17.

What Is the Behavioral Position on Freedom and "Free Will"?

Quick Take

Free will is basically the ability to select a particular course of action in order to fulfill a need or desire. Whether we have free will has been debated for centuries. The ability to control our own destiny or things happening because of fate are ideas that sometimes accompany the debate about free will. There are deep philosophical divides among scholars on this important issue.

> *"We know that aversive control produces escape and avoidance behavior. Aversive control can elicit aggression and cause bad feelings."*

For the behavior analyst, this is a practical question that comes down to how we approach our daily life and how we try to help others with theirs. A person who is under a great deal of aversive control such as a domineering abusive father or a nagging spouse and a saleswoman who has constant pressure to meet deadlines only to discover even more unreachable goals have been set by management are people who might feel as though they have little or no freedom. They could run away from home, divorce the spouse, and quit the job, but these may not be the realistic options. If well-educated people can see that these situations are bad, they might be able to chart a course to freedom from all of this aversiveness. As behavior analysts, we see ourselves as being in an ideal position to accomplish this important goal, and we do this for a living minus all the philosophical baggage. We know that aversive control produces escape and avoidance behavior. Aversive control can elicit aggression and cause bad feelings from living under these insufferable conditions.

To get the ball rolling, the person living under aversive conditions must seek help from someone who understands what it will take to solve the problem. This does not take willpower but rather enough insight into the condition to see that it does not need to be permanent. There needs to be some initial behavior to reverse the conditions. These are skills that can be taught and should be taught to every person approaching adulthood. Behavior analysts support and promote assertiveness training as a method of breaking the chain that is keeping anyone in a situation where a person is constrained emotionally or physically by direct threats of harm or implied threats.

Control by aversive events is fairly obvious, and we take it as a serious obligation to work with our clients to remove these barriers to a happy and productive life. Another, more subtle, challenge to freedom is that which comes from schedules of reinforcement, specifically intermittent schedules of reinforcement. Intermittent schedules can lock people into certain patterns of behavior (such as gambling) that are destructive and harmful to individuals and those around them.

> *"Intermittent schedules can lock people into certain patterns of behavior (such as gambling) that are destructive and harmful to individuals and those around them."*

As we discussed earlier, computer games pose this sort of threat to freedom since they can provide a type of reinforcement that may be far more powerful than what can be derived in the real world. This is especially the case if the person "feels powerless" in a job or domestic situation and can retreat to a world of make-believe where he can control some consequences and where the intermittent reinforcers make life interesting (at least for a couple of hours).

Technically Speaking

It is not useful to say that a person addicted to computer games has the "free will" to discontinue this activity, since it flies in the face of what we know about contingencies of reinforcement. Intermittent schedules of reinforcement (variable interval, variable ratio) can take away a person's freedom just as surely as a controlling boss or domineering spouse.

As behavior analysts, we are committed to trying to enrich the lives of the people with whom we work. We would like to see people enjoy the reinforcers that come from friends and family as well as from those that have been produced by our culture such as art, dance, music, literature, and sports. All of these reinforcers, along with those in nature, give people the freedom to come into contact with a wide range of reinforcers. To this extent, we would say these people have more freedom than those who are not able to make choices to experience these reinforcers. Someone in a working relationship with a controlling boss or a living arrangement with a domineering spouse or partner has far less freedom than is desirable. Behavior analysts believe that it is important to have an expansive repertoire in order to maximize one's reinforcers, and this involves many choices of behaviors and reinforcers.

Behavior analysts, for all their interest in promoting a good life with loads of fun and interesting behaviors and engaging reinforcers, are still *determinists*. We do not believe that people are literally free to engage in just any behavior that they like. We do believe that behavior is controlled by the person's reinforcement history plus the current contingencies that are in place. Understanding that behavior is controlled by its consequences

"We do not believe that people are literally free to engage in just any behavior that they like."

will help everyone understand how important it is to be able to analyze their condition. A personal audit will help someone analyze their condition to determine if they are satisfied with their choices. The act of choosing is an operant behavior just like any other behavior. The extent to which we, as behavior analysts, can contribute to strengthening this key behavior is the extent to which we can expand the freedoms that will make the lives of others worthwhile.

• •

Key Concepts:
Free will, choice, aversive events, determinists

EXERCISES:

1. How do behavior analysts view "free will"? Does this match up with your personal belief?
2. Give an example of how choice can help a person escape an aversive situation.

QUESTION #18.

Are Behaviorists and Behavior Analysts the Same Thing?

Quick Take

The short answer is no. These are two different professions. Behavior analysts are professionals who are highly trained in the basic principles of behavior and have extensive hands-on experience with clients in home, school, clinic, and community settings where they implement behavior-analytic procedures to improve the quality of life of their clients. They know how to take data on a wide variety of behaviors and develop reinforcement-based treatments that are humane and effective. Behaviorists, on the other hand, usually do not get involved in treatment with humans; they tend to be academic-based philosophers or laboratory or field scientists who work with animals. There is a relatively new profession, *applied animal behaviorist*. These are people who work with family pets such as cats, dogs, and parrots where the owners are having difficulty with some behaviors such as urinating indoors on the rugs or furniture; food guarding; aggression; or feather picking, often seen in captive birds.

> *"Some animal behaviorists work in zoos or aquariums where they help maintain the health of the animals."*

Some animal behaviorists work in zoos or aquariums where they help to maintain the health of the animals by teaching them to cooperate with veterinarians who are giving shots or administering examinations. Marine behaviorists may work in aquatic-themed parks to train the animals to do tricks for the entertainment of large audiences (note that there is some controversy surrounding this practice).

Technically Speaking

The term "behaviorist" originated in 1913 with a psychologist, J.B. Watson,[9] who broke ranks with the thinking of his time about how psychology was conceptualized. Back then, *introspection* was the accepted methodology for understanding the content of one's thoughts or consciousness, but Watson believed that "Psychology as the behaviorist views it is a purely objective experimental branch of natural science," and he believed that animals, and man, "adjust themselves to their environment."[10] This is to say that they respond and adapt to their environments, indicating that they can learn. Watson promoted the study of learned behavior and believed that it could be explained by studying the *stimuli* in the environment. Watson's goal was to build a science of behavior that would eventually allow for the prediction of behavior, and this would be followed by the "control" of behavior.[11] This was not meant in any Orwellian sense but rather that we would eventually understand the effect of the environment on behavior so that we could produce reliable changes in behavior. It was hoped that this would lead to more effective therapies and more successful educational settings.

• •

Key Concepts:
Behaviorist, animal behaviorist, applied animal behaviorist, marine behaviorist

EXERCISES:

1. If you own a pet that presents behavior problems, go to the internet and search for any articles written on this topic. If you need help with a pet behavior problem, you may want to search for an

applied animal behaviorist in your community rather than trying to deal with it on your own.

2. J.B. Watson had a huge influence on psychology in general and child-rearing practices. In particular, he is considered "America's first 'pop' psychologist." Go to Wikipedia.org to learn more about this important early psychologist.

QUESTION #19.
You Seem So Skeptical of Other Approaches. Can You Tell Me Why?

Quick Take

Several years ago, at a meeting of the Association for Behavior Analysis in San Francisco, a speaker caught the attention of the behavioral audience when she reported on "some amazing findings" from her work with autistic youths. She had been trying a brand-new technique called "facilitated communication" with teenaged autistic clients, and in her words, she "was simply blown away" by what she had found. Why, they really weren't autistic at all but rather were normal people trapped by their inability to communicate. All they needed was a little help . . . from a *facilitator*. A facilitator who would sit next to them and guide their hands as they typed out messages on a keyboard. The audience was enthralled, but some of us were thinking, "What? This doesn't sound right. You're telling me that these young people who have never shown any acquisition of expressive language are writing poems? I'm not sure believe it." Despite this, it was a compelling story, and there were people who had been trained in behavior analysis crying when she finished reading some of the poems written by the teens with autism.

What was missing from this presentation was any actual data except for the typed poem. By the way, the poem had no spelling errors, no typos, and no grammatical errors. This was amazing considering that plenty of college students who have been educated for 25 years can't produce work as clean as the sample poem we were viewing.

"Extraordinary claims require extraordinary evidence."

If there is one thing we can learn from our friends who are skeptics, it's that, as Carl Sagan was fond of saying, "Extraordinary claims require extraordinary evidence." This was truly the time to apply this standard, but no evidence was offered, and surprisingly, none was asked for by the audience during the question-and-answer period.

Over the next few years, the momentum built surrounding facilitated communication. The technique was also used with adults and children with cerebral palsy who reportedly, through facilitated communication, could now write letters to their parents, create artwork, and write short stories. While many nonverbal individuals with mild mental retardation and cerebral palsy may have the receptive language needed to make choices about how a story should end or what color of paint should be used in a picture, what is at question is the ability of people who have never written a poem or story to suddenly produce one that includes sophisticated concepts, vocabulary, and language.

The popularity of facilitated communication grew until there were more and more dramatic instances of successful breakthroughs, autistic children and youth all over the country were taking regular classes with their facilitators in tow, and school systems were footing the bill. Many experts in autism became skeptical and began designing research using scientific methods to actually test this magical cure. Lo and behold, facilitated communication was a—drum roll please—HOAX.

> *"Lo and behold, facilitated communication was a—drum roll please—HOAX."*

It turns out that in facilitated communication, or "FC" as it is sometimes called, it was actually the facilitators who were writing the poems and the letters and doing the homework. In the end, all of this was made blatantly clear in a TV documentary produced by the Public Broadcasting Service's (PBS) Frontline. *Prisoners of Silence*,[12] produced by Jon Palfreman, showed that when an autistic student is exposed to one stimulus and the facilitator to another, what gets typed is what the facilitator saw. The documentary was dramatic and convincing, the facilitators who were the test subjects were visibly shaken, and shortly after, many left the profession for other lines of work.

Technically Speaking

Behavior analysts are by nature skeptical. We like to refer to our skepticism as critical thinking. Critical thinking can be applied to most claims about behavior that just don't sound right. Radical changes in behavior don't usually sound right. Reports of people engaging in behavior where there are no obvious consequences don't sound right. We know how behavior change comes about. It is not an easy process, and it takes a lot of training and reinforcement. Analyzing the acquisition of behavior can be time consuming, first just to understand what the controlling variables are and then to figure out how to replicate meaningful behavior change. Behavior analysts are skeptical of infomercials that promise "Five Simple Steps to Financial Freedom"; "magic pills" for dramatic weight loss; very expensive, strange diets that supposedly cure autism; or therapies that work without any scientific basis, visible means, or mechanisms for working. "Thought field therapy," for example, supposedly works by "cosmic energy from the cosmos . . . transmitted to a person through the channel of an accomplished healer."[13] Now, does that sound crazy, or what? What kind of person could possibly take such a preposterous claim seriously? Certainly not one with any critical thinking skills.

While we do not claim to have cornered the market on the treatment for autism, what behavior analysis does claim is a significant market share on evidence-based treatments that have passed muster with the leading scientific, peer-reviewed journals. Our critical thinking also applies to approaches that have been "endorsed by well-respected figures" including past presidents, football coaches, and entertainment icons. The Son-Rise Program is just such a treatment approach that behavior analysts would be quite skeptical of, primarily for its lack of an empirical basis, and potentially for its strong association with other questionable fad-like treatments such as auditory integration therapy, vitamin therapy, sensory integration, and the highly questionable gluten/casein-free diet. While vitamins and diets free of gluten may result in some health benefits, the point to remember is there is no empirical evidence that such diets cure children who are autistic.

●　●

Key Concepts:
Skepticism, critical thinking, facilitated communication (FC)

EXERCISES:

1. Describe some treatments for autism for which there are no controlled studies.
2. As a behavior analyst, when you hear about a procedure that supposedly impacts behavior, what are some questions you should ask about the procedure?
3. What is facilitated communication? What does the most current controlled research show about FC?

QUESTION #20.
Do Behavior Analysts Believe in Punishment?

Quick Take

This is a difficult and somewhat touchy subject, but it is a great question that raises lots of issues about how behavior analysts think about certain kinds of problems. First of all, in the culture, there is a lot of confusion about the terms, "punishment" and "punish." People often hear the word "punishment" and think immediately of moral retribution and parents who, in a fit of rage, send small children to bed without their supper. This is absolutely not what behavior analysts are talking about when they use the word "punishment."

Let's start with a definition of punishment. When behavior analysts speak of punishment, they are referring to a scientific term. Generally speaking, we would define a punisher as a consequence: this consequence follows a behavior and decreases the probability that the behavior will occur again in the future. This is what we call a *functional definition*. Punishment is defined by its effects; it decreases future behavior. (Note that punishment can also involve taking away something as well. This is how traffic and parking fines work.) Punishers can be as mild as giving someone a look of disapproval, putting a child in time-out for one minute, or saying "No!" to get a toddler to stop a behavior. We need to remember that, just like reinforcers, punishers are very individualized; what is punishing to one person may not be to another. You might scream at your roommate, partner, or spouse for leaving dirty dishes in the living room. If the behavior stops, your screaming was a punisher. If the roommate continues to leave dirty

> *"Punishment is defined by its effects; it decreases future behavior."*

dishes, your screaming was not a punisher. If punishment is to work effectively, it should be delivered immediately following (or possibly during) the behavior to be reduced. And it's a bad idea to start with a mild punisher and gradually work up to a more severe one, because the person will likely just adapt to the punishment, and it will be ineffective.

Technically Speaking

While some may argue that punishment should not be used because it doesn't work, the research in operant conditioning and in applied research does not support this conclusion. Punishment does work, the question is whether we should use it. That is, are there other alternatives

> *"Punishment, although it works, can have side effects that are very serious."*

that might be a better response? One reason we want to consider alternative ways of decreasing behavior is that punishment, although it works, can have side effects that are very serious. For one thing, punishment is usually delivered by a person, and the person becomes paired with this aversive event. This means they become a *conditioned aversive stimulus*. If your dad beats you with a belt for stealing, you will pair him with the beating and come to dislike or even hate your father. Even though you might think that you deserved to be punished and you should be punished for stealing, ironically, the beating may not even reduce the stealing. Also, punishment can *elicit aggression*. A child who is beaten with a belt might hit a little sister shortly thereafter. Punishment also sets the occasion for *escape and avoidance responding*. Given the earlier scenario, for example, you might start to avoid your father and try to escape altogether by running away. A high percentage of teens who run away each year report that they couldn't stand the punishment they received and were prepared to take their chances on their own in the real world.

There is an extensive literature on the use of punishers in applied behavior analysis. Everything from lemon juice to Tabasco sauce to electric shock have been used to decrease or eliminate certain behaviors. Again, the major concern here is not that punishment doesn't work but rather that it *should be a last-resort method* to change behavior. We now have much more effective ways of reducing or eliminating behavior that primarily involve the use of positive reinforcement for competing or "other" behaviors, known as DROs. So, to eliminate a preschooler's hand biting, for example, we would arrange to reinforce her for playing with toys or brushing her hair. Using reinforcement in this manner side-steps all the negative side effects of punishment.

One further reason for not using punishment is that in clinical settings such as treatment facilities for severely handicapped individuals with very dangerous self-injurious behaviors, the punisher must always be delivered by a specially trained staff member, and the concern is that that person may not be consistent in the use of the punisher. They might make a mistake and punish the wrong behavior, or they may try to use the procedure with another resident. Such unauthorized uses of punishers are unethical in the extreme. For this reason alone, behavior analysts would think seriously about recommending the use of punishment for a client.

At an early point in the history of behavior analysis, it was not uncommon for punishment to be used to decrease behaviors. We have since learned that the side effects of punishment are so great and the risk of misuse so likely that it is only recommended under extreme circumstances where all positive methods have failed. Most behavioral professionals recommend that if punishment is necessary, it should be always accompanied by a reinforcer for appropriate behavior, that staff be given extra training, and that the procedures be evaluated for effectiveness.

In March of 2020, the U.S. Food and Drug Administration banned electrical stimulation devices (ESDs) used for self-injurious or aggressive behavior. The devices are used at one facility in the country—Judge Rotenberg Educational Center (JRC), a special needs day and residential school in Canton, Massachusetts.[14]

Key Concepts:

Punishment, functional definition, side effects, escape and avoidance responding, conditioned aversive stimulus, elicited aggression, DRO (differential reinforcement of other response)

EXERCISES:

1. Think back on a time when you were punished for something. Did you repeat the behavior? Did you have any hard feelings toward the person who punished you? Did you try to avoid that person?
2. Have you had occasion to punish someone for a bad behavior? How did the punishment work? Do you now wish you would have thought of another course of action?
3. Go to BACB.com and search for the Ethics Code for Behavior Analysts and look for Code 2.15 to look for the limitations on the use of punishment.

SUMMARY

The philosophy behind behavior analysis is behaviorism. Behaviorism includes an assumption of determinism of all phenomena in the universe, including human behavior, the methodology of empiricism for data collected via observation and experimentation, the logic of rationalism, the perspective of operationalism, and the questioning of scientific skepticism. Watson excluded private events from his methodological behaviorism, but Skinner insisted that feelings, sensations, ideas, and mental life in general be included in his theory of radical behaviorism. For Skinner, *free will* meant that people "feel free" if they are not under aversive control, and he promoted the idea of designing environments based totally on positive reinforcement. Behaviorists are considered different from behavior analysts; the former are usually academics with a philosophical bent, whereas behavior analysts use behavior principles to improve the human condition. Behavior analysts rely on data for decision making and challenge any treatments that are not based on evidence. As a field and collectively, behavior analysts follow Skinner's lead and avoid the use of punishment, primarily due to the numerous side effects that almost always appear as soon as it is used.

NOTES

1. B.F. Skinner (1976). *About Behaviorism*. New York: Vintage Books.
2. D. Royse, B.A. Thyer, & D.K. Padgett (2016). *Program Evaluation: An Introduction to an Evidence-Based Approach*, 6th Edition. Boston: Cengage.
3. B.F. Skinner (1974). *About Behaviorism*. New York: Vintage Books, p. 18.
4. www.fda.gov/consumers/consumer-updates/be-aware-potentially-dangerous-products-and-therapies-claim-treat-autism
5. J.B. Watson (1913). Psychology as the behaviorist views it. *Psychological Review*, 20(2), 158–177.
6. B.F. Skinner (1957). *Verbal Behavior*. Englewood, NJ: Prentice-Hall.
7. B.F. Skinner (1953). *Science and Human Behavior*. New York: Macmillan; B.F. Skinner (1957). *Verbal Behavior*. Englewood, NJ: Prentice-Hall.
8. B.F. Skinner (1957). *Verbal Behavior*. Englewood, NJ: Prentice-Hall.
9. J.B. Watson (1913). Psychology as the behaviorist views it. *Psychological Review*, 101(2), 248–253.
10. J.B. Watson (1913). Psychology as the behaviorist views it. *Psychological Review*, 101(2), 250.
11. J.B. Watson (1913). Psychology as the behaviorist views it. *Psychological Review*, 101(2), 248.
12. J. Palfreman (Producer) (1993, October 19). *Frontline: Prisoners of Silence*. Boston, MA: WGBH Public Television.
13. J.W. Jacobson, R.M. Foxx, & J.A. Mulick (Eds) (2005). *Controversial Therapies for Developmental Disabilities*. Mahwah, NJ: Lawrence Erlbaum Associates, Publishers, pp. 265–277.

14. www.masslive.com/news/2020/03/after-fda-bans-judge-rotenberg-center-from-using-electric-shock-devices-advocates-seek-public-apology-reparations.html

REFERENCES

Jacobson, J.W., Foxx, R.M., & Mulick, J.A. (Eds) (2005). *Controversial Therapies for Developmental Disabilities*. Mahwah, NJ: Lawrence Erlbaum Associates, Publishers, pp. 265–277.

Palfreman, J. (Producer) (1993, October 19). *Frontline: Prisoners of Silence*. Boston, MA: WGBH Public Television.

Royse, D., Thyer, B.A., & Padgett, D.K. (2016). *Program Evaluation: An Introduction to an Evidence-Based Approach*, 6th Edition. Boston: Cengage.

Skinner, B.F. (1953). *Science and Human Behavior*. New York: Macmillan.

Skinner, B.F. (1957). *Verbal Behavior*. Englewood, NJ: Prentice-Hall.

Skinner, B.F. (1976). *About Behaviorism*. New York: Vintage Books.

Watson, J.B. (1913a). Psychology as the behaviorist views it. *Psychological Review*, 101(2), 248–253.

Watson, J.B. (1913b). Psychology as the behaviorist views it. *Psychological Review*, 101(2), 250.

Watson, J.B. (1913c). Psychology as the behaviorist views it. *Psychological Review*, 101(2), 248.

Watson, J.B. (1913d). Psychology as the behaviorist views it. *Psychological Review*, 20(2), 158–177.

Five

Applications of Behavior Analysis

DOI: 10.4324/9781003160915-6

QUESTION #21.
Who Provides Behavior-Analytic Services?

Quick Take

Depending on the setting, behavioral services are usually delivered by a small team of behavior analysts. In the area of autism, where approximately 75% of behavior analysts are employed, the team is made up of behavior analysts with different degrees of training, from those with a minimum of a high-school degree to those with a master's or PhD. The typical pyramid of service delivery is shown in Figure 5.1. The primary contact, the person that the family and the client see almost every day, is the Registered Behavior Technician.

> The Registered Behavior Technician® (RBT®) is a paraprofessional certification in behavior analysis. RBTs assist in delivering behavior analysis services and practice under the direction and close supervision of an RBT Supervisor and/or an RBT Requirements Coordinator, who are responsible for all work RBTs perform.[1]

This individual is the one-to-one provider who has been trained by a board certified behavior analyst and is under their direct or indirect supervision. The board certified assistant behavior analyst may also provide some direct supervision to the RBT, but not all agencies have BCaBAs on their staff. As the person who has the most contact with the client and their family, the RBT needs to have excellent social skills and must be sensitive to family needs and able to negotiate with ease. In addition to their behavior training skills, behavior techs need to follow the guidance of their RBT Ethics Code and be able to apply the code on the spot as situations arise. They should be friendly with clients but cannot become friends with them. Additionally, they should be aware of and respect the client's cultural practices but cannot accept food, drink, or gifts over $10 from them.

This pyramid applies if the services are being delivered in the home, a school, or a clinic. The RBT does almost all of the hands-on work with the

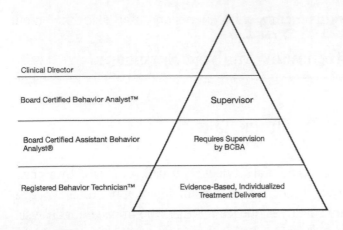

Clinical Director

Board Certified Behavior Analyst™

Supervisor

Board Certified Assistant Behavior Analyst®

Requires Supervision by BCBA

Registered Behavior Technician™

Evidence-Based, Individualized Treatment Delivered

FIGURE 5.1 The pyramid of behavior analysis service delivery for autism treatment.

client and might be in the home 3–4 days a week for 3–5 hours at a time, depending on what is needed. RBTs require at least 5% of their hours to be supervised by the BCaBA® or the BCBA®. This supervision should be by direct observation and involve suggestions for improving behavior-analytic skills as well as positive comments on what the RBT is doing well.

One other aspect of "who provides behavior-analytic services?" should be noted. Behavior analysts are a wonderfully diverse group of professionals. They are women and men of different ages. They come from a variety of different ethnic backgrounds and they represent a number of races. There are individuals who have gender identities and marital/relationship statuses that vary from one behavior analyst to the next. Behavior analysts practice different religions or they have different beliefs related to religion, and they come from a variety of national origins. The richness in the diversity of behavior analysts and all other people makes us all better and should be celebrated.

Technically Speaking

The RBT, often referred to as a *behavior tech* or just *tech*, is a paraprofessional whose scope of work is defined by the *RBT Task List* (2nd ed.) issued by the Behavior Analyst Certification Board. These 37 tasks are divided into six categories: measurement, assessment, skill acquisition, behavior reduction, documentation and reporting, and professional conduct and scope of practice. The tech is the frontline person who is trained to conduct skills training with clients and may also implement behavior-change programs and take data.

The *Task List* (5th ed.) for BCaBAs, which is for those with a BA/BS degree, includes a whopping 91 tasks in nine categories and includes determining the need for behavioral services, experimental design, interpreting data from graphs, assessing behavior, and using contingency contracting. The BCaBA implements more complicated behavior plans, such as the matching law, errorless learning, precision teaching, and direct instruction.

Finally, the *BCBA Task List* (5th ed.), which is for those with a master's or PhD, includes nine categories and 95 items, including most of the earlier-mentioned items plus philosophical underpinnings, concepts and principles, data display and interpretation of data, selecting and implementing interventions, personnel supervision, and ethics. The BCBA will generally be the person who conducts the client assessment of behavior, designs data collection procedures that are used by RBTs, monitors and supervises the behavior tech, and evaluates that data to determine if the outcomes are successful. They will also implement some of the more complex behavior-change procedures such as extinction, token economies, and group contingencies, among others.

● ●

Key Concepts:
Registered Behavior Technician, Board Certified Assistant Behavior Analyst, Board Certified Behavior Analyst, Pyramid of Services, Task List

EXERCISES:

1. If you think you might be interested in working as an RBT, go to BACB.com and look for the task list for RBTs. Read through the items there to decide if this sort of work appeals to you.
2. To learn more about the BCaBA job, again, go to BACB.com and look at the task list for this job position to determine if this is something you think you might like to do.

QUESTION #22.
Can I Use Behavioral Procedures to Improve My Health or Enhance My Athletic Ability?

Quick Take

"You can apply the basic principles yourself to help you lose weight, increase your exercise, stop smoking, study more effectively, improve your public speaking, or even enhance your inter-personal skills."

Absolutely! The way that behavior analysts think about improving one's own behavior is that you can use behavioral procedures to improve almost any human performance. Many of the basic principles of behavior are easy to use, and you do not need to be a behavior analyst to employ them. You can apply the basic principles yourself to help you lose weight, increase your exercise, stop smoking, study more effectively, improve your public speaking, or even enhance your inter-personal skills. This area of application is generally referred to as "self-management," which is far more effective than making a New Year's Resolution. Self-management requires you to set realistic goals, measure your performance regularly, and establish reinforcers to maintain the hard job of changing your own behavior.

Let's say another new year is approaching, and this time you want to make a resolution to get healthy and actually keep fit. This time you're determined to go to the gym, lose that extra 25 pounds, and achieve scores on your annual physical exam that will make your doctor smile. You've identified the target behaviors: 1) go to the gym at least three times a week for a full workout and 2) lose one-half pound per week

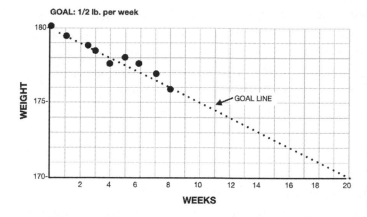

FIGURE 5.2
A sample behavior
analysis weight-loss
chart.

in the next 20 weeks. Your next step is to find a reinforcer for going to the gym and set up a contingency system to maintain that behavior. You might establish the following rule, for example: "If I go to the gym, I can watch my favorite TV show when I get home from class." For losing weight, you will first need to establish a reasonable short-term goal such as losing a pound every other week. For this, you will prob-ably need to start weighing three times per week and graphing your results, as shown in Fig. 5.2. Here, again, you will need to establish a reward/reinforcer for meeting your goal. If you are a movie buff, you might have a reward such as going to a movie on Saturday night if you have met your goal for the past two

"For the behavior analyst, 'Behavior change begins at home' is a commonly accepted value."

weeks. Of course, you will need to start watching your calories and carb intake as well, since exercise alone is usually not enough to lose weight.

Technically Speaking

For the behavior analyst, "Behavior change begins at home" is a com-monly accepted value. We take seriously the notion that professionals in this field should "walk the walk," not just "talk the talk." By analyzing their own behavior, specialists in this new technology can not only model for others how behavior change can be done, but they can also gain some sense of how difficult it can be to change behavior. As a behavior analyst, changing one's own problem behaviors will result in a greater understanding of what clients are experiencing. There are a significant number of studies that have been published to establish concrete steps you can take.[2] These include defining the target behavior, doing a functional assessment, setting a goal, choosing and implementing the appropriate self-management strategy, and evaluating the change.

If you have set goals in the past and were unsuccessful in meeting them, you should do an informal analysis to determine why you failed. Is it the time of day you were trying to exercise? If you're not a morning person, setting a goal of going to the gym at 5:00 a.m. may not be a good idea. If you have three children who need to be transported to every activity under the sun after work, your taxi duties may interfere with your gym time, so you will need to look carefully at your weekly calendar to find a time that is open. Another consideration is distance. Ask yourself if the gym is too far away and if you need to take up walking in your neighborhood instead or invest in your own modest home gym. You get the idea. In troubleshooting your previous exercise failures, you next need to think about the consequences. Did you fail to build in a strong reinforcer for exercising or for actual weight loss? Every time you lose 5 pounds, you could buy yourself a new clothing item, or you could involve your spouse, partner, or a friend as a support team and go out to a special dinner (within your diet, of course). Using a graph with a criterion line, as shown previously, will give you a visual picture of how you're doing.

B.F. Skinner himself was a great model of self-management.[3] Since he was so committed to writing, Skinner modified his office space to increase his productivity. To decrease fidgeting, he modified the seat cushion on his chair, and he installed timers and invented a "thinking aid"[4] to improve his output. Long before this equipment was common at every gym, to get himself to engage in the unpleasant task of riding his exercise bike, Skinner installed a holder to position reading materials so he could read while improving his cardiovascular fitness. Skinner was pleased that he had developed a theory of behavior that had practical implications, "It is not enough to live your life . . . you also need to analyze it and make changes in it frequently and regularly."[5] B.F. Skinner lived to be 90 and was active professionally to the very end.

As a behavior analyst, you've got the skills to change your own behavior or enhance your own performance. All you need to do is decide you are ready to put an organized plan in place that involves the consistent application of behavioral principles.

• •

Key Concepts:
Self-management, human performance, short-term goals

EXERCISES:

1. Select a personal behavior that you would like to improve. Next, develop an easy way to count the behavior that you've selected.
2. Now, try to *think like a behavior analyst* and see if you can figure out what sets the occasion, that is, what the *trigger* is for the behavior. What changes do you need to make to increase the likelihood of the behavior occurring? Try to implement a change in your behavior to see if you can make an improvement.
3. Here are two articles to review if you are interested in the research on using behavioral procedures to improve your performance:

Quinn, M.J., Miltenberger, R.G., & Fogel, V.A. (2015). Using TAGteach to improve the proficiency of dance moves. *Journal of Applied Behavior Analysis*, 48, 11–24.

Wack, S.R., Crosland, K.A., & Miltenberger, R.G. (2014). Using goal setting and feedback to increase weekly running distance. *Journal of Applied Behavior Analysis*, 47, 181–185.

QUESTION #23.

Can You Use Behavior Analysis in "Real Life"?
My Roommate (Spouse, Partner, Boyfriend, Child,
etc.) Is Driving Me Crazy; Can Any of This Help Me
Get Along With Them?

Quick Take

> *"Blaming people just doesn't work; it does not produce any change in behavior."*

Behavioral procedures are ideally suited for changing the behavior of your roommate, friends, in-laws, spouses, partners or other significant others. Frank was a student in one of first author Jon Bailey's psychology classes. Frank frequently complained in class that his roommate never took out the trash, even though that was one of several chores he had agreed to take on. "He will just walk right by the trash can and head out the door, totally oblivious." After letting him vent for several minutes, Bailey said, "Okay, let me see if I have this right. You're saying that your roommate should want to take out the trash." Frank nodded, "Yep, I shouldn't have to remind him; it's his responsibility. He agreed to do it." Bailey replied, "A lot of people feel that way about the behavior of others. They think, 'My partner should *want* to quit smoking,' 'My husband should *want* to lose weight,' but that kind of thinking is nonproductive. The only place you can go with this kind of thinking is to Blamesville. Blaming people just doesn't work; it does not produce any change in behavior. So, let's move on. How about putting your behavior analyst hat on? Let's look at this problem behaviorally."

Bailey then proceeded to suggest that the trash can did not yet have stimulus control over the roommate's behavior. He made the following suggestion, "How about this: take the trash can and put it directly in front of the front door, so that he would have to stumble over it to get out. He'll see it and take out the trash. Now what do you do?" Frank looked puzzled. "Well, I don't know. Reinforce him?" "Yes, exactly, and then what?" Frank tentatively replied, "wait until the next day and see what happens?" "Well, you could do that, but that's not the best plan," said Bailey. He then proceeded to remind Frank about stimulus fading—gradually reducing a stimulus that, through manipulation has gained some control and continuing this until the environment is back to normal. "So, the next day you want me to pull the trash can back just a little bit, is that right?"

"Right, about an inch, and then the next day, add another inch—this is going to take a few days; you'll have to be patient." A week later, Bailey saw Frank and his roommate at a fundraiser. "Hi, Dr. B. Good to see you here. This is my roommate . . ." Before he had a chance to introduce us, the roommate stuck out his hand and said, "Hi, I'm Ben, you know . . . the 'trash can guy.' I understand that little experiment was your idea. That was funny, actually. I'm not exactly sure what kind of psychology you teach, but it sure worked, and it was pretty much pain-less. Basically, Frank got me to break a bad habit without insulting me or ticking me off."

Students and families experience scenarios just like this one all the time. Roommates won't do the dishes; girlfriends, boyfriends, part-ners, spouses, or children won't pick up their clothes. Even behavior analysis graduate students have been so conditioned to complain and get so much pleasure out of being outraged that they completely forget to analyze the behavior. And in most cases, a simple rearrangement of the environment does the trick—enhancing some stimulus or adding a prompt; shaping on small behaviors using immediate, personal reinforc-ers; and then gradually fading out the extra cues and add-on reinforcers. Changing someone's behavior can be a delicate matter if people think you are trying to manipulate them. Manipulation is a nasty term that suggests you are trying to get something out of a person for your bene-fit. We would never suggest this practice, and we push hard for the idea that human relations would be much improved if everyone understood the basic principles of behavior. There is an extremely good chance that if you have to deal with uncomfortable situations on a regular basis, with a friend, acquaintance, relative, or coworker, you are a part of the problem. You are probably accidentally reinforcing the behavior that is annoying, grating, irritating, or rude.

Technically Speaking

It is not manipulation to use your reinforcers wisely to produce a behavior that is comfortable for all parties. A recent letter to one of the syndicated self-help columns in the local paper described a situation where a neighbor would stop over every morning, invite herself in, and suggest, "Why don't we have some coffee and chat?" The columnist advised the letter writer, Samantha, who was known as "Sam," to talk to the neighbor and explain that she is a busy person and doesn't have time for coffee-klatching. Behavior analysts object to simplistic recommendations such as this because they do not really deal with the "cause" of the problem. If you *think like a behavior analyst* about this, you will realize that the neighbor just finds Sam's company and conversation reinforcing (and has time on her hands). The best treatment for the behavior is for Sam to first have a conversation where she explains that she works at home and has deadlines to meet every week, for example. Then Sam could suggest that they both find a day and time every couple of weeks where she will make herself available and would be happy to chat for 30-minutes or so. This is called bringing a behavior under stimulus control. If the neighbor comes calling on the wrong day or time, Sam does not have to apologize or feel guilty. She simply does not reinforce the behavior (called extinction).

> *"Behavior analysis can help people improve their interpersonal relationships."*

Behavior analysis can help people improve their interpersonal relationships. With a greater knowledge of human behavior, you can change things for the better.

Key Concepts:
Analyzing behavior, stimulus fading, extinction

EXERCISES:

1. If you have a friend or acquaintance who has an annoying behavior, play close attention to the dynamics of your interaction with this friend. Try to determine what the controlling variables (cues, triggers, stimuli) might be for the behavior to occur. Pay attention to possible reinforcers and take a few days' data on the frequency of the behavior.
2. If it turns out that you are reinforcing the behavior, consider making a change. Choose an alternative, replacement behavior that you find acceptable and begin to reinforce that behavior instead.
3. Keep track of the behavior by continuing your frequency count.
4. After two weeks, evaluate your personal intervention plan and see if it worked for you.

QUESTION #24.

I've Been Told That Behavior Analysis Is the "Gold Standard" for Treatment of Children With Autism. Why Is That?

Behavior analysis has been used with children with autism spectrum disorder (a neurodevelopmental disorder) since the mid-1960s.[6] However, it has only caught on with parents since the publication of Catherine Maurice's best-seller *Let Me Hear Your Voice: A Family's Triumph Over Autism*.[7] This very readable, first-person account describes how Maurice discovered ABA and found a behavior analyst to treat her two children using proven behavior-analytic methods. Both children improved so dramatically that once the treatment was completed, they were able to go to school with no need for any extra support.

> *"Thirty years of research demonstrated the efficacy of applied behavioral methods in reducing inappropriate behavior and in increasing communication, learning, and appropriate social behavior."*
> —The Surgeon General

The term *gold standard* refers to some system that is the best, most reliable, or most prestigious[8] method available. Currently, applied behavior analysis is considered the gold standard among dozens of other types of treatment, primarily because it has such a strong applied research base, going back nearly six decades. Applied behavior analysis was recognized by the US Surgeon General who declared: "Thirty years of research demonstrated the efficacy of applied behavioral methods in reducing inappropriate behavior and in increasing communication, learning, and appropriate social behavior."[9] The American Psychological Association, the National Institute of Mental Health, the Autism Society of America, the National Institute of Child Health and Human Development, and many other state and federal agencies[10] have endorsed ABA as an evidence-based, best-practice treatment. Published, peer-reviewed research has clearly shown that behaviors associated with autism such as

> *"Two unique features stand out with ABA: 1) The therapy is tailored to the needs of each individual child, and 2) data are taken every day on every behavior to determine if the procedures are working."*

lack of social skills, severe language deficits, an obsession with self-stimulation, and sometimes dangerous self-injurious behaviors can be effectively treated, often with amazing outcomes when intensive, long-term therapy is implemented.[11] ABA is so well known as an effective treatment that it is usually the first treatment that is recommended by physicians and pediatricians for ASD children. It is considered a comprehensive treatment that is delivered intensively from 25–40 hours per week depending on the needs of the child.

Two unique features stand out with ABA: 1) The therapy is tailored to the needs of each individual child, and 2) data are taken every day on every behavior to determine if the procedures are working. If they are not working, the procedures can be modified, again based on best-practice research, and a different method employed. ABA treatments can be employed in the home or clinic setting as well as special classrooms in elementary schools. The early work in this area was carried out with young children, and it is currently in use with adolescents and adults[12] as well. ABA treatment is so widely respected and accepted that all Medicaid plans that include physician-prescribed, medically necessary treatment are required to include this form of therapy.

● ●

Key Concepts:
Proven behavior-analytic methods, gold standard, surgeon general endorsement, peer-reviewed research

EXERCISES:

1. Go to the internet and search for *ABA gold standard autism* and look at the many sites that appear. Choose any that look interesting and pay attention to how they describe behavior analysis treatment.
2. If you are interested in autism treatment, look for Catherine Maurice's book on Amazon. Every behavior analyst should read this book.

QUESTION #25.
Can Parents or Foster Parents of a Child Be a Client?

By Yamilex Molina

Quick Take

Biological parents, adoptive parents, foster parents, and even grandparents can be clients! Behavior analysts working in the child welfare system have one main goal, and that is to provide children with stability and decrease the chances that the child's placement will be disrupted due to challenging behaviors. It is no secret that being separated from your parents and sibling(s) and removed from the place you have known as "home" can be traumatic, frustrating, confusing, and terrifying. The foster or adoptive parents welcoming these children and teenagers into their homes might not be prepared

> *"Behavior analysts train foster and adoptive parents on how to identify the function(s) of the problem behavior(s), the skills necessary to manage these behaviors, and how to teach children more appropriate replacement behaviors."*

to manage the behaviors that come with readjustment. Children who are constantly being moved from home to home due to placement disruptions have a hard time succeeding and finding happiness. Thus, behavior analysts train foster and adoptive parents on how to identify the function(s) of the problem behavior(s), in the skills necessary to manage these behaviors, and on how to teach children more appropriate replacement behaviors. Behavior analysts also work with biological parents during visitations and reunifications to assist with the transition and ensure the safety of the children.

Technically Speaking

Challenging behaviors can be seen before or after visitations because it may be difficult for children to understand why they are not going home with their biological parents and/or siblings after spending time with them for an hour. In this common situation, behavior analysts work with both the biological parents and foster parents to develop *antecedent manipulations* such as providing the child with a timer, warnings, and even a visual schedule. Biological and foster parents are taught how to become *conditioned reinforcers* and use *reinforcement* to modify their children's behavior rather than using punishment and *aversive stimuli*. They are also trained to use *differential reinforcement* to manage disruptive behavior and redirection for more serious and dangerous behaviors.

A child who has been neglected can engage in many inappropriate attention-seeking behaviors or *escape-maintained* behaviors when they are presented with demands. Transitions, bedtime, hygiene, and mealtimes are common areas of challenging behaviors for children in the child welfare system. Parents need to teach their children or those they are fostering appropriate alternative behaviors using behavioral interventions such as functional communication training, positive reinforcement, *behavior chain interruption*, and *shaping*. Behavior analysts train foster and adoptive parents on how to use these behavioral principles using another behavioral principle, behavioral skills training.

A parent fostering a child who comes from an environment with no rules or expectations could benefit from *contingency contracting*; a parent fostering a child who refuses to brush his teeth, eat her vegetables, or take a shower could use the *Premack Principle*, a token economy, or *demand fading*. And a parent fostering a child who engages in self-injurious behaviors after visitations with his siblings can use response interruption/redirection.

An adoptive parent of a 4-year-old with limited language who tantrums for hours when access is denied could use *functional communication training, differential reinforcement,* and *extinction* to teach an alternative behavior. An adoptive parent of a teenager who engages in property destruction or elopement can implement *antecedent manipulations* to decrease the chances of the behavior occurring and learn to identify precursors to intervene and de-escalate the situation. An adoptive parent can use *forward or backwards chaining* to teach daily living skills to their child.

A biological parent whose toddler is not complying with requests could use *stimulus fading*, a biological parent recently reunified with his four children could use an *interdependent contingency* such as the Good Behavior Game to address challenging behaviors, and a biological parent whose son just started overnight visits and could use a *response cost* program on Wi-Fi time to increase compliance.

Key Concepts:
Child welfare system, foster parents, challenging behaviors, escape-maintained behavior, behavior chain interruption, contingency contracting, forward chaining, backward chaining, response cost

EXERCISES:

1. Type "antecedent manipulations ABA" into your search engine to find further information on this very useful and user-friendly method of changing behavior.
2. Type "Premack Principle ABA" into your search engine to find further information on another very useful and user-friendly method of changing behavior.
3. Can you think of ways of using these methods to change your own behavior?

QUESTION #26.
What Do Behavior Analysts Think About Changing Behavior in an Organization or Business Setting?

Quick Take

Behavior analysts are often asked this question, and the standard reply when it comes to changing behavior is, "Changing behavior in an organization or business is very much like changing the behavior of a person. We can analyze the behaviors that go on in a business and find ways of improving them. In businesses and organizations, it is just a matter of scaling up the interventions." The application of behavior analysis in organization and business settings is referred to as performance management.[13] This area has been around since the early 1970s and is currently a vigorous and active area of consulting practice and applied research. The basic principles of behavior that work in homes, schools, and rehabilitation facilities are also effective in for-profit and non-profit organizations as well as businesses and industry. The additional benefit in business and industry is that changes in behavior can have an economic payoff in terms of work efficiency, improving safety, saving money, and improving the bottom line.

Applied research has been conducted in a wide variety of settings, from small, family-owned businesses to non-profits to Fortune 500 corporate giants. The range of problems that have been tackled include improving warehouse dock sorting and loading procedures, behavior-based safety to reduce accidents and injuries, to improving leadership in the boardroom. In our increasingly service-oriented economy, improving customer service is essential for restaurants, hotels, and retail chains to remain competitive, and here there has evolved a very clear strategy for managers to employ.

Rather than assuming that the solution to every performance problem is to provide more training, a behavior analyst will ask, "I wonder why the service is so poor here? I know they've all been through training, but they still don't reliably attend to customer needs, they don't offer to answer questions, and they don't do any follow up." As they deal with restaurants and businesses in their communities, behavior analysts will always be thinking of ways that performance can be improved in these settings.

"A behavior analyst consulting with a business will start by asking diagnostic questions."

Technically Speaking

Thinking like a behavior analyst yields questions about whether the performance that is desired has been prompted, whether the supervisor gives any feedback or praise when the behavior does occur, and whether there is some competing behavior actually being reinforced (e.g., talking on the phone when the sales associate should be waiting on customers). A behavior analyst consulting with a business will start by asking diagnostic questions and then determine which is most appropriate depending on the answers and baseline data. Working directly with management, a performance improvement plan (PIP) will be drawn up that is custom designed for the setting. Then, the PIP will be implemented over days or weeks and evaluated to determine if it is effective in achieving pre-established goals and objectives. In business, industry, and organizations, it is important to focus on both the performance of the employees and the results of their behavior. Other approaches to improving business practice often stress only the "results" and are likely to fail since they don't treat the underlying behavior that produces the results.

There are some behavior analysts who consult with Fortune 500 companies on industrial safety, instructional design, and training in giving and receiving peer feedback as well as larger projects such as organizational change and transformation of organizational culture.

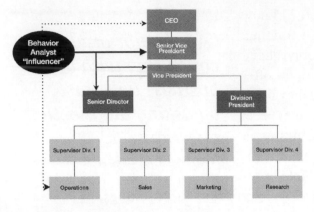

FIGURE 5.3   Behavior analyst consultant "influencer" in an organization.

This might include those with a BA/BS with a background in business who are trained in ABA and are embedded within the company full time for up to a year. Behavior analysts most often will consult a few days per month with these large corporations, where they interact and "influence" middle management, as shown in Figure 5.3. This sort of consultation is usually done on six-month to one-year contracts, with the behavior analysis consultant traveling to other companies the other days. Many behavior analysts are flying around the country 40+ weeks per year, living out of a suitcase.

A good example of improving safety behaviors using performance management in a food processing plant is shown in Figure 5.4.

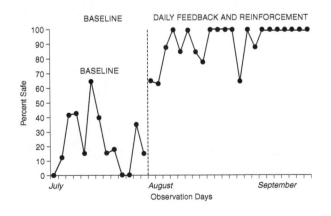

FIGURE 5.4   Improving safety behaviors in a food processing plant.

Key Concepts:
Performance management, performance improvement plan, diagnostic questions, feedback

EXERCISES:

1. Find a manager in a business in your town and ask if you may conduct an interview regarding employee performance.
2. Ask questions about any employee performance problems that seem to affect the bottom line; that is, they cut into profits, increase costs, are not optimal for employees, and so on.
3. Go to your local library and look for the *Journal of Organizational Behavior Management* (JOBM) and look for any articles that address problems that resemble those you learned about in your interview.
4. Prepare a mock performance improvement plan based on your reading of JOBM and the text by Daniels and Bailey.

QUESTION #27.

What About Other Areas of Application Such as the Community? Does Behavior Analysis Work There, Too?

Quick Take

"There are forward-thinking behavior analysts who are looking at the behavioral aspects of climate change and how citizens around the world can do their part to conserve natural resources and protect our natural environment."

Behavior analysts live and work in communities across America and around the world, and they observe problems in their community that can be analyzed using the same basic principles of behavior described in Chapter 1. Their way of thinking in this case is just on a larger scale and with more participants in anticipation of a greater impact. Early in the development of *behavioral community psychology*,[14] behavior analysts worked on consulting with community boards, setting up community recycling systems, increasing access to health services, decreasing electricity consumption by encouraging homeowners to lower their thermostats, and encouraging commuters to form carpools to save on gas. More recently, behavior analysts have taken on problems such as improving pedestrian safety at crosswalks and encouraging drivers to buckle up and maintain safe speeds in school zones. Additional work is ongoing in teaching children to avoid touching firearms if they find them in the home and training them how to respond should there be an abduction attempt in their neighborhood. Finally, there are forward-thinking behavior analysts who are looking at the behavioral aspects of climate change and how citizens around the world can do their part to conserve natural resources and protect our natural environment; sustainability is a goal that can be reached only if there are widespread changes in human behavior, and it will take behavior analysts to figure out how to make this happen.

Each of these applications addresses problems faced on a large scale by communities everywhere. The benefits that result from the use of behavioral technology to solve community problems includes improving and protecting the environment in a sustainable way for future generations.

Technically Speaking

Another area in which behavior analysis has played an important role is in the area of animal welfare and training (behavior.org/help-centers/animal-behavior/). There are nearly 90 million pet dogs and 95 million pet cats in the United States. Each year, in animals shelters across the country, millions of animals are euthanized, many because of behavior problems that are easily treatable. Excessive barking, jumping on company, snapping at children, and urinating on the new white carpet are behaviors that earn many animals a one-way ticket to an over-crowded animal shelter that will ultimately have no choice but to euthanize the animal.

Behavior analysts who have *species-specific training and expe-rience* are making a difference by making animal training technologies and behavioral assistance available in their communities. Dog owners can attend classes at dog clubs, go to seminars, or attend class at a local pet superstore.

"Dolphins can be trained to swim into a net to receive medical assessments and care, and in most settings that have captive animals, behaviorally based enrichment programs are now in place."

Also, in the animal world, behavior analysts are involved in improving the lives of animals in settings from A to Z, aquaria to zoos. Elephants are trained to raise their massive feet to receive routine foot care that can save their lives. Dolphins can be trained to swim into a net to receive medical assessments and care, and in most settings that have captive animals, behaviorally based enrichment programs are now in place.

From infants to geriatrics, work behaviors, employees, at home, in the community, every kind of disability, animal training, pets, non-pet animals, specialized skills such as sports and flying jet planes, health and exercise, getting along with others, improving relationships . . . if it involves behavior, behavior analysts can help.

• •

Key Concepts:
Behavioral community psychology, safety, conservation, sustainability, animal training and welfare

EXERCISES:

1. Describe a community problem in your community (e.g., litter at the playground). Assuming city officials provided the needed resources, describe a behavior plan to fix this.
2. You've either grown up with pets or seen the pets or neighbors or relatives. What are some of the pet behavior problems you've seen or know about? Describe one animal behavior problem and give a description of a behavior plan to address the problem.
3. Take a look at the Animal Behavior section of the Cambridge Center for Behavioral Studies. Briefly list several applications of behavior analysis with animals (https://behavior.org/help-centers/animal-behavior/).

QUESTION #28.

I Took My Dog to Obedience School, but He Still Jumps on People When They Come in the House. Does This Mean That Behavior Shaping Doesn't Work With Pets?

From where we sit as behavior analysts, we have to say that *behavior is behavior*, regardless of the organism: canine or coach, feline or florist. It doesn't matter from our perspective; the principles always apply.

One thing we know for sure is that animal behavior has been thoroughly explored by professionals in many areas. For decades, animal behavior has been the subject of study from many different perspectives, including experimental psychology, ethology, veterinary medicine, animal trainers, police and military K-9 units, and behavior analysts.[15]

"From where we sit as behavior analysts, we have to say right off the bat that behavior is behavior, regardless of the organism."

It is amazing to us how so many people trained in behavior analysis have such little knowledge when it comes to training or managing the behavior of their own pets. Related to the dog question previously, one of the first things every responsible dog owner should do after finding a veterinarian is locate a dog training class. This even pertains to behavior analysts, who may think they know all they need to know about training a dog. Dogs are a different species than children with autism, and you will need some species-specific education and training. When your dog is a puppy, you should begin training him in the basics of sit, stay, down, come, and walking on a leash. In a six-to-eight-week class that meets once per week, each week, you will learn how to train a new behavior and will be given homework exercises. The purpose of the homework is not only to reinforce the new behaviors but also to *train for generaliza-tion* to your home setting and neighborhood.

This generalization from your dog's obedience class in a local recreational center or gym probably will not be automatic. You should expect that you will have to practice the skills you learned in dog training classes over and over at home until your pup can sit, stay, down, come, and walk on a leash just as nicely at home as he does with your instructor present. You should not expect that because your dog can sit at school, he will generalize this to a *down* at home—it doesn't work that way unless you *train for generalization*. This means prompting and reinforcing the behavior in each setting that you frequent during a given week.

In the situation described in the previous question, the problem was not that "Behavior shaping doesn't work," the problem was that the owner did not engage in generalization training to other settings. You need to practice what you learned in the obedience training class at home in your living room, in your yard, and at the local pet supply store. If your dog jumps on people who come in the house, teach an alternative behavior such as *sit-stay* or *down-stay* ahead of time and practice it several times per day until this behavior is solid and reliable. The release command from a down stay is usually, "Free dog."

The routine, then, is that when you see the FedEx worker or your mother-in-law coming down the driveway, you should position Duke about ten feet from the door and say, "Down," then "Stay," and provide a treat. When the doorbell rings, repeat the command "Stay" and provide another treat. Take the package from the delivery person, say, "Thank you," close the door, turn to Duke and say, "Free dog," and then give lavish praise and a treat.

For not coming when called, if your dog gets loose, first, invest in a better fence and teach family members to always close the door and gate when they are coming and going. Remember, a part of managing behavior is analyzing the environment. Then, start with calling your dog from short distances and provide a tasty treat when your dog comes to you. Next, lengthen the distances from 5 feet to 10, then 20. You may want to do this training on a "long line" so you can give a gentle tug on the line to prompt the behavior.

Key Concepts:
Generalization, train for generalization

EXERCISES:

1. In everyday life, the failure for skills to generalize happens frequently with motor skills. People often have a hard time adjusting to novel golf courses, tennis courts, and computer equipment or from their home piano to the one at the piano teacher's house. ("I swear, I practiced two hours every day!") Think about something you might have learned or been taught in the past. Were there any problems with the generalization of your newly acquired skills?
2. If you teach a client with developmental disabilities how to do a specific leisure skill at a day training program, what should you do to ensure the client uses the skill at home?

For details on basic dog training, see:

Burch, M.R. (2013). *AKC STAR Puppy: A Positive Behavioral Approach to Puppy Training*. Dogwise Publishing. Wenatchee, Washington.

Burch, M.R. (2021). *Canine Good Citizen: Ten Essential Skills Every Well-Mannered Dog Should Know*. Fox Chapel Publishing. Mount Joy, Pennsylvania.

Burch, M.R., & Bailey, J.S. (1999). *How Dogs Learn*. Howell Book House, Macmillan Company. New York, New York.

QUESTION #29.

It Seems That Many Behavior Analysts Are Saying They Want to Start Working With Animals. Is Animal Behavior Consulting Something Behavior Analysts Could Do?

Many people, including behavior analysts, have experience as pet owners. They love dogs or cats, have always been fascinated by parrots or zoo animals, or have a history of riding horses. Once they have discovered the powerful technology of behavior analysis, they realize that the basic principles of behavior can be used to change any behavior—including that of animals. However, *animal behavior consulting* requires special training and expertise regarding species-specific behavior. An organizational behavior management (OBM) consulting behavior analyst should not start consulting in a preschool classroom for children with autism without training on autism, and the same goes for making the switch from human to animal consulting.

"A behavioral solution for a dog-related problem might not be appropriate for a horse, and what one knows about people and parrots certainly does not always apply to cats."

For behavior analysts who want to move into the area of animal behavior consulting, it is critical that the behavior analyst have experience, knowledge, and training related to the specific species. A behavioral solution for a dog-related problem might not be appropriate for a horse, and what one knows about people and parrots certainly does not always apply to cats.

The importance of knowing and having experience with a particular species before providing behavioral consultation is illustrated by the following example.

> A behavior analyst who had worked only with children volunteered to help a first-time cat owner and their new adopted companion. The cat would cry and wander around the house, keeping the owner awake at night. The cat owner would hold out until about 3:00 a.m., then get up and feed the cat. The cat would stop crying, and all was well until the next night, when the routine was repeated. The behavior analyst (who had zero experience with cats) listened to this and concluded the owner was reinforcing crying at night by giving the cat food. She instructed the owner to use extinction, and the cat then developed other behavior problems. Long story short, the behavior analyst lacked feline knowledge, and as a result, missed extremely important information about the eating habits of cats. The cat owner was feeding the cat once a day in the early morning. Cats have higher metabolisms than dogs and need to eat more frequently. Cats are often fed twice a day, with dry food left for grazing in between. Young kittens eat as often as six times a day. The cat in this story was crying because it was hungry, not because, as the no-cat-experience behavior analyst said, the behavior had been "shaped up." To put this behavior on extinction was inappropriate and unethical. Once the cat had been put on an appropriate feeding schedule, the problems disappeared.

Just as there are board certified behavior analysts who work with humans, there are certifications for animal behavior consultants.

- Veterinarians with a specialty in animal behaviors are certified through the American Veterinary Society of Animal Behavior (AVSAB). These veterinarians and research professionals treat animal behavior problems. For more information, see: https://avsab.org
- Applied animal behaviorists are certified through the Animal Behavior Society as certified applied animal behaviorists (CAABs). These animal behaviorists are scientists, researchers, educators, or

other animal professionals with an advanced background in the principles of animal behavior. For more information, see: www. animalbehaviorsociety.org/web/applied-behavior.php

- The International Association of Animal Behavior Consultants (IAABC) certifies animal behavior consultants who not only have theoretical training but in-depth experience with a particular species also. Applicants must pass exams, demonstrate that they have applied experience, and demonstrate core competencies. For more information, see: https://m.iaabc.org

• •

Key Concepts:
Animal behavior consulting, applied animal behaviorists, core competencies

EXERCISES:

1. If you have a cat or dog, the next time you are at your veterinarian's office, ask about applied animal behaviorists.
2. If you have an interest in working with animals using behavior analysis, look up the Animal Behavior Society (animalbehaviorsociety.org) and read what is required to become an applied animal behaviorist.

SUMMARY

In this chapter, we present a sample of the range of applications of behavior analysis beginning with Registered Behavior Technicians. RBTs are on the front line of delivery of behavioral treatment of children with a diagnosis of autism spectrum disorder, developmentally delayed (DD) individuals, and a whole host of other diagnostic categories in the human services. These *techs*, as they are often called, are sometimes supervised by a BCaBA and more often by a BCBA, with a clinical director at the top of the chain of command. All of these professionals come under a very specific task list that outlines their scope of practice. Behavioral procedures are not only used to improve the lives of people who have disabilities. They can also be used by an individual to improve their own health or enhance their athletic ability. There are many other personal applications of behavior analysis, including shaping on the behavior of close acquaintances to improve social relationships. ABA is considered the gold standard for treatment in autism because of the 50+ years of applied research showing its effectiveness in increasing language and social skills and reducing aberrant behaviors. Behavior analysis is also used to train parents and foster parents to cope with child behavior problems and to inform executives on how to improve safety practices and work productivity in their companies. In addition, behavior analysis has been shown to provide an effective solution in communities to encourage homeowners to conserve energy and drivers to buckle up and drive safely. In more recent years, a whole field of applications with dog training has exploded in including a positive reinforcement approach that is increasingly popular with dog owners and professional animal trainers alike.

NOTES

1. For more information go to: www.bacb.com/wp content/uploads/2020/05/RBTHandbook_200917.pdf
2. R.G. Miltenberger (2019). *Behavior Modification: Principles and Procedures*. Belmont, CA: Wadsworth/Thompson Learning.
3. R. Epstein (1997). Skinner as self-manager. *Journal of Applied Behavior Analysis*, 30, 545–568.
4. B.F. Skinner (1987). A thinking aid. *Journal of Applied Behavior Analysis*, 20, 379–380.
5. R. Epstein (1997). Skinner as self-manager. *Journal of Applied Behavior Analysis*, 30, 545–568.
6. M. Wolf, T. Risley, & H. Mees (1964). Application of operant conditioning procedures to the behavior problems of an autistic child. *Behavior Research and Therapy*, 1, 305–312.

7. (Maurice, 1993).
8. Oxford Languages via Google for "What does gold standard mean?"
9. United States Surgeon General. (1999). *Mental Health: A Report of the Surgeon General*. Washington, DC: Author.
10. The American Association on Intellectual and Developmental Disabilities, American Academy of Child and Adolescent Psychiatry, Association for Science in Autism Treatment, Centers for Disease Control, National Institute of Mental Health, California Senate Select Committee on Autism and Related Disorders, and New York State Department of Health.
11. O.I. Lovaas (1987). Behavioral treatment and normal educational and intellectual functioning in young autistic children. *Journal of Consulting and Clinical Psychology*, 55, 3–9.
12. L. Bishop-Fitzpatrick, N.J. Minshew, & S.M. Eack (2013). A systematic review of psychosocial interventions for adults with autism spectrum disorders. *Journal of Autism and Developmental Disorders*, 43, 687–694. https://doi.org/10.1007/s10803-012-1615-8.
13. A. Daniels & J. Bailey (2014). *Performance Management: Changing Behavior That Drives Organizational Effectiveness*, 5th Edition. Atlanta: Performance Management Publications.
14. R.V. Briscoe, D.B. Hoffman, & J.S. Bailey (1975). Behavioral community psychology: Training a community board in problem solving behaviors. *Journal of Applied Behavior Analysis*, 8, 157–168.
15. M.R. Burch (2013). *AKC Star Puppy: A Positive Behavioral Approach to Puppy Training*. Washington: Dogwise Publishing.

REFERENCES

Bishop-Fitzpatrick, L., Minshew, N.J., & Eack, S.M. (2013). A systematic review of psychosocial interventions for adults with autism spectrum disorders. *Journal of Autism and Developmental Disorders*, 43, 687–694. https://doi.org/10.1007/s10803-012-1615-8

Briscoe, R.V., Hoffman, D.B., & Bailey, J.S. (1975). Behavioral community psychology: Training a community board in problem solving behaviors. *Journal of Applied Behavior Analysis*, 8, 157–168.

Burch, M.R. (2021). *Canine Good Citizen: Ten Essential Skills Every Well-Mannered Dog Should Know*. Mount Joy, PA: Fox Chapel Publishing.

Burch, M.R., & Bailey, J.S. (1999). *How Dogs Learn: The Science of Operant Conditioning*. New York: Howell Books.

Daniels, A., & Bailey, J.S. (2014). *Performance Management: Changing Behavior that Drives Organizational Effectiveness*, 5th Edition. Atlanta: Performance Management Publications.

Epstein, R. (1997). Skinner as self-manager. *Journal of Applied Behavior Analysis*, 30, 545–568.

Lovaas, O.I. (1987). Behavioral treatment and normal educational and intellectual functioning in young autistic children. *Journal of Consulting and Clinical Psychology*, 55, 3–9.

Maurice, C. (1993). *Let Me Hear Your Voice: A Family's Triumph Over Autism*. New York: Fawcett Columbine.

Miltenberger, R.G. (2019). *Behavior Modification: Principles and Procedures*. Belmont, CA: Wadsworth/Thompson Learning.

Skinner, B.F. (1987). A thinking aid. *Journal of Applied Behavior Analysis*, 20, 379–380.

United States Surgeon General. (1999). *Mental Health: A Report of the Surgeon General*. Washington, DC: Author.

Wolf, M., Risley, T., & Mees, H. (1964). Application of operant conditioning procedures to the behavior problems of an autistic child. *Behavior Research and Therapy*, 1, 305–312.

The Behavioral Take on Other Fields of Psychology

DOI: 10.4324/9781003160915-7

QUESTION #30.
What Do Behavior Analysts Think of Counseling?

Quick Take

Counseling is a form of treatment that relies almost entirely on talking as a means of reducing "emotional turmoil," improving "communication," strengthening "self-esteem," and promoting changes in behavior. There are certainly times when people need to have someone to talk to and counseling is appropriate. For example, when children have been sexually abused, there is no doubt that counseling can be a valuable therapy.

However, when it comes to behavior problems, sometimes counseling is not the treatment of choice. Some people are in counseling for *years*. If you have been in counseling to work out simple problems with your spouse for seven years and you still have "issues," you need to ask yourself Dr. Phil's famous question, "How's that workin' for ya?"

Counseling is the single most frequently recommended solution to problems of everyday life by newspaper self-help columns. A distraught person wrote in and said,

> I have lived with my partner for two years. My partner is very bright and is working on a graduate degree. This is a person who can be very theatrical and dramatic, using weird voices at times and always wanting to be the center of attention. These behaviors are getting on my nerves more and more often. Our families are eagerly awaiting a wedding. I see things getting worse over time. What should I do?

The answer from the newspaper columnist: "You and your partner should start couples counseling as soon as possible."

Another letter from the same column a few days later reads: "My spouse has become addicted to computer games. He comes home from work, eats without saying much, and goes straight to his office where he stays on the computer most of the night—I never see him. If I ask him to spend time with me, he says, 'I need to unwind from my job'." The answer from the newspaper advisor: "You should both go to counseling to learn to communicate."

So, how would a behavior analyst who is reading these scenarios be likely to respond? For the most part, behavior analysts are skeptical of counseling to solve behavior problems such as the two mentioned previously. There's no question that there are some wonderful drug counselors, marriage counselors, and family counselors who can counsel people in some situations and help them get their lives on track. Sometimes a person just needs to have someone else confirm his or her thinking. However, the main concern with advocating counseling for "Engaged to Dramatic Partner" and the "Computer Gamer couple" is that the counseling approach may very well ignore some basic facts about human behavior, which is that immediate stimuli and consequences in a person's life exert a great deal of control.

Technically Speaking

The Computer Gamer seems to have become hooked on a very powerful *conditioned reinforcer*. Think about how computer games work—the same powerful *intermittent reinforcement schedule* that is provided in casinos by their rows and rows of slot machines is being delivered right in the comfort of his very own office. This all could have started as a function of escape and avoidance behavior. Maybe Computer Gamer's significant other has become an un-reinforcing person. After all, this person also has a stressful job, along with many family related jobs. Talk therapy alone is not going to change things for this couple.

Someone needs to get to the bottom of why Computer Gamer does not want to spend time with his family. Maybe family members need to learn to deliver a variety of reinforcers and Computer Gamer needs to adopt the Premack Principle[1] and use access to the video games as reinforcer for spending time with the family and helping around the house.

A behaviorally oriented counselor would probably make a recommendation like this to this troubled couple. It could be that behavior management is needed for the children as well; both parents need to learn child-behavior management techniques so that the children play quietly, complete their chores happily, and do their homework willingly with little to no prompting. With these routines in place, Computer Gamer will not feel the need to come home from work and immediately run for cover.

How about the Academy Award-winning partner? This was a person who started out okay in the relationship. What happened? The Tired-of-the-Drama partner needs some help analyzing this. Is anyone providing reinforcement for dramatic behavior? Do friends at work find this behavior wildly entertaining? Is the drama increasing because Tired-of-the-Drama is now showing flat affect and does not respond in the same way as when they first met?

Many other problems that are frequently addressed by counselors can also be addressed with a behavior analysis approach that involves analyzing the cause of the problem and implementing a treatment plan. One example is behavioral researchers who have used their analytic procedures with patients who have sexual disorders and dysfunctions. Because of our cultural conditioning, sex is an area that can make many people uncomfortable, including some professionals trained in psychology. But this is an important part of life, and it is important to know that a behavioral approach can be used to solve this kind of relationship problem. Another letter to a newspaper self-help columnist was from a husband who signed the letter as "Lonely in Lexington." The man bared his soul and wrote in to say he loved his wife, he tried to be a good husband, and he could not understand why she had avoided having sex with him for the past three years. He wanted to know if the columnist thought his wife had a secretly found someone else. As with the other letters previously mentioned, the columnist recommended, "You and your wife should start counseling as soon as possible to put the spark back in your love life."

From a behavior analysis perspective, something has gone seriously wrong in this relationship, and mere talk-therapy will be unlikely to change it. One possibility is that all of the behaviors Romeo engaged in when they were courting are long gone. Essentially, the "romance" is now missing, and when you take away the Hallmark cards, long-stemmed roses, and passionate statements of, "I love you," plus all of the other behaviors that led up to sex in the beginning of a relationship (candlelight dinners, shared laughter, warm and tender hugging and snuggling, holding hands during a stroll in the park, compliments galore, and more), one shouldn't be surprised that there is no sex now. This relationship problem is about more than sex; if they no longer have anything in common, this may be a couple that will soon be on their way to the divorce attorney's office. A couple that finds themselves in a situation like this needs to undergo a very complete analysis of their behaviors, looking at the conditions that existed when they met and were madly in love and consider those antecedent stimuli (actually, most are *antecedent behaviors*) to determine what it would take to bring the romance back into their lives.

A functional assessment of Romeo's lack of lovin' could identify some other causes that have nothing to do with cards and kisses. There could be other circumstances such as the wife having a medical problem she is embarrassed to talk about.

This particular case was presented in a self-help column in a newspaper. It should be noted that all couples, not just those that are heterosexual, can have intimacy and relationship problems for which help is needed.

If marriage counselors had training in behavior analysis, they could conduct a behavioral assessment of the problems and help the troubled couple change their behavior or identify and seek treatment for medical issues. This would be a more successful approach to solving this problem. Counseling sessions that involve talking alone without an analysis of the problem and a behavior change plan are unlikely to succeed.

• •

Key Concepts:
Counseling, talk therapy, conditioned reinforcer, intermittent reinforcement schedule, antecedent behaviors

EXERCISES:

1. What are some situations for which traditional counseling (involving mainly listening to the client) would be appropriate?
2. What is the problem with getting only "talk-therapy" for a behaviorally based problem?

QUESTION #31.

What Is the Behavioral Position on Depression, Schizophrenia, Obsessive Compulsive Disorder, and Other "Mental" Disorders?

Quick Take

Behavior analysis is an approach that is directed specifically at operant or learned behaviors. Knowing that some forms of mental illness are biologically caused, there are absolutely times when the behavior analyst should refer the client to relevant medical experts. However, some aspects of mild, short-term depression, called situational depression, do appear to have a behavioral cause, for which non-pharmacological treatment is recommended. An elderly, widowed pet owner who loses her furry canine companion of 15 years is very likely to go into depression in the sense of feeling deep sadness, finding no joy in other activities, having no interest in being around others, and experiencing a general feeling of "being lost and abandoned." This should be expected considering that Snuggles provided a significant amount of reinforcement for Memaw hour by hour every day. A spaniel, Wyn, that fills a professor's life with joy from that first wake-up kiss on the nose and wagging tail at daybreak that says, "Let's go have some fun," until the last walk of the evening when they share a sunset together is going to be greatly missed. All of the behavior that was prompted and maintained by Snuggles and Wyn is much less likely to occur when they are gone; there is little reason to get up in the morning and no reason to go for a walk. This condition could be analyzed essentially as situational depression caused by the dramatic loss in reinforcement and the subsequent loss of all the behaviors prompted and maintained by that faithful, loving creature. Similar "operant depressions" can easily be seen when a person loses a job; gets divorced or separated from a partner; or has a vintage, lovingly restored Porsche 911 stolen from his garage.

Technically Speaking

Some depression is thought to be caused by biological factors such changes in the function of neurotransmitters in the brain, fluctuations in hormones related to pregnancy, thyroid problems or menopause, and possibly inherited traits from blood relatives.[2] Behavior analysts respect well-controlled research in any field, and to the extent that severe and chronic depression can be attributed to biological causes, we would concur with this approach to what may otherwise appear to be a *behavior* problem.

Schizophrenia is another "mental" disorder that appears to have a biological basis. Although the *behavior* of a schizophrenic patient is quite bizarre (hallucinations, delusions, and disordered thinking) and some think that elements of schizophrenia are learned, it is reasonable to believe that the fundamental issue is biochemical in nature. Some research on schizophrenia is pointing toward an imbalance of the chemical systems in the brain specifically involving the neurotransmitters dopamine and glutamate. This is not to say that some behavior of a schizophrenic person might be operant; however, at this time, the consensus among behavior analysts is that the analysis and treatment of this population is best left to those whose expertise is in the fields of medicine and biochemistry.

Obsessive-compulsive disorder (OCD) involves patterns of unwanted thoughts and fears that can lead to repetitive or compulsive behaviors resulting from changes in body chemistry, genetics, and even learning from family members.[3] This is another disorder where there is some research pointing at low serotonin levels in the brain as a key element in the cause. It is difficult to believe that such strange behaviors as excessive hand washing; checking to see if a door is locked over and over again; or a powerful need to hoard, pray, or repeat a phrase could be anything but operant behaviors; however, at this time, there is no evidence that supports this. Behavior analysts have not been involved in developing treatments for OCD, but some behavior therapists have reported success with an extinction procedure referred to as "exposure and response prevention." Basically, the client is presented with the stimulus that elicits the compulsive behavior and then prevented from engaging in the behavior so that extinction can take place.

While the treatment of some mental health problems is best left to professionals in other areas, behavior analysts can play an important role in the treatment of these populations by setting up systems-level programs to manage data, train staff, and ensure that daily activities are carried out in mental health facilities. An example of a behavioral approach to verbal tics related to Tourette syndrome can be found in Woods et al.'s[4] research in JABA and is shown in Figure 6.1. The authors took data on the number of verbal tics that occurred during therapy sessions where the clinician in some sessions brought up topics related to tics (e.g., "Do you have any feelings right before you have the tic behavior?") versus other sessions where non-tic topics were discussed (e.g., "Tell me about your family pet."). Their data clearly showed the stimulus control exerted by the topics—that is, "tic-talk" resulted in up to five times the frequency of tics over non-tic topics!

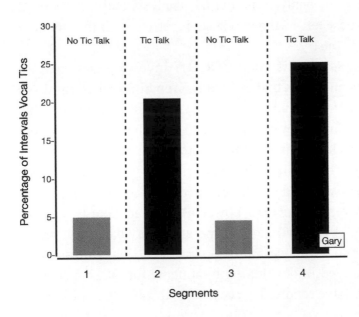

FIGURE 6.1 The percentage of intervals when Gary had vocal tics when there was no discussion of the tics (no tic talk) vs when there was discussion of his tics (tic talk).

Key Concepts:

Mental disorders, depression, situational depression, reactive depression, biological factors in depression, tic, Tourette syndrome

EXERCISES:

1. What are some mental disorders that are best treated by medical professionals? Why should behavior analysts not provide the primary treatment for people with these disorders?
2. How would a behavior analyst explain the depression that follows the death of a loved one?

QUESTION #32.
Can ABA Fix Problems Like Drug Addiction and Alcoholism?

Quick Take

Both alcoholism and drug addiction appear at first blush to be behavior problems. They involve a person repeatedly engaging in injection or consumption of a substance that has behavior-altering effects and that ultimately is self-destructive if used to excess. From a behavioral perspective, we could hypothesize that drinking alcohol or using opioids[5] is an escape response to some aspect of an aversive environment; that is, it dulls some significant physical pain or alters the senses and makes the pressure of a job or relationship go away for at least a period of time. Alcoholism and drug use could also be viewed as behaviors that are socially reinforced by peers. If peers are involved, the behavior is likely to be under some stimulus control, such as, drinking with friends as you watch "The Big Game" or as part of a social event such as a wedding, birthday, or graduation celebration. Opioid use in particular may start with a legitimate prescription from a physician for back or other pain from an injury and then rapidly expand to illegal drugs that basically consume the person's life as they become addicted.

Surprisingly, alcoholism, although it has been written about and studied for over 200 years, is still not well understood. The American Medical Association concluded in 1987 that alcoholism was an illness,[6] but a survey of doctors[7] in 1996 found that only 25% of them believed it was a disease. One of the most visible methods of treating alcohol and drug abuse in our culture is Alcohol Anonymous, which was formed in 1935 and has since spun off other self-help groups such as Narcotics Anonymous, but there is disagreement as to whether these 12-step programs are actually significantly effective.[8] An alternative approach is to deal with alcoholism via medication; both naltrexone and Antabuse have been used successfully by reducing the reinforcing "high" that comes with alcohol by creating a toxic reaction; that is the person becomes sick when consuming alcohol. This could be interpreted as a behavioral approach since it involves the concept of *punishment* (i.e., a consequence that decreases the likelihood of a behavior).

The research on behavioral tactics in the treatment of alcohol addiction is quite limited, and ABA is currently not a widely adopted approach, so the short answer to the question about ABA fixing problems like drug addiction and alcoholism is that we do not have a viable approach at this time; for more information, please see the "Technically Speaking" section.

Technically Speaking

As mentioned, considering alcohol consumption or opiate injection a behavior in need of reduction suggests two strategies: 1) *reinforce an incompatible behavior* or 2) apply an *aversive consequence* immediately following the behavior. To study the former possibility, a therapeutic workplace was set up at Johns Hopkins University School of Medicine where cocaine-addicted individuals could be paid for typing, keypad, and data entry on computers if they showed they were not using by providing a clean urine sample each day. On their home page, participants could see how much they earned each day and the total amount earned, which constituted the immediate reinforcer for abstaining from drug use. The authors concluded that, "This study provides firm experimental evidence that employment-based abstinence reinforcement can increase cocaine abstinence."[9] It should be noted that although the employment-based requirement showed that drug users had three times greater cocaine-negative samples during treatment than during their baselines, this was still a small effect, from 10% to 29%. The overwhelming majority, that is, 70%, were not phased in the least by this reinforcement contingency, suggesting that much more powerful reinforcers would have to be offered to lure these individuals away from their cocaine addictions.

This study was recently replicated with unemployed, homeless, alcohol-dependent adults and showed very similar results. These authors concluded, "Overall, the results confirm the benefit of payment contingencies in increasing *achievement* in a job-skills training program, *engagement* in a job-skills training program, and *performance quality* while on task in a job-skills training program" (italics added).[10]

One final study replicates the previous two but extends the findings to not only alcohol-dependent but also problematic methamphetamine users.[11] In this study, which evaluated the effects of contingency management with vouchers as the reinforcer, the researchers found that there was a near doubling (35% to 69%) of participants who had negative tests for alcohol relative to their baseline levels. One interesting feature of this experiment was that the authors used an *escalating schedule of reinforcement* that started out at $5 for the first visit with a negative alcohol test and then increased by $2 for each subsequent test; this reinforcement for abstinence produced clinically significant reductions in alcohol use.

One experiment that was conducted in the mid-1970s explored the use of aversive consequences to directly reduce drinking. Wilson et al.[12] set up a simulated bar at the Behavior Research Laboratory at Rutgers where they could study alcohol consumption on a 24-hour basis in a four-bed inpatient research facility. Participants were hooked up via electrodes on their index and middle fingers to a shock apparatus (the shock was mild, and they were all volunteers who were paid $15 per week with a bonus at the end). There were several experiments with a number of participants; in the last experiment, the number of ounces of whiskey or bourbon consumed was reduced from approximately 20 ounces per 24-hour period to near zero when the experimenter administered the shock; this level maintained for all four participants in a final baseline condition. These studies support the idea that "loss-of-control drinking" is a learned behavior rather than being just an involuntary loss of control.

• •

Key Concepts:
Punishment, reinforce an incompatible behavior, aversive consequence, escalating schedule of reinforcement

EXERCISES:

1. Look up "evidence-based treatment for alcoholism" in Google to find articles that you might find interesting.
2. Can you think of other uses for the concept of *reinforce an incompatible behavior*? Could you use this to reduce or eliminate a compulsive behavior that you might have such as biting your nails or popping your knuckles?

QUESTION #33.

Do Behavior Analysts Believe in Psychotherapy? Is It Evidence Based?

Quick Take

Psychotherapy consists almost entirely of "talk therapy" and is a much different practice than ABA. Whereas behavior analysts observe behavior in the setting where the behavior is problematic, psychotherapists listen to the "patient" describe the problem they are having and observe them while they are in the office. Depending on their background and training, the therapist will arrive at a diagnosis and proceed with their dialogue, the actual *talk therapy*, to resolve the issue the patient reported. In behavior analysis, we are primarily dealing with *clients* who have observable behavior problems that are severe enough to cause parents, teachers, group home staff, or other caregivers to seek expert assistance. By the time the problem rises to the level of discomfort for someone to report it, there have usually been other attempts at resolution, including talking to the person, threatening them with consequences, applying actual punishment procedures, and so on.

In psychotherapy, the person is almost always an adult of some means (i.e., they have a job, a car, an education, social and coping skills sufficient to know they need help, and the ability to find a therapist), and they are aware of their problem, which involves some internal discomfort. Psychotherapists deal with a wide range of mental illnesses and emotional difficulties, including mood, personality, and anxiety disorders, as well as substance abuse, trauma, and depression, which are dealt with in sessions usually lasting 50 minutes conducted in the therapists' office.

Since the types of problems that psychotherapists deal with are so dramatically different from those that a behavior analyst will encounter, our standard method of evaluation is not appropriate. The therapist may see changes in the verbal behavior of the patient, but without following the patient around and observing throughout their day, it is not possible to know if there has been any impact as a result of talk therapy. As behavior analysts, we know that talking and doing are two different behaviors. A person can describe how they are handling a stressful situation that has possibly been shaped by the therapist over the course of several sessions. However, the person can react in a totally differently manner when encountering the demands of the stressful situation. As behavior analysts, we can perfectly understand this disconnect, since we know that it is the contingencies in the environment that actually control behavior.

A patient may have anxiety over work because their boss is constantly looking over their shoulder and making occasional critical comments. As behavior analysts, we would ask questions that the therapist would probably not. We would want to know about the nature of the work, the preparation and training the patient has to do that work, exactly how the supervisor responds with her remarks, and, of course, how the patient responds to the criticism. If we were observing the patient at work, we might see that he is somewhat sloppy in his production, spends time off-task talking with colleagues, and takes personal calls while on the job. These details are not be likely to be revealed to the therapist. One other detail has to do with how the patient responds when the supervisor makes comments about his work. Rather than say, "I'm so sorry; I can see that that was a mistake on my part. I will fix it immediately," he says, "It's not my fault; Jane gave me the wrong instructions. Why don't you go criticize her?" Seeing the patient be defensive could be a big reinforcer for the supervisor, which means the criticism will likely continue in the future.

The direct answer to the question, "Do behavior analysts believe in psychotherapy?" is that we believe that many problems in a person's life can cause them to be anxious or depressed, have mood swings, and so on, but unless there are changes in the environment, the therapist is not going to be successful in alleviating the patient's suffering. There is one type of psychotherapy that comes close to ABA, and that is *cognitive behavioral therapy*. In cognitive behavioral therapy, psychologists who are also behavior analysts work to identify those things in a person's daily life that are causing trouble. Parents with children who are presenting problems at home with school avoidance, oppositional behavior, lying, sibling conflict, and so on will want to look for a professional who specializes in *behavioral pediatrics* will work with them on practical solutions to behavior problems like these and more.

Technically Speaking

The question about the evidence to support psychotherapy is difficult to answer directly, at least to our satisfaction as behavior analysts. Patients may *self-report* that they *feel* less anxious, depressed, moody, and so on, but that is difficult to verify given the office-based model used by most psychotherapists. A psychotherapist may report that her clients are greatly improved and that they show less anxiety or fewer mood swings, but that is entirely based on observations in her office. In fact, she does not know what actually happens at home, at work, or in the community.

Evidence-based practice means that those techniques that a therapist uses are based on scientific evidence. This concept was first introduced in medicine in the early 1990s and then spread to other fields such as education, psychology, and social work. It should be noted that ABA has been evidence based since the onset of the field in 1968 with the first publication of the *Journal of Applied Behavior Analysis*. For behavior analysts, evidence-based treatment means two things: 1) there is substantial behavioral research, utilizing single-case design, published in peer-reviewed journals, replicated several times, which shows socially, educationally, or clinically significant changes in behavior, and, 2) those evidence-based procedures produce observable,

"Given the intangible nature of psychotherapy, it has been difficult to establish its scientific validity."

measurable, socially significant changes in behavior for *their* client. The standard for evidence-based practice for psychotherapy is not as strict. It includes "the best-available research, with clinical expertise in the context of the patient's culture, individual characteristics and personal preferences."[13]

Psychotherapists have carved out their own areas of practice that are quite different from behavior analysts. For the most part, they work on the outpatient treatment of psychiatric disorders using talk therapy that involves a conversation with patients. As Howard et al., have stated succinctly, "Given the intangible nature of psychotherapy, it has been difficult to establish its scientific validity."[14] We hesitate to criticize another profession such as psychotherapy for not meeting our standards for evidence-based treatment, especially since these professionals work with such different human behavior problems under vastly different circumstances. We believe that a significant segment of our population finds solace in the psychotherapy that they receive, and we are content to live with this.

• •

Key Concepts:
Talk therapy, talking vs doing, contingencies in the environment, cognitive-behavioral therapy, self-report, behavioral pediatrics, evidence-based practice/treatment

EXERCISES:

1. There are many different versions of psychotherapy. Look for some of these on the internet and see if you can determine the type of problems addressed by each one.
2. Search the internet for information on evidence-based practice for an area in which you are interested. Ask: What is the status of that effort at this point in time? Identify the standards for the evidence.

QUESTION #34.
What Do Behavior Analysts Think About Cognitive Psychology?

Quick Take

The so-called "cognitive revolution" has not impressed most behavior analysts. As a convergence of several wildly different theoretical fields, including philosophy, cybernetics, and psycholinguistics, as well as the basic research specialties of anthropology, neuroscience, and computer science, cognitive science is all about basic research and is about as far afield from our applied approach to behavior as one can get. Cognitive psychologists study "perception, attention, memory, language, reasoning, decision-making and problem solving"[15] and attempt to develop theories about these cognitive processes. *Applied cognitive psychology*, on the other hand, is defined as, "the science of the cognitive processes involved in activities of daily living"[16] in complex situations. One clear similarity to behavior analysis is that applied cognitive psychologists often use a task analysis as part of their work so they can determine exactly how many individual steps, and in what order, are necessary to complete a task. Some examples of the work in applied cognitive psychology include training risk perception in new drivers, analyzing the multitasking demands on a driver who is talking on a cell phone, training baggage screeners to detect images of threatening objects, determining how to improve a quarterback's ability to read the pattern of the opposing players on the field before throwing the football, and understanding how seniors can be assisted in remaining independent in their activities of daily living.[17]

The field of applied cognitive psychology, also referred to as engineering psychology or applied experimental psychology, appears to have many of the same goals as behavior analysis, except that in behavior analysis, we are looking to make a socially significant difference in

the behavior of the participants rather than to "develop general principles that will have relevance to a range of problems and to specify the
boundary conditions under which such principles will be valid."[18]

Technically Speaking

Skinner, in his difficult-to-read and greatly underappreciated work *Verbal Behavior*,[19] devoted a whole chapter to "Thinking." For behavior
analysts, this approach has served them well when dealing with complex
human behaviors ordinarily thought of as speech, language, communications, cognitions, or private events. One way to study these events is
through a procedure called "think aloud," which was invented by J.B.
Watson, an early behaviorist.[20] *Think aloud* is used in an updated, mod-
ern form in cognitive labs around the country[21] to study thinking and
problem solving.

For the behavior analyst, cognitive *behavior* involves "self-talk" that
might include self-instructions ("First I turn the red knob to the right, and
then I pull the lever . . ."), paranoid thoughts ("Oh my, there they go talking
about me again") or other similar covert verbal behaviors such as statements of self-confidence ("I know I can do this . . .") that may in some
way increase or decrease the likelihood of a later *overt* behavior. Behavior
analysts are very interested in complex human behaviors, but there is not
a great deal of research published on this topic just yet. Perhaps the most
significant contribution to the general area of complex human behavior
involves the recent advances in teaching language to autistic children.[22]
This work, which has taken the applied field of autism by storm, has
become the "bible" for behavior analysts who teach language to autistic
children. In what has come to be called "*applied verbal behavior*," these
authors have shown what can be done with Skinner's concepts of verbal
behavior in a very practical and necessary way. This work is supported by
an extensive body of basic research on language acquisition that is published in the peer-reviewed journal *The Analysis of Verbal Behavior*.[23]

Most of the time, changing the way one *thinks* about personal difficulties will be unlikely to fix them (although effective thinking comes

first). The solution to personal troubles does not involve just thinking positive thoughts, it involves having a plan of action and engaging in different behavior. Dealing with a verbally abusive spouse or partner does not just require putting up with the verbal abuse, taking yoga classes, or memorizing daily affirmations. To be effective, some action is required. If you were working with a behavior therapist, they would probably start by asking about any "triggers" for the abusive behavior (we call them antecedents) and also the consequences that follow. From there, the behavior therapist would probably recommend some specific steps you could take, including finding reinforcers for the person and asking what behavior you would like to see in place of the verbally abusive behavior (differential reinforcement of incompatible behavior).

• •

Key Concepts:
Cognitive psychology, applied cognitive psychology, motivation, emotions, verbal behavior, "thinking," differential reinforcement of incompatible behavior

EXERCISES:

1. Look at any recent general psychology text and review the section on cognitive psychology. Find some examples of applied cognitive studies that might appear to overlap with applied behavior analysis.
2. How do behavior analysts talk about motivation?
3. What role does understanding someone's emotions play in behavioral treatment?

QUESTION #35.

What Do Behavior Analysts Think About IQ? What About "Motivation" and "Emotions"?

Quick Take

Behavior analysts are not involved with standardized testing, so they don't make much use of IQ scores. We are, however, very much interested in knowing about an individual's level of practical functioning if this will help us develop effective behavioral programs. As members

> *"One topic that is very much at the heart of behavior analysis has to do with motivation."*

of habilitation teams, behavior analysts are often involved with conducting assessments of adaptive behavior. Does this person have any leisure skills? Can she wash her hair? Can this young client with developmental disabilities feed himself with a spoon? These are functional, real-world behaviors that are needed to get through the day regardless of a score they got on a paper-and-pencil intelligence test.

One topic that is very much at the heart of behavior analysis has to do with *motivation*. You might even say that we consider motivation a prime focus of the field, a topic that is present in almost every study of human behavior and certainly every clinical behavior plan. For behavior analysts, motivation has to do with reinforcement, and reinforcement has to do in a major way with a lack of that reinforcer for some period; that is, unless the person has some lack of the reinforcer (they haven't eaten in a while, are sad because their pet fish died, or are lonely because their best friend did not come to school that day), then basically there is no reason for the behavior to occur. Dr. Jack Michael of Western Michigan University introduced the expression "establishing operation"[24] as a term to help behavior analysts describe, understand, predict, and provide treatment for behavior. In 2003, in a major theoretical paper, Michael and his colleagues suggested using the more generic term "motivating operation" to describe "environmental events that influence the effects of operant consequences."[25] With the term "motivation" as a centerpiece of operant theory, it is clear that behavior analysts consider understanding what motivates people to engage in certain behaviors at certain times a paramount feature of our field. Figure 6.2 shows the relationship between motivational operations such as deprivation of food or presence of something painful such as missing a friend and how they can directly affect the person, who will then engage in some behavior to reduce the deprivation or pain.

Technically Speaking

As we mentioned earlier, the first question that a behavior analyst asks upon being presented with a behavior problem is, "Why? Why does

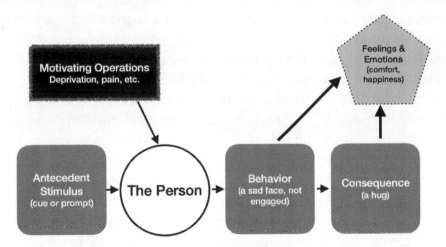

FIGURE 6.2   Graphic showing how motivating operations, such as hunger or pain, can affect the person and cause behaviors (and consequences), which may produce certain feelings and emotions. A child who is sad and lonely receives a hug from her pre-school teacher; this can produce feelings of comfort and happiness.

the behavior occur? What are the controlling variables?" When we understand what motivates a person to engage in a behavior, we can then proceed to develop an ethical and effective behavior plan.

> *"The behavioral position is that emotions accompany certain behaviors and certainly result from consequences."*

As behavior analysts, we do not usually work on emotions or emotional behavior, but that does not mean we are not concerned with a person's emotions. The behavioral position is that emotions accompany certain behaviors and certainly result from consequences, but emotions alone are probably not responsible for behavior. This can be seen in Figure 6.2. We suggest focusing on the environmental change that produced the troubling emotion. A person who is sad or angry feels that way for some reason—something has happened to cause this feeling, and we are concerned about that; we don't like to see a person being miserable. Focusing too long on the emotion itself, however, can be a major distraction from identifying the cause.

Behavior analysts use emotions and emotional behavior as indicators of satisfactory or unsatisfactory contingencies of reinforcement in a person's life; they are important and a key to understanding what needs to be done to help the person improve their condition.

• •

Key Concepts:
Motivation, emotions

EXERCISES:

1. How do behavior analysts talk about motivation?

2. What role does understanding someone's emotions play in behavioral treatment?
3. How could feelings be used to determine what a person needs to do in order to improve their emotional well-being?

QUESTION #36.

Do You Believe in "Brushing" Therapy and Weighted Vests?

Quick Take

Therapies such as sensory diets, brushing, weighted vests, and more are often recommended by occupational therapists for children with autism spectrum disorder. The use of such methods is derived from a complex theory of brain functioning proposed by Dr. Jean Ayres, an occupational therapist, in 1972.[26] Known as *sensory integration*, the theory proposes that, "the neurological processes that organizes sensation from one's own body and from the environment and makes it possible to use the body effectively within the environment" (Ayres, 1972, p. 11). Theoretically, then, this information goes to the brain, where it is "organized and interpreted," and this allows the person to respond to their environment. Allegedly, this should result in "improved behavior, learning, and social participation."[27] These latter outcomes fit right in with the types of goals and objectives that behavior analysts strive for, but most behavior analysts look skeptically at this approach. The reason we are skeptical is that we have a huge body of research showing that *behavior, learning, and social participation* are primarily affected by contingencies of reinforcement. It seems very unlikely to us that using a "weighted vest, brushing, bouncing on a ball, and using adapted seating devices" would in any way improve those categories of behavior. In a recently published review of the sensory integration literature,[28] the authors found one study that used brushing seven times per day for five weeks on a child with SIB.[29] They found no effect of the brushing and found similar results for the use of weighted vests; that is, there is no evidence. After carefully reviewing 25 studies that used weighted vests, it was not clear that they have any positive effect on measurable child behaviors.[30]

The original neurological theory that is driving all of these sensory integration methods (weighted vests, brushing, bouncing on a ball, kneading bread, aromatherapy, etc.) has been challenged and found wanting. In their review of the science supposedly behind the sensory integration model, Smith et al.[31] conclude that, "In actuality, there is no sound scientific basis for any of these assertions."

Technically Speaking

Behavior analysts will tell you that they are not surprised at these findings, since they would appear to be indirect uses of irrelevant antecedent stimuli to change behavior. We would take a different tack that involved conducting an functional behavior assessment (FBA) to understand the controlling variables, followed by a *reinforcer assessment* and a *task analysis*. Having broken the task down into small parts, we would teach each one using chaining if appropriate, along with a strong reinforcer, as determined by the reinforcer assessment.

Another issue with the research that has been done on sensory integration is that the studies for the most part are group statistical designs; that is, participants are randomly assigned to two or three different groups, and the results for each group are analyzed statistically to determine if the groups' data are "significant." By *significant*, they do not mean *important*, *vital*, or *impressive* but rather that they are *statistically* significantly different from chance. Statistics are okay to prove a theory, but when it comes to evaluating a treatment, the effects need to be important to the individual. This is why we use *single-case experimental designs*. Single-case research is done in a very straightforward manner by first taking a baseline of a behavior of interest, followed by the treatment, then finally by a return to baseline. This model was followed in a study by Davis et al.,[32] who wanted to test the effectiveness of brushing on stereotypy, with the results published in the journal *Research in Autism Spectrum Disorders*. As shown in Figure 6.3, the 4-year-old boy, Aiden, who was an ASD child, spent a high percentage of his time engaging in stereotypy consisting of hand flapping,

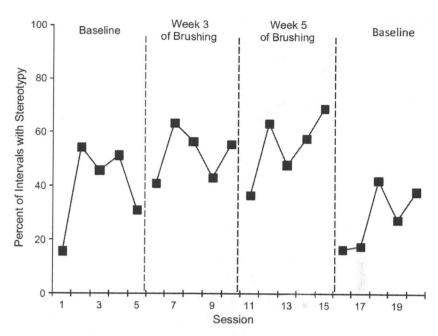

FIGURE 6.3 Stereotypy during (a) baseline, (b) week three of the brushing protocol, (c) week five of the brushing protocol, and (d) a return to baseline.

finger flicking, and body rocking. His occupational therapist (OT) had diagnosed him with sensory deprivation, and the prescription was the Wilbarger brushing protocol to meet his sensory diet needs (the theory was that he engaged in stereotypy because he needed more stimulation than he was getting on a daily basis). It seems clear from the data that Aiden's hand flapping, finger flicking, and body rocking actually increased during the two weeks of brushing rather than decreasing.

The snug vest is similar to a weighted vest in that it provides firm pressure to the child's torso. It is alleged to "relieve anxiety as well as increase focus and attention" and is sold on the internet in several sizes for children with ASD.[33] Researchers Watkins and Sparling[34] set out to see if it was actually effective in changing the behavior of stereotypy of several children with a diagnosis of ASD. They involved three children in their study, and the data for one 6-year-old child, Carl, and his vocal stereotypy are shown in Figure 6.4. This study used a different

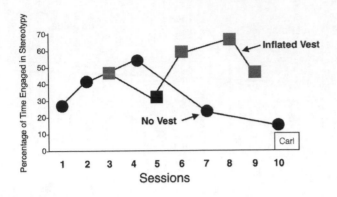

FIGURE 6.4   Percentage of time Carl engaged in stereotypy during no-vest and inflated vest conditions.

single-case design called a *multielement design*. A multielement design is where the intervention is alternated randomly from session to session to see if there was any difference from when the snug vest minus air was worn versus when it was actually inflated. Carl's data show that when the vest was inflated so that it provided pressure on his chest, the vocal stereotypy actually increased. The other two children in the study showed similar results, which were that the inflated vest did not appear to relieve any anxiety that might have been shown by the stereotypic behaviors.

Behavior analysts are skeptical of brushing and weighted (inflated) vests because we do not feel that the theory behind them is appropriate; that is, a deprivation of sensory input, the sensory diet theory, is not the cause of the self-stimulatory stereotypic behavior, and providing brushing or the vest is not a solution.

• •

Key Concepts:
Sensory integration, reinforcer assessment, task analysis, statistically significant, single-case experimental designs, multielement design, stereotypy

EXERCISES:

1. Look up snug vest on the internet. Try to find any research supporting its use with children with ASD.
2. To learn more about sensory integration theory, look this topic up on the internet. Try to find any additional single-case design studies.
3. If you are interested in learning more about stereotypy, type this in as a keyword to the JABA search engine at: https://online library.wiley.com/journal/19383703

QUESTION #37.

What About Alternative Treatments in General for Children Diagnosed With ASD, Such as Facilitated Communication, Magic Mineral Solution, Camel Milk, and Hyperbaric Oxygen Therapy?

Quick Take

In the past decades, autism spectrum disorder has become increasingly pervasive. The CDC now estimates that 1 in 54 children have ASD (National Center on Birth Defects and Developmental Disabilities. Center for Disease Control and Prevention, 2021).[35] Autism spectrum disorder has such potentially profound effects that it is no wonder that desperate parents will jump at any fad treatment, including those that are very expensive, exotic, or dangerous, to help their child. This great need is compounded by a huge vacuum in understanding of the possible causes of this developmental disorder. ASD was initially thought to be the result of the "refrigerator mother theory," which was promoted by psychiatrist Leo Kanner in 1943.[36] As behavior analysts, we view these *pseudoscientific* "treatments" with disdain and worry about both their lack of effectiveness and their potential for harm. Further, we have concern for those that adopt them without questioning their scientific basis.

One larger consideration is that we are apparently living in a time of anti-science bias, or science denial, as it is sometimes called. Vyse[37] puts it this way, "In this environment that devalues evidence and critical thinking, it is easy to see how nonscientific treatments for children and adults with developmental disabilities can flourish." This situation is further compounded by a burgeoning, accessible internet communication system which allows purveyors of dubious, questionable, and even fraudulent products and services to connect directly with naive and desperate consumers. These consumers most often have no easy way to determine if what they have just bought into will have any effect or not. These same consumers are also subject to lottery, banking, charity, and telephone scams as well as Ponzi schemes[38] that rob them of millions and millions of dollars yearly. This situation constitutes a virtual perfect sociological storm of desperate consumers, deliberate misinformation, and callous profit-making by aggressive entrepreneurs who care little for the welfare of their clients or the truth. The supportive role of the media deserves some mention as well. In their aggressive drive to fill 24 hours per day of attention-grabbing programming, some media sources will promote the strange and unusual without the least concern for credibility. Parents in search of effective treatment have their work cut out for them, since it appears that even respected professionals can be fooled into recommending worthless remedies:

> When her daughter was diagnosed with autism in 2004, Ariane Zurcher threw herself into researching a condition she knew nothing about. She and her husband took Emma to neurologists, gastroenterologists, behavioral, speech and occupational therapists, nutritionists, naturopaths, a shaman and homoeopath, a craniosacral therapist, and a Qigong master. A developmental pediatrician who had a months-long waiting list and didn't take insurance charged the parents least $200 per visit and recommended they call a psychic in Europe. The psychic, ironically, refused payment because she didn't pick up a "signal" from the Zurchers. They tried dozens of treatments that claimed to have "recovered" children with autism, including numerous vitamin supplements, topical ointments, restrictive diets, chelation, hyperbaric oxygen therapy, brain scans, a so-called detoxification system and stem cell therapy.[39]

Technically Speaking

The best protection against these treatment rip-offs is skepticism, common sense, and a healthy respect for science. It helps if consumers also have some background in statistics so they can analyze the marketing language that always accompanies these trendy treatment scams.

Having a reference work that catalogues these dubious treatments for easy reference is also recommended. In this regard, we highly recommend Foxx and Mulick's[40] timely and comprehensive work, *Controversial Therapies for Autism and Intellectual Disabilities: Fad, Fashion, and Science in Professional Practice* (2nd ed.), which contains 30 chapters on the history of fads and unvalidated treatments. Beyond this, we urge anyone interested in the development of effective treatment methods to peruse the *Journal of Applied Behavior Analysis*, where they will find study after study demonstrating the power of single-case designs that demonstrate ways to transform the behavior of children and adults with ASD and other developmental disabilities. Here is a sampling of these pseudoscientific "treatments" with cautionary comments:

Facilitated communication—This is a fad treatment which emerged in the 1980s in Australia and was later brought to America. It is a form of assisted typing where a facilitator guides the hands of the ASD child or adult, who then purportedly types out long sentences, poetry, and short stories. With the assistance of the facilitator, the child or adult with the disability can supposedly solve math problems and answer questions that are put to them. Well-controlled research has shown that it is the facilitator who is typing the answers rather than the client.

Miracle Mineral Solution—This is the industrial chemical chlorine dioxide that was first advertised in 2006. It has been promoted as a cure for HIV, hepatitis viruses, and autism, among many other diseases, maladies, and genetic disorders. Miracle Mineral Solution has caused life-threatening responses in many individuals, and the FDA has advised against its use because of a rise in health-related issues: "Miracle Mineral Solution and similar products are not FDA-approved, and ingesting these products is the same as drinking bleach. Consumers should not use these products, and parents should not give these products to their children for any reason."[41]

Raw camel milk—"Raw camel milk has been alleged to cure autism-related ills with benefits ranging from improved eye contact and motor skills to decreased inflammation. Although it may be nutritious, there is no scientific research that upholds claims that raw camel milk is an autism 'cure-all'."[42]

Hyperbaric oxygen therapy (HBOT)

HBOT has been proven effective for treatment of gangrene, carbon monoxide poisoning, 'the bends' and various other conditions related to oxygen in blood. There is no evidence to support ASD as an insufficiency of oxygen in the blood. Evidence also fails to support HBOT as safe or effective for the treatment of autism. Furthermore, the benefits of hyperbaric oxygen delivered in a soft-shelled chamber are no different than with a less expensive oxygen tent, or nasal cannula.[43]

This is just a sampling of non-evidence-based treatments, and there are more being added almost every week. It is difficult, if not impossible, to keep up with the growing number of non-evidence-based treatments. In fact, there is usually a two-to-five-year lapse between the time a fad comes on the scene and researchers can gear up to test its effectiveness. Even then, it is not always possible to get the information to consumers since the results are presented in peer-reviewed journals rather than the popular media. Even when the word does spread, there can be a strong resistance to new information by people who have become true believers in the therapy or treatment. One group that stays on top of these fads is the Autism Science Foundation (Autism Science Foundation, 2021), which we recommend as a starting point if you need to research any "too good to be true" treatments for ASD.

* *

Key Concepts:
"Refrigerator mother theory", pseudoscientific, science denial, Ponzi schemes, facilitated communication, Miracle Mineral Solution, hyperbaric oxygen therapy

EXERCISES:

1. Using your favorite browser, search for "cures for autism." Can you guess which treatments are fads or bogus or both?
2. Go to the Autism Science Foundation and look at the treatments that they have reviewed. Have you have heard of any of these treatments? If you find a treatment that sounds interesting, go to Google and look it up to see if you can distinguish between marketing and research for this treatment.

SUMMARY

This chapter presents our position on other fields of psychology. One of these areas is counseling, which is commonly recommended when people are having difficulty coping with life's problems. We explain how a behavior analyst might think about this and the solutions they would offer. Behavior analysis has not yet seriously addressed the field of mental health, but there is ongoing research on drug addiction and alcoholism. We are unconvinced by the existing research in psychotherapy, but applied cognitive psychology appears to be a viable area of research and practice. Traditional cognitive psychology does not seem appropriate to treat common behavior problems. Most behavior analysts include motivational variables in their treatment plans, but we do not typically focus on IQ to develop these plans. Another area about which we have skepticism involves the theory of sensory integration as it is applied to autism. Research shows that brushing, weighted vests, and other related treatments for children with autism do not improve behavior. Alternative treatments such as facilitated communication and so-called Miracle Mineral Solution can be not only useless but also possibly dangerous (USAGov, 2021; U.S. Food and Drug Administration, 2019), and we strongly advise against their use. These treatments are considered pseudoscientific rather than evidence based by behavior analysts.

NOTES

1. The Premack Principle advises to make the following arrangement: high-probability behaviors always follow low-probability behaviors, also known as Grandma's rule: Eat your vegetables before you have dessert.
2. www.mayoclinic.org/diseases-conditions/depression/symptoms-causes/syc-20356007
3. www.mayoclinic.org/diseases-conditions/obsessive-compulsive-disorder/symptoms-causes/syc-20354432
4. D.W. Woods, T.S. Watson, E. Wolfe, M.P. Twohig, & P.C. Friman (2001). Analyzing the influence of tic-related talk on vocal and motor tics in children with Tourette's syndrome. *Journal of Applied Behavior Analysis*, 34(3), 353–356.
5. Including heroin, morphine, fentanyl, codeine, oxycodone, and hydrocodone.
6. A. Leshner (1997). Addiction is a brain disease, and it matters. *Science*, 278(5335), 807–808.
7. S.I. Mignon (1996). Physicians' perceptions of alcoholics: The disease concept reconsidered. *Alcoholism Treatment Quarterly*, 14(4), 33–45. https://doi.org/10.1300/j020v14n04_02.
8. G. Glaser (2015). The irrationality of alcoholics anonymous. *The Atlantic*. Retrieved April 15, 2016.
9. K. Silverman, C.J. Wong, M. Needham, K.N. Diemer, T. Knealing, D. Crone-Todd, M. Fingerhood, P. Nuzzo, & K. Kolodner (2007). A randomized trial of employment-based reinforcement of cocaine abstinence in injection drug users. *Journal of Applied Behavior Analysis*, 40, 387–410, p. 402.
10. M.N. Koffarnus, C.J. Wong, M. Fingerhood, D.S. Svikis, G.E. Bigelow, & K. Silverman (2013). Monetary incentives to reinforce engagement and achievement in a job-skills training program for homeless, unemployed adults. *Journal of Applied Behavior Analysis,* 46, 582–591, p. 589.
11. McDonell, M.G., Howell, D.N., McPherson, S., Cameron, J.M., Srebnik, D., Roll, J.M., & Ries, R. K. (2012). Voucher-based

reinforcement for alcohol abstinence using the ethyl-glucuronide alcohol biomarker. *Journal of Applied Behavior Analysis*, 45, 161–165.

12. G.T. Wilson, R.C. Leaf, & P.E. Nathan (1975). The aversive control of excessive alcohol comsumption by chronic alcoholics in the laboratory setting. *Journal of Applied Behavior Analysis*, 8, 13–26, p. 25.

13. S.C. Cook, A.C. Schwartz, & N.J. Kaslow (2017). Evidence-Based Psychotherapy: Advantages and Challenges. *Neurotherapeutics*, 14, 537–545. https://doi.org/10.1007/s13311-017-0549-4.

14. K.I. Howard, R.F. Krasner, & S.M. Saunders (2017, November 30). Evaluation of psychotherapy. In B.J. Sadock, V.A. Sadock, & P. Ruiz (Eds.), *Kaplan and Sadock's Comprehensive Textbook of Psychiatry*, 10th Edition, Vol. 2. Philadelphia, PA: Lippincott Williams & Wilkins.

15. W.A. Rogers, R. Pak, & A.D. Fisk (2007). Applied cognitive psychology in the context of everyday living. In F.T. Durso (Ed.), *Handbook of Applied Cognition*, 2nd Edition. New York: Wiley & Sons, Ltd., p. 4.

16. W.A. Rogers, R. Pak, & A.D. Fisk (2007). Applied cognitive psychology in the context of everyday living. In F.T. Durso (Ed.), *Handbook of Applied Cognition*, 2nd Edition. New York: Wiley & Sons, Ltd., p. 4.

17. W.A. Rogers, R. Pak, & A.D. Fisk (2007). Applied cognitive psychology in the context of everyday living. In F.T. Durso (Ed.), *Handbook of Applied Cognition*, 2nd Edition. New York: Wiley & Sons, Ltd., pp. 11–18.

18. W.A. Rogers, R. Pak, & A.D. Fisk (2007). Applied cognitive psychology in the context of everyday living. In, F.T. Durso (Ed.). *Handbook of Applied Cognition*, 2nd Edition. New York: Wiley & Sons, Ltd., p. 5.

19. B.F. Skinner (1957). *Verbal Behavior*. New York: Appleton-Century-Crofts.

20. J.B. Watson (1920). Is thinking merely the action of language mechanisms? *British Journal of Psychology*, 11, 87–104.

21. K.A. Ericsson & H.A. Simon (1993). *Protocol Analysis: Verbal Reports as Data*. Cambridge, MA: Bradford Books/MIT Press.

22. M.L. Sundberg & J.W. Partington (1998). *Teaching Language to Children with Autism or Other Developmental Disabilities*. Danville, CA: Behavior Analysts, Inc.

23. Published by the Association for Behavior Analysis: International. To see recent topics, go to: www.abainternational.org/avbjournal/currentissue.asp

24. J. Michael (1982). Distinguishing between discriminative and motivating functions of stimuli. *Journal of the Experimental Analysis of Behavior*, 37, 149–155.

25. S. Laraway, S. Snycerski, J. Michael, & A. Poling (2003). Motivating operations and terms to describe them: Some further refinements. *Journal of Applied Behavior Analysis*, 36, 407–414.

26. A.J. Ayres (1972). *Sensory Integration and Learning Disorders*. Los Angeles, CA: Western Psychological Services.

27. www.cl-asi.org/about-ayres-sensory-integration

28. R. Watling & S. Hauer (2015, September). Effectiveness of Ayres sensory integration® and sensory-based interventions for people with autism spectrum disorder: A systematic review. *American Journal of Occupational Therapy*, 69. 6905180030. https://doi.org/10.5014/ajot.2015.018051

29. T.N. Davis, S. Durand, & J.M. Chan (2011). The effects of a brushing procedure on stereotypical behavior. *Research in Autism Spectrum Disorders*, 5, 1053–1058. http://dx.doi.org/10.1016/j.rasd.2010.11.011.

30. R. Watling & S. Hauer (2015, September). Effectiveness of Ayres sensory integration® and sensory-based interventions for people with autism spectrum disorder: A systematic review. *American Journal of Occupational Therapy*, 69.

31. T. Smith, D.W. Mruzek, & D. Mozingo (2016). Sensory integration theory. In R.M. Foxx & J.A. Mulick (Eds.), *Controversial Theories for Autism and Intellectual Disabilities*, 2nd Edition. New York: Routledge, p. 249.

32. T.N. Davis, S. Durand, & J.M. Chan (2011). The effects of a brushing procedure on stereotypical behavior. *Research in Autism Spectrum Disorders*, 5, 1053–1058.

33. https://specialneedstoys.com/usa/proprioception/snug-vest-small-sizes.html?gclid=Cj0KCQiA_qD_BRDiARIsANjZ2LDEy2HprgqUn_NsqlDqmmF04K3SXOiY45B1HmmkBoVT6zyefV6NvHcaAk7pEALw_wcB

34. N. Watkins & E. Sparling (2014). The effectiveness of the snug vest on stereotypic behaviors in children diagnosed with an autism spectrum disorder. *Behavior Modification*, 38(3), 412–427.

35. www.cdc.gov/ncbddd/autism/addm.html

36. L. Kanner (1943). Autistic disturbances of affective contact. *The Nervous Child*, 2(2), 217–250.

37. S. Vyse (2014). Where do fads come from? In R.M. Foxx & J.A. Mulick (Eds.), *Controversial Therapies for Autism and Intellectual Disabilities*. New York: Routledge, pp. 3–16.

38. www.usa.gov/common-scams-frauds

39. www.spectrumnews.org/features/deep-dive/the-seekers-parents-who-find-fringe-therapies-for-autism/

40. R.M. Foxx & J.A. Mulick (Eds.) (2016). *Controversial Therapies for Autism and Intellectual Disabilities*. New York: Routledge, pp. 3–16.

41. www.fda.gov/news-events/press-announcements/fda-warns-consumers-about-dangerous-and-potentially-life-threatening-side-effects-miracle-mineral

42. https://autismsciencefoundation.org/what-is-autism/beware-of-non-evidence-based-treatments/

43. https://autismsciencefoundation.org/what-is-autism/beware-of-non-evidence-based-treatments/

REFERENCES

Autism Science Foundation. (2021). *Beware of Non-Evidence Based Treatments*. Retrieved June 5, 2021, from https://autismsciencefoundation.org/what-is-autism/beware-of-non-evidence-based-treatments/

Ayres, A.J. (1972). *Sensory Integration and Learning Disorders*. Los Angeles, CA: Western Psychological Services.

Cook, S.C., Schwartz, A.C., & Kaslow, N.J. (2017). Evidence-Based Psychotherapy: Advantages and Challenges. *Neurotherapeutics*, 14, 537–545. Retrieved June 1, 2021, from https://doi.org/10.1007/s13311-017-0549-4

Davis, T.N., Durand, S., & Chan, J.M. (2011). The effects of a brushing procedure on stereotypical behavior. *Research in Autism Spectrum Disorders*, 5, 1053–1058. Retrieved June 1, 2021, from http://dx.doi.org/10.1016/j.rasd.2010.11.011

Ericsson, K.A., & Simon, H.A. (1993). *Protocol Analysis: Verbal Reports as Data*. Cambridge, MA: Bradford Books/MIT Press.

Foxx, R.M., & Mulick, J.A. (Eds.) (2016). *Controversial Therapies for Autism and Intellectual Disabilities*. New York: Routledge, pp. 3–16.

Glaser, G. (2015, April). The irrationality of Alcoholics Anonymous. *The Atlantic*. Retrieved June 1, 2021, from www.theatlantic.com/magazine/archive/2015/04/the-irrationality-of-alcoholics-anonymous/386255/

Howard, K.I., Krasner, R.F., & Saunders, S.M. (2017, November 30). Evaluation of psychotherapy. In B.J. Sadock, V.A. Sadock, & P. Ruiz (Eds), *Kaplan and Sadock's Comprehensive Textbook of Psychiatry*, 10th Edition, Vol. 2. Philadelphia, PA: Lippincott Williams & Wilkins.

Kanner, L. (1943). Autistic disturbances of affective contact. *The Nervous Child*, 2(2), 217–250.

Koffarnus, M.N., Wong, C.J., Fingerhood, M., Svikis, D.S., Bigelow, G.E., & Silverman, K. (2013). Monetary incentives to reinforce engagement and achievement in a job-skills training program for homeless, unemployed adults. *Journal of Applied Behavior Analysis*, 46, 582–591, p. 589.

Laraway, S., Snycerski, S., Michael, J., & Poling. A. (2003). Motivating operations and terms to describe them: Some further refinements. *Journal of Applied Behavior Analysis*, 36, 407–414.

Leshner, A. (1997). Addiction is a brain disease, and it matters. *Science*, 278(5335), 807–808.

McDonell, M.G., Howell, D.N., McPherson, S., Cameron, J.M., Sreb-nik, D., Roll, J.M., & Ries, R. K. (2012). Voucher-based reinforcement for alcohol abstinence using the ethyl-glucuronide alcohol biomarker. *Journal of Applied Behavior Analysis*, 45, 161–165.

Michael, J. (1982). Distinguishing between discriminative and motivating functions of stimuli. *Journal of the Experimental Analysis of Behavior*, 37, 149–155.

Mignon, S.I. (1996). Physicians' perceptions of alcoholics: The disease concept reconsidered. *Alcoholism Treatment Quarterly*, 14(4), 33–45. https://doi.org/10.1300/j020v14n04_02

National Center on Birth Defects and Developmental Disabilities. Center for Disease Control and Prevention. (2021). Autism and developmental disabilities monitoring (ADDM) network. Retrieved June 1, 2021, from www.cdc.gov/ncbddd/autism/addm.html

Opar, A. (2016, September). The seekers: Why parents try fringe therapies for autism. *Spectrum*. Retrieved June 5, 2021, from www.spectrumnews.org/features/deep-dive/the-seekers-parents-who-find-fringe-therapies-for-autism/

Rogers, W.A., Pak, R., & Fisk, A.D. (2007a). Applied cognitive psychology in the context of everyday living. In F.T. Durso (Ed.), *Handbook of Applied Cognition*, 2nd Edition. New York: Wiley & Sons, Ltd., p. 4.

Rogers, W.A., Pak, R., & Fisk, A.D. (2007b). Applied cognitive psychology in the context of everyday living. In F.T. Durso (Ed.), *Handbook of Applied Cognition*, 2nd Edition. New York: Wiley & Sons, Ltd., p. 5.

Rogers, W.A., Pak, R., & Fisk, A.D. (2007c). Applied cognitive psychology in the context of everyday living. In F.T. Durso (Ed.), *Handbook of Applied Cognition*, 2nd Edition. New York: Wiley & Sons, Ltd., pp. 11–18.

Silverman, K., Wong, C.J., Needham, M., Diemer, K.N., Knealing, T., Crone-Todd, D., Fingerhood, M., Nuzzo, P., & Kolodner, K. (2007). A randomized trial of employment-based reinforcement of cocaine abstinence in injection drug users. *Journal of Applied Behavior Analysis*, 40, 387–410, p. 402.

Skinner, B.F. (1957). *Verbal Behavior*. New York: Appleton-Century-Crofts.

Smith, T., Mruzek, D.W., & Mozingo, D. (2016). Sensory integration theory. In R.M. Foxx & J.A. Mulick (Eds.), *Controversial Theories for Autism and Intellectual Disabilities*, 2nd Edition. New York: Routledge, p. 249.

Snug Vest. Retrieved June 1, 2021, from https://specialneedstoys.com/usa/proprioception/snug-vest-small-sizes.html?gclid=Cj0KCQiA_qD_BRDiARIsANjZ2LDEy2HprgqUn_NsqlDqmmF04K3SXOi-Y45B1HmmkBoVT6zyefV6NvHcaAk7pEALw_wcB

Sundberg, M.L., & Partington, J.W. (1998). *Teaching Language to Children with Autism or Other Developmental Disabilities*. Danville, CA: Behavior Analysts, Inc.

USAGov. The official guide to government information and services, updated June 2, 2021. Retrieved June 5, 2021, from www.usa.gov/common-scams-frauds

U.S. Food and Drug Administration. (2019, August 12). FDA warns consumers about the dangerous and potentially life threatening side effects of miracle mineral solution. Retrieved June 5, 2021, from www.fda.gov/news-events/press-announcements/fda-warns-consumers-about-dangerous-and-potentially-life-threatening-side-effects-miracle-mineral

Vyse, S. (2014). Where do fads come from? In R.M. Foxx & J.A. Mulick (Eds.), *Controversial Therapies for Autism and Intellectual Disabilities*. New York: Routledge, pp. 3–16.

Watkins, N., & Sparling, E. (2014). The effectiveness of the snug vest on stereotypic behaviors in children diagnosed with an autism spectrum disorder. *Behavior Modification*, 38(3), Figure 1 p. 419.

Watling, R., & Hauer, S. (2015, September). Effectiveness of Ayres sensory integration® and sensory-based interventions for people with autism spectrum disorder: A systematic review. *American Journal of Occupational Therapy*, 69.

Watson, J.B. (1920). Is thinking merely the action of language mechanisms? *British Journal of Psychology*, 11, 87–104.

Wilson, G.T., Leaf, R.C., & Nathan, P.E. (1975). The aversive control of excessive alcohol comsumption by chronic alcoholics in the laboratory setting. *Journal of Applied Behavior Analysis*, 8, 13–26. p. 25.

Woods, D.W., Watson, T.S., Wolfe, E., Twohig, M.P., & Friman, P.C. (2001). Analyzing the influence of tic-related talk on vocal and motor tics in children with Tourette's syndrome. *Journal of Applied Behavior Analysis*, 34(3), 353–356.

Chapter
Seven

Myths and the Media

DOI: 10.4324/9781003160915-8

QUESTION #38.

Some People Refer to Reinforcement as a Form of Bribery; Do You Agree With That?

Is reinforcement bribery? Absolutely not! A bribe is defined as "money or favor given or promised in order to influence the judgment or conduct of a person in a position of trust" (Merriam-Webster online, 2021). Behavior analysts abhor the notion that a powerful generalized positive reinforcer such as money would be used to persuade someone to engage in dishonest or illegal behavior. We *do* like the idea of using powerful generalized reinforcers to strengthen *appropriate* behaviors. Many parents who have difficulty convincing their children to complete school homework use money or privileges as a reinforcer

> *"Behavior analysts abhor the notion that a powerful generalized positive reinforcer such as money would be used to persuade someone to engage in dishonest or illegal behavior."*

for getting the assignments done on time. This is similar to adults being paid by their employers for the work they do. Either way, it only seems fair. Some parents provide a bonus for grades on report cards. In neither case is money or favorite activities used as a *bribe* since the target behavior is highly appropriate. Another feature of bribes that the dictionary does not seem to mention is that bribes are usually offered *in advance* as an incentive for the illegal behavior. An example of a bribe would be, "I can guarantee you a $50,000 payoff if you just sign that resolution from the county commission." As you know by now, reinforcers are always made contingent on a behavior. This means that reinforcers *follow* a behavior. Behavior analysts strongly discourage the idea of holding up the reinforcer as an antecedent for behavior.

We've All Witnessed Scenes Like This in the Grocery Store

Scene One: "Mommy, I want that, right there, I want it. I want it." This 4-year-old cutie-pie is standing in the grocery basket pointing at the sugar-coated cereal she saw on this morning's children's television show. Mom initially refused, saying in a matter-of-fact voice, "No, not today. You don't need that; we already have cereal."

Scene Two: "Please, please, mommy, I want it, I want it!" Now she's screaming and crying. Several customers pause to see what is going on, mom takes a quick look around and sees the gathering crowd. There is more crying, and cutie-pie now looks like she might be holding her breath. Mom gives up, saying, "Okay, okay. If you stop crying and sit down, I'll get it for you, but you have to stop crying."

Scene Three: Our little moppet is sitting in the cart and, having opened the box, is eating the chocolate-coated bites of cereal. Quietly. There is a satisfied little grin on her face that says, "There; I showed you who's boss." In this case, the food *was* used as a bribe: not that ceasing the crying was an illegal behavior, but mom essentially promised a reward, under duress, to stop an aversive event. You might ask, "What should mom have done under the circumstance?" The way this should be handled may be awkward, but sometimes parents must swallow their pride and do what is in the best behavioral interest of their children. In this case, when the screaming and wailing started, mom should have taken her little darling out of the store (saying to the nearest clerk, "I'll be right back to finish my shopping," not talking to her daughter at all, just walking briskly straight to the car. Put the little screamer in the car-seat and let her go at it until she stops (extinction). Although it is hard to do this, mom needs to maintain her composure and not show any signs of anger or being emotional. Then, as soon as the child is calm and quiet, it's back to the store and right down that same cereal aisle again. If cutie-pie repeats her tantrum, it's back to the car. It shouldn't take more than two or three repetitions for her to get it. On future trips, mom could establish the rules before they leave the house, "We're going shopping in a little while. I want you to be good today with no asking for anything and no crying. If you cry, we will leave the store." This is the appropriate way to use reinforcers. Reinforcers are planned in advance by the parent who sets the rules and who will not be blackmailed into giving a *bribe* to a screaming child.

• •

Key Concepts:
Reinforcement as bribery, bribes, extinction

EXERCISES:

1. What are bribes? How is a bribe different than a reinforcer?
2. You are at a social gathering. Someone finds out you are a behavior analyst. They say, "So do you believe in paying off kids for doing their chores and things like that? I think all these new child-rearing techniques are ridiculous. We did our chores because we had to. I don't think you should bribe kids with money and toys to do what they are supposed to do." How would you respond?

QUESTION #39.

If You Use Behavioral Procedures Like Food Treats and Tokens With Your Kids, Will They Get to Where They Only Work for Reinforcers?

Quick Take

> *"It is important to fade out the tangible rewards in favor of the natural consequences of the behavior."*

There is really no reason for children to become dependent on food treats and tokens unless the parents don't properly manage the consequences. One very important rule of positive reinforcement with children and adults is that it is important to fade out the tangible rewards in favor of the natural consequences of the behavior.

When it came using behavior procedures, Betty was a grandmother who was a natural. When her daughter had to enter a residential treatment program for substance abuse, Betty began raising Wyatt and Jacob, her five-and six-years old grandsons. Betty had some in-home behavioral services when her grandsons were first moved into her home and with the assistance of a behavior analyst, she learned how to teach new skills, use reinforcement, and set up a very basic token system.

Betty decided that the boys needed to learn some basic household chores. After learning about "Grandma's Rule" (also called the *Premack Principle*), from the behavior analyst, she started by having them clean up their rooms to gain access to other reinforcers. Clean up your room and you can go outside, clean up your room and you can come down to dinner, and clean up your room and you can watch TV or play a video game. That went fairly well, and the boys learned the routine in a few weeks. Betty went to work one day and announced to her friends she was going to teach the boys to do their own laundry. Her co-workers (many who couldn't get their spouses or children to do laundry) laughed and said, "Good luck."

In the first session to teach Wyatt and Jacob to use the washing machine, Betty discovered they could not reach the controls. She took the boys to the store and let them choose a small stepstool for doing the laundry. Then came the hands-on instructions and the step-by-step, "this is what you do next" training with Betty modeling the behaviors as the boys practiced. When each boy completed his first load of laundry, Betty gave him a quarter. In the beginning, Betty was present every time the children used the washer and dryer, but she was eventually able to fade her presence. Before long, the boys washed their own clothes and instead of getting a quarter each time, Betty transitioned them to a small weekly allowance. Throughout the entire process, as the boys learned new skills, Betty praised the quality of their work, bragged on them to friends and neighbors, and let them know how proud of them she was that they were growing into fine young men who could be counted on to help when needed.

There are many possible ways to cause problems a system like this. Not fading out the money very gradually, or not pairing the money with praise will soon cause trouble. It is important to point out the natural consequences, which were in this case having clean clothing to wear to school. Anyone who decides to use tangible rewards should start with a plan in mind for eventually fading them for naturally occurring reinforcers.

Technically Speaking

Quite a few years ago, some researchers came up with the idea that reinforcers not only don't work but that they have negative side effects. They conducted some laboratory research with 4th and 5th graders that demonstrated a reduction in behavior rather than an increase *after* the incentives were withdrawn. They called this the "over justification effect."[1] A behavior analyst colleague of ours, Dr. Matt Normand of the University of the Pacific, was asked to comment on this in an article published in *The Atlantic* magazine, "Stop Worrying About Free Beer and Doughnuts. We're in the Middle of a Pandemic." The article had to do with rewarding citizens for getting their vaccine shots.[2] "There are major problems with that literature. The *over justification effect* was seen only in repetitive tasks, and only in the first few repetitions, after which the effect went away. Plus, it seemed to act only on people who were happy to do the job in the first place," said Normand.

There was an unfortunate subtitle to this article, "For too long, we've believed the myth that incentives backfire. But there's nothing wrong with bribing people to get vaccinated." As we pointed out in Question 38, when reinforcers are used for positive, principled, morally correct, law-abiding behaviors, the term bribery is simply not appropriate

• •

Key Concepts:
Premack Principle, "grandma's rule", token system

EXERCISES:

1. You have been asked by a parent how she can get her 8-year-old son who hates homework to get his homework done before 10:00 p.m. By then, she is frustrated and yelling at him. What are some basic suggestions you could give?
2. What is the Premack Principle?
3. Is it appropriate to use token systems (or token economies) with young children? If you had a seven year old whose had a basic

chore list including clean her bedroom, do her homework, and clean the hamster cage every day, how could you use a token system for these behaviors? What would you do first?

4. Do you feel it is appropriate to reward citizens for engaging in socially appropriate behaviors? What do you see as the pros and cons?

QUESTION #40.

Can You *Cure* Autism With ABA? Is Your Goal to Make Children With ASD "Normal?"

When we think about autism, we do not think of ABA as a way to *cure* this bio-neurological developmental disability. Behavior analysis is a *treatment*, not a *cure*, for autism, As far as we know, there is no cure. We do know that based on six decades of ABA treatment and research, many of the symptoms (including a lack of social and communication skills and little to no play repertoire) can be overcome so that the children with this diagnosis can eventually lead relatively normal lives. Critics of behavior analysis like to portray children who have received ABA treatment as robot-like, but this is simply not true. Advances in school and community treatment approaches emphasize individualized treatment methods based on caregiver input and parent training, and this is a significant part of the approach. Pivotal response treatment (PRT) is another behavioral approach specifically designed to improve communication and social skills. This method uses a naturalistic approach to skill development that emphasizes self-initiation and motivation through the use of intrinsically reinforcing activities. In most cases, children in the 2–3-year-old range arc treated in the home setting, and as they move through treatment, they are prepared to enter pre-school, where therapists and teachers will

> *"Behavior analysis is a treatment, not a cure, for autism."*

> *"The goal of behavior analysis is not to make children 'normal' but rather to give them the tools necessary to enjoy a normal life."*

equip them with the skills necessary to succeed in regular classrooms as they get a little older.

The goal of behavior analysis is not to make children "normal" but rather to give them the tools necessary to enjoy a normal life, engaging actively with their family, participating in school activities, and fulfilling their needs for regular leisure and play activities with neurotypical children. Our broader goal, of course, is for them to become independent, make their own choices, and live their lives as fully as possible. Some parents who were early adopters of behavior analysis treatment are now able to see their ASD offspring successfully navigate their way through college and graduate with their peers. What a joy this must be for their parents, who may have been told early on that their newly diagnosed child might have to be institutionalized.

As has been said before, behavior analysts do *not* believe that autism can be cured with ABA. We can assess behavior deficits such as the lack of language and social skills, and we can determine if there are behaviors that stand in the way of the child being able to interact with teachers and other children. When we are successful, we would *not* say that the child is "cured," since we know that whatever caused the autism is still there in the DNA and the nervous system. We believe that it is only possible to find a "cure" for autism once scientists and physicians understand the cause. The cause of autism is still a mystery. Autism is similar to the common cold in that since we don't know exactly what causes it, we can only try to manage the *symptoms*. At this point, we know that cold symptoms are caused by a virus, a rhinovirus to be precise, but a "cure" for the common cold still may be years away.

We also know that certain science-sounding cures such as stem cell therapy, neurofeedback, brain-stimulating implants, and special diets are no cure for autism either, although they may relieve some symptoms on a temporary basis.[3] What we do know is that we have a behavioral technology to teach the behaviors that have been lost. Based on 60 years of applied research, we know this technology can be delivered by well-trained therapists in an effective, reliable, and ethical manner. We also know that alternative medical/biological interventions do not work and may cause harm. The FDA has issued a warning on false claims for treatments or cures for autism that should assist parents in understanding that these often bizarre interventions are truly dangerous, including chelation, hyperbaric oxygen, clay baths, camel's milk, Miracle Mineral Solution (bleach), and essential oils.[4]

• •

Key Concepts:
Bio-neurological developmental disability, cure vs treatment, pivotal response treatment, false claims

EXERCISES:

1. Go to your favorite browser and look up "cures for autism." Read more about this concept.
2. Look up pivotal response treatment to learn more about the possibility of changes in the brain as the result of behavioral treatment that show up as biomarkers.

QUESTION #41.

I Heard That Behavior Analysts Were Like the Tin Man From *The Wizard of Oz*—Heartless—Is That True?

This is another myth that borders on ridiculous. Behavior analysts feel strongly about their clients. They go to great lengths to provide excellent professional services that will help clients grow and function in their communities and society. The notion that behavior analysts are heartless may come from the technical language or jargon used by some behavior analysts. Scientific jargon can be viewed as cold and hard for the lay person (such as parents) to understand. Our code of ethics (i.e., the Ethics Code for Behavior Analysts) requires behavior analysts to use language that is *reasonably understandable* when working with clients.

The code of ethics also cautions behavior analysts not to develop multiple relationships with our clients. This means behavior analysts are not allowed to become friends with their clients. Our motto is *Friendly but not friends*. Even though we would love to, we are not allowed to go to a client's birthday party and help them celebrate, because this would be a slippery slope toward a friendship with the client. The same goes for a weekend trip to the beach or to Aspen for a week of skiing with the idea the behavior analyst will be informally shaping on the behavior of the client while splashing in the ocean.

In the *Wizard of Oz* novel, the Tin Man was greatly misunderstood. Given an unfair bad rap for being cold and heartless, he was one of the most sensitive, kind, and compassionate characters in the story. These traits, we believe, describe the sympathetic nature of most behavior analysts. Behavior analysts are kind and caring individuals who only want the best for their clients. They will protect the rights of their clients at all times, and they will work hard to ensure that their clients are safe from harm.

The codes of ethics for both BCBAs and RBTs is clear. We are obligated to watch out for our clients' best interest; to use safe, least restrictive procedures; and to protect client confidentiality and privacy. In the treatment mode, we only use evidence-based procedures and constantly take data to make sure those treatments are working. We know of behavior analysts who care so much for their clients that they will put their employment at risk to protect them from harm. We have seen behavior analysts brought to tears describing a youngster's successes in learning to utter the words "I love you" to a parent or seeing them play with another child for the first time.

• •

Key Concepts:
Friendly but not friends, jargon, Do no harm

EXERCISE:

1. Check online for behavioral treatment agencies or clinics in your community. Contact an agency and ask if it would be possible to interview a behavior analyst. In the interview, ask the behavior analyst to describe some of their experiences with their clients and to describe some client successes. Does the behavior analyst seem heartless to you?

QUESTION #42.
Do You Only Work With Children With Bad Behavior?

Quick Take

The mayor of Madison, Wisconsin, was interviewed recently and asked about their reputation for bad weather (Madison has an average of 42 inches of snow per year and average winter temperatures of 27° highs and 8° lows). She responded, "We have a saying about that—there is no bad weather, just bad clothing." Behavior analysts feel

> *"We feel the same about the kids we work with: they don't have bad behaviors; they are just stuck in bad environments."*

the same about the children and adults who are our clients. They don't have bad behaviors; they are just stuck in bad environments. Unfortunately, some of these environments set the stage for aggressive, destructive, noncompliant, and elopement behaviors.

Behavior analysts do specialize in the treatment of these disruptive behaviors, probably more so than any other human services profession. Most children who engage in these disturbing patterns and actions are referred for behavior analysis services. However, behavior analysts are not limited to working with maladaptive behaviors. We have a very broad reach in terms of other behaviors, including teaching social skills, fluent verbal behaviors, essential academic competences, distinctive athletic ability, and life-saving safety behaviors. Behavior analysts work with coaches to develop strategies for producing top performance from their teams and with teachers to help children master essential educational skills. They also work with parents to devise home-based routines that guide their children to make the right choices, show initiative, and help others in their family and in their community.

Behavior analysts can work with basically any behavior in any setting with people of any age. This is known professionally as our *scope of practice*. All we need is a request for assistance and consent from the parties involved for us to proceed with an intake and assessment so we can develop an ethical behavior plan. One limiting condition is that we must have the full cooperation of the individuals in the setting, whether it is a school, clinic, hospital, home, or the community. In the current situation with a flood of children with ASD, most of our requests are from parents who are desperate for treatment. The vast majority of behavior analysts are working with those children, who often have challenging behaviors along with severe social and language deficits.

Technically Speaking

One of the most creative and fascinating series of studies on teaching safety in children using behavioral procedures has been carried out at the University of South Florida by Dr. Ray Miltenberger and his colleagues. It is not well known how many school-age children die from firearms each year. In 2017, for example, there were a staggering 2,462 children who were killed by guns.[5] Dr. Miltenberger, a behavior analyst professor, has developed a solution. He teaches children how to respond if they should find a gun in their home or at school. His methodology involves behavioral skills training (BST) to prevent children from playing with guns.[6] Miltenberger starts by recruiting preschool children and taking baseline measures of how they react to finding a gun. Parents must give informed consent, and the gun is deactivated, of course. In one study, three target safety behaviors were taken via hidden video cameras. Following a short baseline, the children receive two BST sessions on three safety skills in the home or classroom setting.

The procedure involved instruction on the three skills related to what to do if you find a gun: 1) do not touch it, 2) get away from the gun, and 3) tell an adult you found a gun. Sometime within the next 30 minutes, the children had an opportunity to go into the area where the disabled gun was stashed. If the child did not exhibit the three skills, an experimenter entered the room and conducted additional training. Within two days, a second assessment was conducted. If the child followed the three rules, they were praised, and if they did not follow the rules, they were given additional training.

As you can see from Figure 7.1, the "in situ," meaning on site, training using BST was extremely effective in a very short period of time. It basically took just two sessions to teach the children all three safety

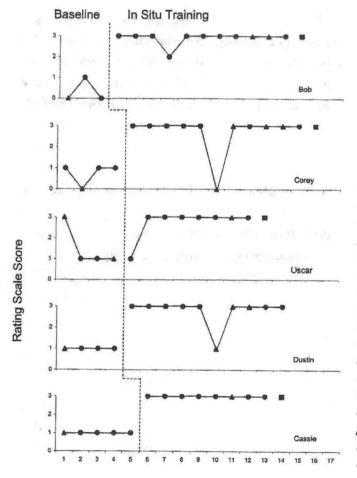

FIGURE 7.1 Rating scale scores for 5 participants during baseline and in situ training phases. Circles are daycare assessments, triangles are home assessments, and squares are dyad assessments. The last home or daycare data point for all participants is a three-month follow-up assessment.

behaviors. Most important was the maintenance of these behaviors. The children still knew the skills and acted safely three months later!

• •

Key Concepts:
Scope of practice, BST, gun safety behaviors, in situ, maintenance of behaviors

---

EXERCISES:

1. In your travels around your community, observe the behavior of people that you encounter. Ask yourself if a behavioral approach might be used to improve those behaviors.
2. Now, using the internet, go to the webpage for the *Journal of Applied Behavior Analysis* (https://onlinelibrary.wiley.com/journal/19383703). Using key words, find an article describing a treatment for a behavior that you have observed.

QUESTION #43.

I Saw Dr. Phil on TV One Time and He Sounded Like a Behavior Analyst. He's Known for Asking, "How's That Workin' for Ya'?" and Promotes "Commando Parenting." What Do You Think of Him?

First Author, Jon Bailey, Writes

Dr. Phil McGraw is a clinical psychologist, talk show host, author, and marketing genius who has the best PR people in the business working for him. Backed initially by Oprah Winfrey, he took the world by storm with his jovial Oklahoma drawl and his seeming directness, warmth, and sincerity. His degree is in psychology, his specialty was in behavioral medicine, and rumor has it that he took a behavioral psychology course at the University of North Texas, where he earned his PhD. He is not specifically trained as a behavior analyst, and it shows. Most of the time Dr. Phil comes across as a common-sense, compassionate, but blunt professional who likes to throw out catchphrases that sound sort of behavioral, "How's that workin for ya'?" being one of the most famous. The question implies that the consequences for a behavior that the guest is describing are just not there. Many of those guests have outrageous personal goals. "I want to be a YouTube influencer," pops up regularly,

> *"Most of the time Dr. Phil comes across as a common-sense, compassionate, but blunt professional who likes to throw out catchphrases that sound sort of behavioral, 'How's that workin for ya?' being one of the most famous."*

but the person is not willing to put in the work that would take, has no fashion sense, is usually not well groomed, and is still living off his mother's largesse in the basement of her home.

Dr. Phil tends to dramatize the problems that people have using staged video clips that are repeated at the beginning of each segment following a commercial break (about every 6 minutes or so). There is a buildup with teasers to keep the viewers glued to their TV sets, "When we come back, Julie tells us a secret that she's never told anyone, and it explains why she has no backbone."

People report that they think Dr. Phil is a behavior analyst or a behavioral psychologist because he occasionally suggests what appear to be operant procedures or alludes to the role of consequences in child rearing: "If a kid chooses the behavior, he chooses the consequences," and "Don't reward bad behavior."

"If a kid chooses the behavior, he chooses the consequences."

He emphasizes the need for children to follow their parent's directions, attend school, complete their homework, and do their chores and wants the parents, who are usually intimidated by their own children, to provide consequences to make this happen. In general, he supports a sort of benign authoritarian model of parenting but lately has been pushing his Commando Parenting model, which seems to involve doing whatever it takes to gain control over their child. "Take away his toys, take away his covers, take away his blanket." Instead of talking about punishment or response cost, Dr. Phil says, "Remove your child's currency."

The cases that make it to his stage are so dramatic that it's easy to see what the solutions are, and many of them are behavioral but vague. "You have exactly 50% of what it takes to take charge in this family and get Montana under control. [Montana was a 4-year-old who ruled the roost with her screaming fits and aggressive behavior.] You dearly love your children; that's very important. Now you need the other 50%—a plan. And I'm going to give you that plan when we come back." When he comes back, Dr. Phil repeats the footage we've already seen two or three times, and now the parents are sitting in the audience waiting for "The Plan." Dr. Phil says, "You need to strip her room of everything, including the TV, the video games, the bed, everything. You take everything away but the minimum, a mattress on the floor. Now she must earn everything back. She will scream, but you won't give in. She will whine and plead, but she gets nothing back until she asks for it nicely and politely, do you understand?" The parents, with dazed eyes staring at their guru, all nod "yes." They will strip the room, they won't give in, they promise. Does this sound like 1960s-style behavior modification to you? It does to us, and there is essentially no behavior *analysis* in Dr. Phil's approach. It's dramatic and draconian, but it's not the way a behavior analyst would approach the problem. And, if this is all the parents are going to get, we'd predict that it's going to fail. Miserably. As a concept, the notion that you will strip a 4-year-old of all her worldly possessions and then make her earn them back sounds like powerful medicine, but how are the parents to carry this out exactly? How much good behavior does Montana have to engage in? What if she gets a few things back and then falls back into her old routine? Without someone there to help them through what could be a mighty big conflict, we doubt that the parents will be able to navigate these troubled waters alone. Perhaps the most perplexing aspect of this particular show was that when viewed carefully, the film clips do not show that Montana was at all responding to possessions as related to her severe tantrums. She wasn't interested in watching TV or playing with video games. The video clips clearly show that Montana was aggressive related to not getting her way, to not being the center of attention, and that it was primarily the mother's attention that she was seeking. In other words, Dr. Phil, because he was not a behavior analyst, did not see what was very obvious from his own film clips. Mom would make a request, "Montana, it's time to pick up your toys." Montana says, "Nooo," and raises her hand with a toy in it, threatening mom. Then there is a loud scream, and mom leaves the room. In another clip, two children are playing together, ignoring Montana. Montana approaches with a toy and hits one child right in the face. The child falls over and starts crying. Mom comes in off camera and grabs

Montana. Cut. "When we come back, I'll tell you what we're going to do about this; don't touch that dial."

Second Author, Mary Burch, Writes

There are 70 questions in this edition of *How to Think Like a . . . Behavior Analyst*. As authors, we agree on the answers to every single question but this one. Dr. Phil is a good guy. Nope, he doesn't take data on his show, and he doesn't use words like *functional analysis*. And it is correct that he doesn't always look for the cause of the behavior. But here's what he has done. He's managed to get the American public interested in thinking about behavior. He talks about solving behavior problems in an unemotional way and in finding solutions that work. He uses "plain English," just like behavior analysts should be doing. He refers people to state-of-the-art treatment programs. He does explain behavioral concepts so people can understand them, "Well, you understand she's doin' that because there is some pay-off, right?" He talks about time-out and explains if the child is being sent to a bedroom full of toys and electronic gadgets, she has not been sent to time-out. Dr. Phil may be bringing us "Behavior Lite," but by golly, he's bringing it to millions of people.

Dr. Phil has brought the topic of behavior to the public, and that is something we as behavior analysts have failed at miserably. Years ago, at the Association for Behavior Analysis International (ABAI) conference, Paul Chance encouraged behavior analysts to take our message to mass media outlets in addition to the scientific journals. We haven't done it yet. As behavior analysts, we spend too much time preaching to the converted. Far too few of us have been media trained. You can't go on television or the radio with a crying parent and talk to her about stimulus control and the contingencies of reinforcement and expect to be invited back. Dr. Phil has taken a very important first step, and while he may not adhere to the experimental rigor we would like, as a field, we have a lot to learn from him. Tell me that Dr. Phil has not made a significant contribution, and I have only one response. As the bald guy from Oklahoma says, "That dog won't hunt."

Key Concepts:
Dr. Phil, Commando Parenting, behavior modification vs behavior analysis

EXERCISES:

1. Watch an episode of Dr. Phil. What are the behavior problems discussed on the day you watch the show? Can you identify any behavioral solutions offered by Dr. Phil?
2. Read an article in the *Journal of Applied Behavior Analysis*. If you were hired as a media consultant, how would you write a press release to report the findings to the general public.
3. Select an article on autism from a behavioral journal. Describe (you don't have to actually do this) how you would re-write the scientific article and the points you would cover if you were to submit this article to *Parenting Magazine*.

QUESTION #44.

What About TV Shows That Depict Behavior Analysts? Is That an Accurate Picture of What They Do?

This is an interesting question. Since actual behavior analysis therapy sessions have not been shown on broadcast television, we do not have a direct answer to this question. ABA shows up as a topic on many YouTube videos, and there are some clips of therapy, but at present, after a perusal of what is available at this point, we do not have any to recommend. Some videos posted on the web do not demonstrate best practice for one-on-one therapy. Most of them violate our code of ethics with regard to confidentiality, since the face of the child is clearly visible and his or her name is used repeatedly. It may be that the parents have given consent for these videos to be made and shown to the public, but we have serious concerns about the potential for harm for the children who are displayed.

There is one clip of the actress Minka Kelly portraying a behavior therapist on an episode of the NBC drama *Parenthood* (Parenthood, 2010). In this episode, the therapist is working for the first time with a child named Max. It shows her attempting to get Max to cooperate with playing a board game. She does hold fast on the contingency she has established, but it doesn't really represent a whole session, and of course it is "acting" and not a real therapy session. (A reference for this episode is provided under "References" at the end of the chapter. You can type the specifics into your search engine to locate the video).

There are several TV shows about "behavioral" analysis which involve criminal profiling and forensic psychology. This has nothing to do with *behavior* analysis or ABA. The shows profiling criminal behavior have a completely different approach from ABA. *Criminal Minds*, for example, has an FBI department called the Behavioral Analysis Unit that gathers anecdotal data from similar crimes and attempts to generalize to the one featured on the current episode. It should be noted that this approach, which is popular in the media, has no empirical evidence to back it up. It makes for good TV, though, and even though it is not necessarily based on science as ABA is, it probably encourages the audience to at least think about behavior as a topic for study.

Operant conditioning is shown in a humorous way as portrayed by Sheldon on *The Big Bang Theory*. We have previously mentioned this example where Sheldon attempts to modify Penny's "correct behavior" by offering her chocolate contingent on talking less. Later, he punishes Leonard with water mist for forbidding his use of this "harmless scientific protocol." We don't recommend Sheldon's methods, since they are obviously manipulative and would clearly be seen as offensive, but it does get people talking about behavior, in this case the use of consequences to change everyday behavior.

● ●

Key Concepts:
Behavioral analysis vs behavior analysis, criminal profiling, operant conditioning on TV

EXERCISES:

1. While we don't have any good video clips to recommend on YouTube regarding behavior-analytic procedures in therapy, you may want to take a look and see what you think.
2. For a good, legitimate presentation on behavior analysis by one of the foremost experts on behavior analysis, we recommend searching on YouTube for Dr. Mark Sundberg. He has several videos that are very worthwhile.

QUESTION #45.
Are Behaviorists the Ones That Don't Believe in Feelings and Emotions?

As behavior analysts, we do not usually target emotions, but that does not mean that we are not concerned with emotional behavior. The way we think about this is that emotions accompany certain behaviors and certainly result from consequences, but emotions alone are probably not responsible for behavior. We suggest focusing on the environmental change that produced the troubling emotion in the first place. A person who is sad or angry feels that way for some reason. Something has happened to cause this feeling, and we are concerned about that because we don't like to see a person being miserable and very much want to help them. Focusing too long on the emotion itself can be a major distraction that could keep the behavior analyst from identifying the cause. Behavior analysts generally discount programs to enhance feelings, such as the failed 1986 "California Task Force on the Importance of Self-Esteem" (Foxx & Roland, 2005).[7]

The goal of this program was to improve reading by enhancing "feelings of self-esteem" in school children. There are other similar programs such as programs in "anger management" that do not deal with the cause of the anger. Learning to breathe deeply, count to 100 slowly, or play mind games with yourself avoids what could be a serious impediment to happiness. As an example, when a person is extremely angry or depressed over a work situation (e.g., the person is being sexually harassed by her supervisor), it would be far better to deal with this by filing a complaint against the boss with Human Resources than going to counseling for anger management or seeing a therapist for the depression. As behavior analysts, we would like to see people be more analytical about their feelings and would urge them to learn how to determine what the causal variables are and make the necessary adjustments to produce more desirable outcomes *and* feelings.

A troubling personal problem or difficult work environment that produces destructive, angry feelings cannot be fixed by simply learning to control your reactions to these situations. Although you may feel you are at the mercy of these emotions, you are not. From

> *"Although it may feel like you are at the mercy of these emotions, you are not."*

a behavioral perspective, determining what those variables are is the first step, and the next is to make some changes with those individuals or those environments before the anger turns into rage. You can choose to remove those things or people from your life or modify their behavior so that you can live a peaceful life. The solution involves having a plan of action and engaging in active behavior-change strategies.

Behavior analysts use emotions and emotional behavior as indicators of satisfactory or unsatisfactory contingencies of reinforcement in a person's life. Emotions are important and a key to understanding what needs to be done behaviorally to help the person improve their condition.

• •

Key Concepts:
Anger management, file a complaint with Human Resources

EXERCISES:

1. Using your browser, look up anger management. What strategies can you find for handling anger and rage?
2. Then think in terms of changing the environment so that those unpleasant emotions are removed or greatly reduced.
3. To look at this another way, think of situations that give you positive feelings such as joy, gratitude, hope, pride, and love. Now see if you can find ways to increase the occurrence of those situations, which may involve people, animals, or different environments.

QUESTION #46.
ABA Stands for "Autism Behavior Analysis," Right?

Wrong! The answer to this question is a resounding, "No." As we have mentioned several times previously, ABA stands for *applied* behavior analysis. The notion that the "A" stands for autism would lead some to believe that behavior analysis principles and procedures are only used with children with ASD, and this is certainly not true. For more than 50+ years of research and application, the science of behavior and the methods of operant conditioning have been used in every conceivable setting. Some of the many applications of ABA have included:

- *Pre-schools* where children have been taught to walk, use words, identify objects, perform early self-care skills (such as dressing, putting on shoes), and play cooperatively with other children.
- *Elementary and high schools* where students have behavioral goals such as staying on task, following classroom rules and the schedule, riding the bus (while behaving appropriately), and completing work on time and accurately.
- *Nursing homes* where behavioral techniques have been used to manage and improve age-related issues with goals such as: walk and exercise throughout the day, attend therapy sessions, eat on schedule, improve balance and use safety procedures, self-care, and interaction with others.
- *Sports*, which is one of the less frequently studied areas in behavior analysis. Researchers have studied behavioral procedures for improving performance in soccer, golf, horseback riding, gym attendance, and ballet.
- *Businesses and corporate headquarters* where behavior analysts help with issues such as safety behaviors like using equipment properly and following safety protocols, employee performance such as coming to work on time and completing job assignments, and developing specific skills such as public speaking.

Applied behavior analysts have worked in a wide variety of settings with great success. If it involves behavior, we can help.

● ●

Key Concepts:
"A" stands for applied (behavior analysis)

EXERCISES:

1. Go to the search engine for the *Journal of Applied Behavior Analysis* (https://onlinelibrary.wiley.com/journal/19383703) and, using key words, look for research in educational settings. Are any of these studies related to your area of interest?
2. Go to the search engine for the *Journal of Applied Behavior Analysis* (https://onlinelibrary.wiley.com/journal/19383703) and, using key words, look for research in nursing homes. What are some studies involving seniors (behavioral geriatrics)?

QUESTION #47.

What Is Your Position on Social Media? Is This a Good Way to Learn About ABA?

By Yamilex Molina

Social media is a great way to learn about the different areas where applied behavior analysis and BCBAs are needed. There are special interest groups on Facebook where you can meet other practitioners (e.g., RBTs, BCaBAs, BCBAs) interested in special topics. For example, how to apply ABA in the criminal justice system, how to use ABA in behavior gerontology, or how to approach trauma from an ABA perspective are just a few of the many informative pages. There are even groups on Facebook such as Blacks in Behavior Analysis and Minority Behavior Analysts (Figure 7.2). These groups and the Latino Association for Behavior Analysis teach practitioners and caregivers of color how to navigate the discrimination and racism experienced in the field. ABA Skill Share is a Facebook "collaborative" for those interested sharing evidence-based practices in ABA. They specifically forbid members from asking for clinical advice. These groups create a space for important dialogue and help practitioners network.

Additionally, there are many informative profiles on Instagram. For instance, @behaviorchef teaches their followers how to use ABA to

FIGURE 7.2   Graphic for Minority Behavior Analysts (MBA).

lead a healthier lifestyle (Figure 7.2). Another group, @abavisualized (Figure 7.3), uploads easy-to-follow visuals of ABA strategies for caregivers and practitioners. For those preparing to sit for the BCaBA or BCBA exam, @studynotesaba and @rogueaba is a great place to learn the task list or simply become familiar with ABA.

Furthermore, Facebook has groups like AllDayABA and Balanced Behavior Analysts, where recently certified BCBAs can join and learn from more experienced BCBAs. Meanwhile, Instagram has the @_dobettercollective that focuses on professional development for behavior analysts. Finally, Pinterest has a plethora of resources such as token board ideas, creative programs for food selectivity, and even assessment data sheets and tips that a BCBA can easily access or someone interested in the field can explore.

Social media is great; however, there are at least two big "no"s regarding social media. No one should be learning ethics in ABA from social media! If you are a new behavior analyst or therapist, find a more

H: High P-(usually 2-3) easy tasks followed by a difficult task.

Bxchef Example: having a child take 2-3 bites of preferred foods just prior to a bite of non-preferred food paired with praise could help increase food acceptance

FIGURE 7.3   Graphic for behaviorchef.

Look! There is a dog!

These are dogs

Teach the skill
- With various people
- In various settings
- With various materials
- Using varied language
- At various times of the day

Here, you see a dog

This is a dog

ABA Visualized

FIGURE 7.4   Graphic
for abavisualized.

reliable source (e.g., ABAEthicsHotline.com, BCAB's Ethics Hand-book) to learn how to appropriately approach a situation. Social media platforms are a good place to begin asking others in the field if something that feels wrong is unethical; however, no final decision should be based on social media comments, observations, and feedback. As O'Leary et al. (2017)[8] have pointed out, social media is not the place to seek advice about client treatments or interventions. These authors provide numerous examples where the suggestions from anonymous Face-book readers have caused harm to clients or led to ethical situations that are difficult for all parties concerned, and they strongly advise behavior analysts not to seek treatment recommendations from those who have "limited access to the client."

Finally, there is so much to ABA that even when you graduate from a master's program, you are still learning about the field, which is why BCBAs must keep up with research. Therefore, the best way to truly learn about ABA is becoming a registered behavior technician and experiencing firsthand what it's like to directly work with clients. Anything that puts you closer in touch with ABA is the best way to learn about ABA (e.g., internships, shadowing, becoming an RBT).

• •

Key Concepts:
Social media, Facebook, Instagram, ABAEthicsHotline.com

EXERCISES:

1. Go to Facebook and look for an ABA group that you might possibly want to join.
2. If you are interested in learning the basics of ABA, check @ abavisualized on Instagram and browse through the graphics. Do the graphics help you understand the behavioral concepts that are illustrated?

SUMMARY

In this chapter, we address some of the common myths surrounding behavior analysis and describe what behavior analysts think about these issues. We begin with the misguided notion that reinforcement is just a form of bribery and point out that "bribery" is a method of encouraging a person to engage in illegal or unethical conduct. This is a far cry from what we do in ABA. Next, we discuss the idea that ABA can "cure" autism, which is certainly *not* the objective of a behavior analytic approach. Behavior analysis is simply an effective treatment method that, when applied consistently, allows individuals with an ASD diagnosis to live a fuller life. In the early days of ABA, the field was dominated by many "experimental types" who had less concern for their social skills than the behavior analysts who are predominant now. Our current professionals care about their clients, treat them with dignity and respect, and show their delight when clients achieve new goals. Although ABA is largely known for "fixing bad behavior," behavior analysis is currently the most effective approach for teaching safety behaviors and working with children and adolescents who may be a little behind or "at risk" and who need some extra training to adapt more fully to their environment. We occasionally receive questions about Dr. Phil, the popular television psychologist, and people want to know if he is a behavior analyst. We have a mixed review on this, with one author saying, "No!" and the other saying, "Sometimes his approach seems to be behavioral." To see a humorous cartoon-like version of operant conditioning (not behavior analysis), you can watch Sheldon using chocolate as a reinforcer to shape on Penny in *The Big Bang Theory*. (The Big Bang Theory, 2009. You can type the specifics into your search engine to locate the video.) Behavior analysts do believe in feelings, but we search for the causes of those feelings so we can help people overcome those that are harmful and disturbing. In this chapter, we destroy the myth that ABA stands for "autism behavior analysis," and we show that some good material can be found on social media about ABA.

NOTES

1. https://psycnet.apa.org/record/1978-32529-001
2. https://www.theatlantic.com/ideas/archive/2021/05/lottery-tickets-free-beer-covid-vaccine/618918/
3. www.nationwidechildrens.org/family-resources-education/700childrens/2019/04/autism-and-alternative-treatments; www.sciencemag.org/news/2018/09/can-brain-stimulating-implants-treat-some-severe-cases-autism
4. www.fda.gov/consumers/consumer-updates/be-aware-potentially-dangerous-products-and-therapies-claim-treat-autism
5. www.usatoday.com/story/news/nation/2019/03/21/gun-deaths-school-age-children-study/3231754002/
6. R.G. Miltenberger, B.J. Gatheridge, M. Satterlund, K.R. Egemo-Helm, B.M. Johnson, C. Jostad, P. Kelso, & C.A. Flessner (2005). Teaching safety skills to children to prevent gun play: An evaluation of in situ training. *Journal of Applied Behavior Analysis*, 38(3), 395–398.

7. J. Foxx & C. Roland (2005). The self-esteem fallacy. In J.W. Jacobson, R.M. Foxx, & J.A. Mulick (Eds.), *Controversial Therapies for Developmental Disabilities*. Mahwah, NJ: Lawrence Erlbaum.
8. P.N. O'Leary, M.M. Miller, M.L. Olive, & A.N. Kelly (2017). Blurred lines: Ethical implications of social media for behavior analysts. *Behavior Analysis in Practice*, 10(1), 45–51.

REFERENCES

The Big Bang Theory. CBS TV. *The Gothowitz Deviation*. Season 3, Episode 3. Aired October 5, 2009. Director, Mark Cendrowski.

Foxx, J., & Roland, C. (2005). The self-esteem fallacy. In J.W. Jacobson, R.M. Foxx, & J.A. Mulick (Eds), *Controversial Therapies for Developmental Disabilities*. Mahwah, NJ: Lawrence Erlbaum.

Merriam-Webster Online. Retrieved October 30, 2021, from https://www.merriam-webster.com/dictionary/bribe

Miltenberger, R.G., Gatheridge, B.J., Satterlund, M., Egemo-Helm, K.R., Johnson, B.M., Jostad, C., Kelso, P., & Flessner, C.A. (2005). Teaching safety skills to children to prevent gun play: An evaluation of in situ training. *Journal of Applied Behavior Analysis*, 38(3), 395–398.

O'Leary, P.N., Miller, M.M., Olive, M.L., & Kelly, A.N. (2017). Blurred lines: Ethical implications of social media for behavior analysts. *Behavior Analysis in Practice*, 10(1), 45–51.

Parenthood. NBC TV. *The Big O*. Season 1, Episode 6. Aired April 6, 2010. Director, Adam Davidson.

Part
Two

Becoming a Professional

Eight

Starting Your Career in Behavior Analysis

DOI: 10.4324/9781003160915-10

QUESTION #48.
How Do I Get Started in This Field? Do I Have to Be an RBT First?

This is a great question, and the basic answer is that *Yes, you should become a RBT before you move into the field.* It is possible to take another route which is to get your master's degree in psychology or some related field and complete the requirements for the BCBA. However, many graduate programs require that you have a year or two of hands-on experience, which presumes that you started out as an RBT or were working under another similar job title such as behavior tech, behavior interventionist, or behavior specialist.

If you choose to go the RBT First route, it will be important for you to have some exposure to the type of work typically performed by RBTs. It is probably a good idea for you to start with a little homework on RBT certification so you know what to expect. You can do this by going to BACB.com and clicking on the RBT box, where you will find a lot of information about this hands-on, direct-intervention position.

> *"Most people who try the RBT route after graduating find it incredibly fulfilling."*

Once you've done some reading on the RBT certification, your next step is to search the internet for behavior analysis clinics, agencies, or companies (these terms are used interchangeably) in your area. Contact at least one agency and ask if you could conduct an interview with one of their RBTs. Agencies that provide behavior-analytic services are bound by our code of ethics to protect the confidentiality of their clients, so you may have to go through a screening procedure first. Having made personal contact with the agency and RBT, and assuming the interview went well, you may ask if you can observe a session or shadow an RBT for an hour or two. Again, confidentiality is key here. For the interview to happen, you will probably need a background check, for which the agency will explain the details.

If being able to interview an RBT at a local agency works out, you should consider volunteering at the agency/clinic. This will give you additional exposure to behavior analysis in action and a chance to show the agency that you are a worthy and reliable person who is very interested in learning more about the field. You may be asked to give at least eight hours per week, so be prepared to save time in your busy schedule for this once-in-a-lifetime opportunity. In order for the agency to determine if you might be a suitable candidate, they may require that you volunteer for at least a semester (15 weeks).

Most people who try the RBT route after graduating find it incredibly fulfilling, and they want to stay in the field and move up the professional ladder. Behavior techs work directly, hands-on with clients who desperately need behavioral training, and the procedures work well so that you can see almost immediate results. The outcomes are so dramatic that parents can easily see the difference and will heap praise on the tech for "saving our child's life" or "bringing our little boy back to us."

Be sure to read question #53, a *Day in the Life of an RBT*.

• •

Key Concepts:
BACB.com, interview an RBT, shadowing an RBT, volunteering at an agency

EXERCISES:

1. If you are interested in becoming an RBT, go to BACB.com and read through the RBT Handbook.
2. If you have questions, you can contact the RBT that you interviewed or the clinical director at the agency where you volunteered.

QUESTION #49.

How Do I Become an RBT? Can I Use This Credential to Make Money on the Side Such as Babysitting?

If you have made it this far and are still interested in becoming an RBT, you should go back to BACB.com and download the RBT Handbook. Here you will find everything you need to know about becoming an RBT and maintaining your credential. The basics are that you must be at least 18 years old, have at least a high school diploma, pass a background check, complete the 40-hour training requirement, and complete an initial competency assessment. A very handy flowchart of the process of becoming an RBT is shown in Figure 8.1.

> *"The Behavior Analyst Certification Board has determined that RBTs are not allowed to engage in childcare. Period."*

You can ask the clinical director of the agency where you completed your volunteer work if you could sign up for the 40-hour training with them. Some agencies provide this training in-house, while others may

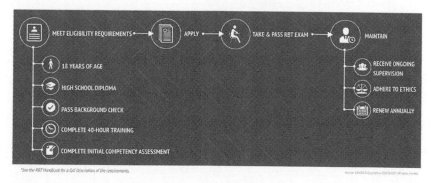

FIGURE 8.1   Overview of RBT requirements flowchart.

send you out to get your training online. At this point, you will proceed with the training and take the exam and then apply for certification as an RBT. Now you are on your way to joining the field.

To answer your second question about using your RBT credential to make money on the side babysitting, the answer is no. The Behavior Analyst Certification Board has determined that RBTs are not allowed to engage in childcare. Period. The reason for this is somewhat complicated, but there are other activities that are not permitted as well. For the details, go to the BACB Newsletter for April 2017 at BACB.com.

• •

Key Concepts:
RBT Handbook, eligibility requirements, no babysitting or childcare

EXERCISES:

1. To learn more about the activities of a registered behavior technician, go to the *RBT Task List* (2nd ed.).
2. To learn even more, while you are on the BACB.com site, click on the RBT Initial Competency Assessment and the RBT 40-hr Training Packet.

QUESTION #50.
Can I Receive This Certification While I Am an Undergrad?

Yes, you can receive the RBT certification while you are an undergraduate, but it would not be through your college or university. Many college students have part-time jobs serving as waiters or Uber drivers. Working as an RBT would also be a part-time job, but you would be providing hands-on, direct therapy to children with disabilities. You could build a resume that might help

> *"ABA agencies . . . are usually looking for smart, ambitious young people who love children, have good social skills, and who are interested in joining the field."*

you get into a graduate program if you decide to go that route. Most behavior analysis organizations employ a few RBTs on a part-time basis, and nearly every college town has one or more of these ABA agencies. They are usually looking for smart, ambitious young people who love children, have good social skills, and who are interested in joining the field. Note that you will need to pass a background check and will probably need to have a car, since some of this work may be in the client's home.

As described in Question #48, you would receive your 40-hour RBT training through an agency or clinic as opposed to your university.

If you are a college student, there are some courses that would be useful for you to take that will prepare you to apply for a graduate program in applied behavior analysis. These include:

- Introduction to Psychology or General Psychology—this is a basic course that outlines all the fields and approaches to psychology.

- Child or Developmental Psychology—this is often required as a pre-requisite for programs that are training students to work in autism or developmental disabilities.
- Learning Theory—this would be most helpful if it covered operant and respondent conditioning, but other theories are likely to be covered as well.
- Applied Behavior Analysis—this course is essential to anyone looking to apply to a graduate program in behavior analysis.
- Research Methods—ideally, this course would cover single-case designs along with group-statistical methods.

• •

Key Concepts:
Certification, part-time RBT work, college courses

EXERCISES:

1. Using your browser, look for behavior analysis agencies in your community. How do they describe their services? Some of them may indicate on their site that they are looking for RBTs and that they offer the 40-hour training.
2. If this looks interesting to you, contact the agency and look into the possibility of applying for RBT training. Be sure to read Questions #47 and #48 to get the full story on entering this field.

QUESTION #51.

What Kind of Jobs/Professional Opportunities Are Available? Where Can I Find Job Openings?

The job market for RBTs appears to be very active. Go to your browser and type in "jobs for RBTs." It is likely that dozens of job postings will pop up for ABA agencies in or near your town as well as in your state and even across the country. Each of these will show whether they offer the 40-hour RBT training and indicate

> *"Job opportunities in this field are booming. There are far more job openings than there are RBTs available to fill them."*

how to contact them for further information. In addition, there may be information on how the ABA company is rated by current or previous employees and how much per hour the agency pays for RBTs.

Job opportunities in this field are booming. There are far more job openings than there are RBTs available to fill them. Within the RBT position, many companies and organizations have designations for those with more experience, such as lead therapist or senior therapist. These might be for RBTs who have one or two years of supervised practice at the agency. Clients in these settings may be young children, or they may also serve adolescents. The types of disabilities may include autism, which is the largest population being treated at this time, as well as clients with Down Syndrome, emotional and behavioral disturbance, and intellectual disabilities. Some hospitals have set up special behavioral treatment units, and there may be employment prospects in these settings for RBTs as well. Some school systems are now requiring teacher aides to receive RBT certification. In these settings, RBTs would be considered paraprofessionals and would be under the supervision of a master's-level teacher who has the BCBA certification.

The *professional* opportunities are somewhat limited for RBTs, since this is the entry-level position in this field. We say "limited" since these positions will all involve direct-hands on therapy with clients or students where you will need to be supervised by a BCBA (see Question #50 for details on supervision). Remember that getting training and experience as an RBT is a gateway to many future professional opportunities. With additional training, you could become a BCBA. Once you've had some experience as an RBT, and you decide you want to continue to grow in this field, you've developed a whole new repertoire of skills that will benefit you when applying to graduate school.

• •

Key Concepts:
Job opportunities, hands-on therapy, work with disabilities

EXERCISES:

1. Go to your browser and type in "jobs for RBTs." What pops up in your area of the country?
2. Got to Indeed.com and search for jobs in different work settings. Click on "Company" and you will see several dozen companies that are advertising for RBTs.

QUESTION #52.

What Is Supervision? Why Do I Have to Be Supervised?

Supervision is a term used to indicate that the RBT is working closely with a BCBA who is serving as a role model, trainer, counselor, and mentor. Your supervisor sets expectations for your clinical performance and will show you how to take data, work with difficult clients, interact appropriately with parents, and prepare case notes for your sessions. In addition, your supervisor will guide you as you learn problem-solving and ethical decision-making skills. RBTs need to be supervised because their BCBA supervisor is totally responsible for their actions on the job. If there is a complaint by a parent, caregiver, or other professional, it will be delivered directly to your supervisor, who is responsible for resolving the problem with you.

It is important to know that your supervisor is totally responsible for the work that you do as an RBT. Supervisors want you to do high-quality work that is delivered precisely according to the behavior plan and is considerate of your client's needs. Supervision is not a behavioral term, so many of us

> *"The purpose of ongoing supervision is to improve and maintain your behavior-analytic, professional, and ethical repertoires and facilitate the delivery of high-quality services to clients."*[1]

> *"It is important to know that your supervisor is totally responsible for the work that you do as an RBT."*

like to refer to it as *behavior shaping*. Shaping involves the gradual improvement of behavior through instruction, modeling, feedback, and practice. Because the essence of supervision involves direct observation of your performance as an RBT, you will need to feel comfortable with someone watching you as you work with your clients. This observation will be followed quickly with feedback. BCBA supervisors are trained to use positive reinforcement as a primary means of helping their RBTs perfect their behavior-analytic service delivery. You should expect to be observed face to face at least twice per month for a total of 5% of the hours that you are working directly with clients.

• •

Key Concepts:
Behavior shaping, behavior plan, ethical repertoire

EXERCISES:

1. Go to BACB.com and type "supervision" into the Search box. Review the Supervisor Training Curriculum to see how BCBA supervisors are trained to do supervision.
2. While you are on this page, scroll down to "Supervising RBTs" and click on the RBT Handbook. Take a look at the Ongoing Supervision section.

QUESTION #53.
Do You Always Work One on One With Clients?

Most of the behavior-analytic work of RBTs is done on one on one since this is the most effective way to train clients and shape on their behavior. Teaching a client to brush their teeth or feed or dress themselves really requires that they have a therapist who is giving their full, undivided attention to the task at hand. This arrangement is even more important when you are dealing with teaching a child to make eye contact, name or match objects, or imitate a gestural move-

> *"There are some circumstances where the RBT therapist may work with two or more clients at a time. These primarily involve teaching social interactions and peer-play activities."*

ment. One skill that many children with ASD are missing has to do with communication. The language of a child with ASD may range from nonexistent to very delayed. The RBT has to imitate the basic elements of language and, using shaping, gradually, step by step, get the child to follow the therapist's cues and produce multi-syllable words.

There are some circumstances where the RBT therapist may work with two or more clients at a time. These primarily involve teaching social interactions and peer-play activities. This is considered small-group instruction. We take both of these "skills" for granted, but in language-delayed or developmentally disabled children, they have to be taught. This generally starts with teaching the child to interact socially with the therapist, and when this repertoire is developed, the therapist may bring in a peer to see if the skills generalize. If the skills don't generalize, the therapist will prompt the peer to ask the client a question such as, "Would you like to play the shopping game with me?" and then prompt the client to respond appropriately. A similar strategy is used in teaching play skills. This usually starts with parallel play and then evolve into interactive play with a peer. The first step is asking the other child if they want to play, then progressing to learning to share toys and taking turns interacting with play materials.

• •

Key Concepts:
Small-group instruction, parallel play, interactive play

EXERCISES:

1. Search the internet for information on small-group instruction, including social interactions and peer play activities.
2. Go to the *Journal of Applied Behavior Analysis* website (https://onlinelibrary.wiley.com/journal/19383703) and look for research on teaching social skills to ASD children.

QUESTION #54.

What Does a Day in the Life of an RBT Look Like?

By Loren Eighmie

Well, it depends. It depends on the type of agency where you are working. An RBT could work at a clinic where the clients are brought to the clinic and then picked up, or they could work for a company that specializes in community-based services. You could be at the clinic, at the client's school, in their home, or even out in the community conducting your session.

> *"BCBAs are like Shakespeare, writing the plays (or programs), but RBTs are the actors."*

Typically, an RBT's responsibilities will look similar no matter where you work. RBTs are responsible for conducting the 1:1 session with a client. This means the RBT implements all the behavior programs (e.g., target goals, probes, acquisition targets, etc.) and records the data from each target. BCBAs are like Shakespeare, writing the plays (or programs), but RBTs are the actors who work directly with clients to implement what the BCBA writes. Being an RBT involves a lot of work on your part. You will see the clients on a daily basis, and depending on where you work, an RBT could potentially work with one to six clients.

As an RBT, you must know each client's behavior support plan, their reduction behavior protocols, preferences, and skill acquisition goals and how to take data for that client. You should be receiving constant training, supervision, and support from your BCBA. The RBT is a very important role in the delivery of behavior analysis services. RBTs are the boots on the ground, and BCBAs depend on them for information, updates, and accurate data collection. You might see a client during a class at school, daycare, in their afterschool program, or at home. As an example of addressing a specific goal, you might go to a "special area" with your client and work on the goal of sitting during non-preferred activities.

Sometimes you might work with adults. As an example, you would meet your client at the grocery store to work on independent living skills. It's important to know what an RBT can and can't do. Along with all the client-centered knowledge an RBT must have, it's also important for the RBT to have a knowledge of their profession. RBTs should become familiar with the RBT Ethics Code. RBTs are ethically responsible to know the code, but the code also provides information about the rights you have as an RBT. If you aren't receiving feedback, if you are being asked to modify some data, or if you are being told to implement a non-behavior analytic procedure, you should know how to ethically behave in these situations.

> *"As the RBT, you are the one teaching your client new skills every session to help increase their independence and quality of life."*

While it can be a lot of work, it can be very rewarding, too! The RBT is the one person that these clients see every day. You build a special relationship with clients so that they are excited to see you. As the RBT, you are the one teaching your client new skills every session to help increase their independence and quality of life. You are the advocate, translator, friend, teacher, and so much more for these clients. There is nothing like the feeling of seeing your client initiate a new conversation with a peer, spotting them playing with other kids in their class, or finding out from a parent that the whole family was able to go out for dinner together for the first time ever!

This job can be a lot of hard work, but you are working to change lives. RBTs get to witness these extraordinary moments and realize that they were a part of helping someone gain their independence and have a better quality of life. RBTs have the remarkable privilege of witnessing these victories on a daily basis.

Sometimes RBTs are the only source of reinforcement a client may receive all day. RBTs see what a client *can* do, and then what they *could* do, and work on teaching the skills a client needs. That is a great responsibility to have, but the rewards are priceless.

● ●

Key Concepts:
RBT responsibilities, behavior support plan, rewards of working with clients

EXERCISES:

1. In your community, check around and see if there are any ABA agencies that employ RBTs. Ask if you could meet with an RBT to do a short interview.
2. If you can make this happen, offer to take the RBT out for coffee or lunch and talk to them about the job of an RBT.

QUESTION #55.
What Does a Day in the Life of a BCBA Look Like?

By Hope McNally

BCBAs have several roles to fill on a daily basis. They are (behavior) analysts, teachers, supervisors, and advocates.

As a behavior analyst, it is your responsibility to look to the data. When working with your clients, you have to review the data being taken on their goals and analyze what the data are showing you beyond the numerical value. Is the client close to mastery on this goal? Why is the client not yet reaching mastery on this goal? Should this goal be discontinued and a modified goal be added? Did I make the current prompt level too high? Do I need to observe the RBT working on this program in order to see what may need to change? After asking these questions, you are expected to look to the research for answers. Behavior analysts implement empirical, evidence-based interventions to help clients learn essential skills.

> *"Behavior analysts implement empirical, evidence-based interventions to help clients learn essential skills."*

As a teacher, you're required not only to teach skills to your clients but also to teach your supervisees how to implement the interventions for your clients. Your supervisees are working one on one with your clients the most, so it is crucial that you effectively teach them how to carry out the interventions. You not only have to teach them how to run these interventions, but you also have to provide ongoing feedback on their performance. On a daily basis, at least one of your scheduled sessions should be for supervision. As crucial as it is to provide your supervisees with feedback, it is just as crucial to receive feedback from them. Ask them questions about how their sessions have been, what some of their questions are regarding interventions, and what questions or concerns they have on your performance as a supervisor.

You are also a teacher for your client's caregivers. BCBAs are required to complete caregiver training in order to help clients maintain and generalize their skills in multiple environments. You could provide this training in the home or out in the community with caregivers. You're expected to set clear expectations with your client's caregivers, typically with a contract, on what their role is while ABA services are provided. Just as you provide feedback to your supervisees, you provide feedback to caregivers on their performance. It's also important to get feedback from them on the interventions and your teaching techniques.

As a supervisor, you're required to provide effective, ongoing supervision to your RBTs. This is not just your typical supervision session in which you provide feedback on the RBT's performance of teaching skills. As a BCBA supervisor, you follow the BACB guidelines for effective supervision, Ethics Code for Behavior Analysts, and RBT Ethics Code. As examples, providing effective supervision could be walking your RBT through an ethical dilemma they are facing with a client or setting clear expectations for what your supervisor-supervisee relationship should look like in a contract.

> *"Every day you are helping someone gain their independence, whether it be a client, caregiver, or supervisee."*

As an advocate, you are ensuring the goals and interventions in your clients' behavior plans are only meant to benefit your clients and not harm them. You should always ask these questions when working with your clients: Am I assisting in improving their quality of life? Am I helping them gain and achieve independence? Are these goals and interventions providing them with essential, age-appropriate skills? Is the client benefitting from the services provided? Not only are you an advocate for your clients when creating their behavior plan and working one on one with them, but you're also their advocate when you're asked to attend school meetings. You will find yourself sitting at a table with other professionals who may not have the information you have on the client's skill level. This is when you step up and speak up for your client by providing the other professionals with the data and information on the client's skills to make sure he or she receives the accommodations needed.

The day in the life of a BCBA can be overwhelming, but the work being done is incredible. You are touching the lives of so many and making positive changes in all of them. Every day you are helping someone gain their independence, whether it be a client, caregiver, or supervisee.

• •

Key Concepts:
Supervision, caregiver training, advocate, improving quality of life

EXERCISES:

1. Go to BACB.com, locate the box that says "BCBA," and click on it. Then double-click on the BCBA Handbook and the BCBA Eligibility Requirements.
2. While you are on this page, scroll down and review the flowchart that shows the overview of BCBA requirements.

SUMMARY

Having a career in behavior analysis usually means starting out as a registered behavior technician. You can get this training while you are in college to earn some money and get great experience working with children or adults. Because there are far more job openings than there are RBTs available, there are probably agencies in your town that will offer the 40-hour initial training and then an entry-level job. RBTs must be supervised, since they have a limited range of skills. The RBT supervisor is a job coach and mentor who is totally responsible for all the RBTs' interactions with clients. RBTs are supervised a minimum of 5%

of their hours and usually work one on one with clients, but they may occasionally run small groups for social skills training. A day in the life of a RBT can be quite varied from one day to the next depending on the number of clients in their caseload and the settings where they are assigned. An RBT could be teaching basic language skills to a new client in the morning and doing generalization training in the afternoon with another client whose services are close to completion. BCBAs have many responsibilities in addition to training and supervising RBTs. In addition to supervision, some of the responsibilities of BCBAs include conducting assessments, writing behavior programs, and screening new potential clients for admission.

NOTE

1. BACB 2020 RBT Handbook, p. 17.

Nine

Advancing Your Career in ABA

DOI: 10.4324/9781003160915-11

QUESTION #56.

If I Get a BS in Psychology, Can I Be a BCBA?

Quick Take

To become a Board Certified Behavior Analyst, it is necessary to have at least a master's degree, but the BACB does offer a Board Certified Assistant Behavior Analyst behavior analyst certification. A BCaBA does require a bachelor's degree, but it does not necessarily have to be in psychology. The degree for a BCaBA could be in other areas such as special education, rehabilitation, or human development. The important thing is that you plan in advance to get the right courses to qualify for this certification. The details regarding coursework are provided subsequently in "Technically Speaking."

"Being a BCaBA is a very important position in the delivery of services. This job entails a lot of responsibility, and it provides a perfect training ground for anyone who is interested in working their way up to the master's-level BCBA position."

A BCaBA needs to be supervised by a BCBA. BCaBAs either provide direct services to clients, or they supervise RBTs who work directly with clients. In many cases, BCaBAs provide both supervision and direct services to clients. The obligations and responsibilities of BCaBAs are lengthy and are contained in what is referred to as a Task List. The BCaBA Task List[1] includes some of the following:

- understand the philosophy underlying behavior analysis;
- can observe, define, and measure behavior in a variety of ways;

- can explain single-case design research;
- follows the code of ethics;
- conducts assessments;
- can use a variety of behavior-change procedures (shaping, chaining, token economies, etc.) in working with clients;
- can recommend goals and strategies for changing client behavior; and
- can train personnel (RBTs) to perform interventions.

As you can see, BCaBAs hold a very important position in the delivery of services. This job entails a lot of responsibility, and it provides a perfect training ground for anyone who is interested in working their way up to the master's-level BCBA position. There is an opportunity not only to work directly with clients and their families but also to learn supervisory skills while working with RBTs. The BCaBA's supervisor will in many cases become their mentor and will help guide them along the path toward a possible career in ABA.

Technically Speaking

There are two ways of preparing to become a BCaBA. The first way involves attending a college or university that offers an *accredited program* through the Association for Behavior Analysis International. The other way is to attend a qualifying institution that offers the necessary behavior-analytic coursework. Both of these approaches involve earning an undergraduate degree; completing coursework in ABA; and getting practical, hands-on fieldwork in applied behavior analysis. Each of these two options is discussed in the following.

Pathway 1: Accredited Program Track

There are only two accredited bachelor's programs, so this is a bit of a stretch. One of them is at Oslo Metropolitan University in Norway, and the other is at the University of Nevada, Reno. The Reno program is in the psychology department, where they offer a bachelor of arts degree in behavior analysis.[2] Once you complete the degree requirements and the fieldwork experience (a minimum of 1,000 hours), you will need to pass an exam administered by the BACB. Then you will become certified as a BCaBA and can begin looking for a position.

Pathway 2: Behavior-Analytic Coursework

This method is by far preferred, since there are many more options available. Here you will need to find a *qualifying institution* that offers the necessary coursework, earn the undergraduate degree, complete the supervised fieldwork, then take and pass the exam. A qualifying institution is one that offers verified coursework. There are 604 of these in the United States, and this includes almost every state. You can find information pertaining to qualifying institutions on the ABAI website under "VCS Directory," as indicated in the endnote.[3]

Because there are many technical details involved in selecting just the right academic program to fit your needs, we urge you to plan ahead. If possible, find a behavior analyst in your area who can help you sort out all the options. Some of the considerations involve making sure that the program you choose matches your personal and professional interests, that the size of the program is suitable (small college vs big university), and that you are comfortable with the mode of instruction, that is, face-to-face vs online vs hybrid classes. One final thing to consider and a way to evaluate the quality of the instruction is to look into the pass rate data for the VCS program in which you are interested. Some programs have a consistent 90% or better pass rate, while others have a dismal 20–30% pass rate. You may have heard the expression, "buyer beware," which totally relates to this situation.[4] Here is the link to the BACB website that describes in great detail.[5] What is involved in getting training to become a BCaBA? Your exciting future awaits![6] You can also find this information by going to BACB.com and using the search engine for key words.

●　●

Key Concepts:
BCaBA Task List, mentor, accredited program, Verified Course Sequence, behavior-analytic coursework, fieldwork experience, pass rate

EXERCISES:

1. Go to the VCS Directory and look at possible programs for your state or a state where you would like to go for your training.
2. Review their offerings, the mode of instruction, and the faculty interests and see if any of this appeals to you.
3. If you find some programs that look good, check out their pass rates to see if this might indicate that you will be receiving a quality instruction there. A high percentage means most people are prepared well enough that they can pass the certification exam.

QUESTION #57.

What Major Do I Need to Have to Be Admitted to an ABA Graduate Program so I Can Become a BCBA?

Quick Take

The answer to this question is that it depends on the requirements of the particular graduate program to which you are applying. Programs vary quite a bit from one to the next. The solution is to review the application form that each program provides online and then look for their "pre-requisites." For some graduate programs, it may be that they require an undergraduate degree specifically in psychology. For others, they might list other undergraduate majors that are allowed such as special education, rehabilitation, or child development.

Something else you might look for in the way of prerequisites are specific courses you might need to have completed as an undergrad. Examples of these include a beginning course in applied behavior analysis, general psychology, developmental psychology, or research methods. Some graduate programs in ABA are now requiring that applicants be RBT certified and that they have a minimum of one year experience, so be sure to also check the experience requirement.

Other considerations besides your major that come into play when applying to a graduate program are your grade point average (most will require a B), your GRE score (not all schools require this, so be sure to confirm it), and three letters of recommendation. For the letters, some schools will want all three to be from faculty that you took courses with, and others will allow one or more letters to come from someone who supervised you in your volunteer or RBT hands-on work.

Technically Speaking

As an applicant to a graduate program in behavior analysis, you should know that not all programs are created equal. Fortunately, there is a way to distinguish the best programs from all the rest. Although it is not widely advertised, the BACB publishes the pass rates of all the graduate programs that produce students who take the BACB comprehensive exam.[7] You can find this by going to BACB.com and typing "pass rates" into the Search box. Then go to "Sorted by percentages of candidates who passed," and you will find a very long list of schools with pass rates ranging from 100% to 13%. Our advice is to look closely at those that have at least an 85% pass rate. There were about 50 of these schools in 2020. The vast majority of these are campus-based programs, although there are a few distance and hybrid programs included on the list.

In addition to reviewing the pass rate of a program in which you are interested, you should also examine the website to see if there is a built-in field-work experience opportunity. This will allow you to accrue your required fieldwork hours while you are in graduate school. Some programs only offer coursework but then leave the students to find an agency where they can accumulate the necessary experience hours after they graduate. This can present serious problems. You might be required to sign a contract indicating that you will work for the agency for one or two years after you receive your BCBA; otherwise, you will have to "pay for the supervision" that you received, which may be estimated to be as much as $100 per hour.

> "Some programs only offer coursework but then leave the students to find an agency where they can accumulate the necessary experience hours after they graduate. This can present serious problems."

A related issue has to do with whether you will receive any form of financial support while you are in grad school. Look at the graduate program websites to see if they offer scholarships, fellowships, or teaching or research assistantships. Find out what the specific requirements are and how you can apply for those. Some ABA programs offer a "full ride," which means that they cover tuition, both in-state and out-of-state, and guarantee support to all students who are accepted. Other programs offer support to only a handful of admitted students. There is a huge difference between graduating with no debt vs suddenly carrying a $20,000–30,000 loan that must be repaid beginning a few months after graduation.

There is one final point to think about when applying to a graduate program. The admissions committee will almost certainly require a "letter of intent" in which you spell out in some detail why you want to go to graduate school and why you have chosen this particular program. You should carefully tailor your letter to each individual school to which you are applying. If you meet all the other requirements listed previously, the final challenge is to demonstrate to the committee that your background and experience matches the program goals and interests of the faculty. If you say in your letter, for example, that you want to work in

> *"The admissions committee will almost certainly require a 'letter of intent' in which you spell out in some detail why you want to go to graduate school and why you have chosen this particular program."*

animal welfare when you graduate but the thrust of this particular program is to prepare students to work with ASD children, you would be seen as "not a good fit." Even if you had a 4.0 GPA and great letters of recommendation, you would probably not be admitted.

A tip on being accepted: If you are serious about a program, it is a good idea to visit (assuming we are talking brick-and-mortar). You should feel comfortable with the campus and the community and have face time with faculty to determine if they are individuals you would like to interact with over a two-to-three-year period of time.

• •

Key Concepts:
Prerequisites, grade point average, GRE, letter of intent, "good fit," "free ride"

EXERCISES:

1. Make a list of graduate programs that you are interested in and search for them on the internet.
2. Determine if there appears to be a good fit between your interests and the goals of the program and faculty.
3. Now, go to the BACB.com website and search for the comprehensive exam pass rates. What are the pass rates for each of the schools in which you have an interest?
4. Next, check out the status of the supervised fieldwork experience. Is it included as part of the program?
5. Finally, check to see if the graduate program offers automatic financial support to students who are accepted or if there is some way you can apply for support.
6. Draft a letter of intent and show it to your faculty supervisor for feedback.

QUESTION #58.

If I Go to Graduate School in ABA, What Degree Will I Receive? Does the Major or Field of Study Matter?

T he degree that a graduate program confers upon graduation depends upon the college where the program is housed. Some programs are situated in a college of arts and sciences, where the likely degree will be a BA or BS in psychology, or possibly in applied behavior analysis. If the program is

"Depending on what your plans are after you graduate, the type of degree does not matter a great deal."

in a college of education, your degree may be in education or special education. Depending on what your plans are after you graduate, the type of degree does not matter a great deal. If you are not planning on going any further with your education, the topic of your degree will probably never come up in an interview. The primary point is that you have a graduate degree and are a bona fide Board Certified Behavior Analyst ready to practice and begin your career in behavior analysis.

If your goal in obtaining a master's degree is to prepare you to apply for a PhD program, it might matter what it says on your diploma. If this is the case, you will definitely want to initiate a discussion with your advisor/major professor while in the master's program and let that person guide you through the next steps. Something you will want to do early on is start examining the web pages of PhD programs to become familiar with their requirements. Some require not only a master's degree to apply but also a completed experimental master's thesis as well. Note that PhD programs are much more selective than MA/MS programs and that it may require special preparation to make you a great candidate. Participating in research and serving as a teaching assistant will be helpful when it comes time to apply to a PhD program. Your advisor can fill you in on the details related to this.

● ●

Key Concepts:
Academic home of the graduate program, post-master's plans, applying for a PhD program

EXERCISES:

1. After you have narrowed down the graduate programs in which you are interested, go to the website of each one to determine the type of degree they award.
2. If you think you might want to go on for a PhD degree, do your research on this as well and meet with your academic advisor/mentor to get further guidance on what steps you need to take to become a viable candidate.

QUESTION #59.

What Does It Take to Become a Board Certified Behavior Analyst and What Do They Do?

A Board Certified Behavior Analyst is someone who has completed a master's degree program, who has met all of the fieldwork requirements, and who has passed the BACB comprehensive exam. A BCBA is an *independent practitioner* who is allowed to supervise BCaBAs and RBTs. BCBAs have a great deal of responsibility in the delivery of behavior-analytic services and are often owners or clinical directors of clinics and agencies. They are responsible for the full gamut of services for clients from admission to assessment, treatment planning, program writing, training staff, and monitoring them to see that the behavior-analytic programs are properly carried out; ultimately, they will be involved in closing a case when a client has met all the goals.

> *"A BCBA is an independent practitioner who is allowed to supervise BCaBAs and RBTs. BCBAs have a great deal of responsibility in the delivery of behavior-analytic services."*

To prepare for all of this responsibility, BCBAs will take a minimum of 270 hours of graduate coursework in the following areas as required by the BACB[8]:

- ethical and professional conduct;
- concepts and principles of behavior analysis;
- measurement (including data analysis);
- single-case experimental design;
- identification of the problem and assessment;

- fundamental elements of behavior change and specific behavior-change procedures;
- intervention and behavior-change considerations;
- behavior-change systems;
- implementation, management, and supervision; and
- discretionary behavior-analytic content.

In addition, as mentioned, BCBA candidates are required to take from 750 to 1,500 supervised fieldwork experience hours so that they have the necessary applied experience in ABA, plus they must pass a rigorous comprehensive exam.

The duties of a BCBA are laid out by the BACB in a Task List that has nearly 100 very specific items. BCBAs will engage in many of these tasks on a daily basis. The complete list of tasks is spelled out in the "BCBA Task List" (5th ed.) on the BACB.com website. Here is just a sampling of these items so you can get some sense of the repertoire that BCBAs must have in order to work with clients:

- define and provide examples of unconditioned, conditioned, and generalized reinforcers and punishers;
- measure temporal dimensions of behavior (e.g., duration, latency, inter-response time);
- identify the defining features of single-case experimental designs (e.g., individuals serve as their own controls, repeated measures, prediction, verification, replication);
- behave in accordance with the *Ethics Code for Behavior Analysts*;
- review records and available data (e.g., educational, medical, historical) at the outset of the case;
- conduct a functional analysis of problem behavior;
- use reinforcement procedures to weaken behavior (e.g., differential reinforcement of alternative behavior, functional communication training, differential reinforcement of other behavior, differential reinforcement of low rate behavior, and noncontingent reinforcement.)
- identify potential interventions based on assessment results and the best available scientific evidence;

- train personnel to competently perform assessment and intervention procedures; and
- use a functional assessment approach (e.g., performance diagnostics) to identify variables affecting personnel performance.

• •

Key Concepts:
Independent practitioner, task list, fieldwork experience

EXERCISES:

1. Go to BACB.com, and on the front page, look for "Master's Level BCBA." Click on that box. Look through the "BCBA Handbook" and the "BCBA 2022 Eligibility Requirements" to get a more in-depth understanding of the roles and responsibility of a BCBA.
2. Go to BACB.com, and in the Search box, type in "BCBA Task List." Review the various sections to see specific skills that a BCBA must master to become a leading professional in this field.

QUESTION #60.
What Skills Are Involved in Being Successful in ABA?

To be a successful behavior analyst, you do not need to be a whiz at statistics, but there are many other skills that *are* essential. First of all, you need to be a "people person," that is, someone who enjoys being around others, noting informally what they do, becoming aware of motivations, and in general trying to understand their behavior. Since your stock in trade is behavior, and behavior is all around you, it pays to be a curious person, someone who is observant, who can engage easily in conversation, who feels comfortable asking questions, and who can remain non-judgmental about the answers.

This is not as much as a skill as it is a value, but a good behavior analyst will also be a person who demonstrates the ability to work with and respect individuals with diverse backgrounds and needs. This relates to clients, colleagues, and other people in your life who are different than you in terms of age, disability, ethnicity, gender expression/identity, immigration status, marital/relationship status, national origin, race, religion, sexual orientation, and socioeconomic status. Recognizing that everyone is valuable and has something to offer is important for all behavior analysts.

Behavior analysts are largely problem solvers, so you have to be comfortable in this role. You have to be able to "Think outside the box," as the expression goes, since you will be almost constantly trouble-shooting some aspect of behavior programming and looking for new, creative solutions. To be a good behavior analyst, you have to be very good at explaining things to people, and sometimes these are people you've just met. Effective

> *"Effective behavior analysts are very good at thinking on their feet."*

behavior analysts are very good at thinking on their feet about how to define a problem behavior and measure it accurately and reliably. You also must be prepared to put your ideas for behavior change to the test of the data and be willing to change your position if your solutions don't pan out.

Another trait that very successful behavior analysts have is that they are able to establish themselves as quickly as reinforcers. *Friendly, charismatic*, and *trustworthy* are words often used to describe successful people, and these terms apply to good behavior analysts as well. You need to be very comfortable in giving people positive feedback, praising their work, noticing little things that they do that are perfect or darn near perfect, and being able to describe the behaviors objectively and sincerely. It is a given that behavior analysts accept feedback on their professional behaviors and modify them accordingly.

Other skill sets that are essential are an ability to write quickly and effortlessly; to manage your time wisely with little supervision; and meet daily and weekly deadlines for reports, behavior programs, and related memos. Behavior analysts are often the chairs of treatment committees, so you will need to feel comfortable running a meeting, delegating work to others, and asking them to present their results to your committee. Again, all of this must be done in a very friendly fashion, with you showing no signs of stress or fear of failure.

Finally, behavior analysts must be able to think analytically; that is, they must be able to think in terms of a logical series of steps and options confronted each day. Behavior analysts set priorities for things that need to be done using a to-do list, check them off, and then proceed to the next step without being sidetracked. You will need to constantly evaluate your own performance. Many behavior analysts take data on their

"The rewards for being a behavior analyst are great; this has to be one of the most satisfying jobs in the world today."

own behavior, set goals, reward themselves when they meet a particularly challenging objective, and then shape on themselves for higher goals.

This may seem like a tall order, but it is clear that anyone going into this profession who has any significant deficits in any of these areas is going to find this a very frustrating business indeed. The rewards for being a behavior analyst are great; this has to be one of the most satisfying jobs in the world today. As a behavior analyst, you can set children on the road to success with language and social skills, help adolescents turn their lives around, train a supervisor to be more effective with employees, or train a teacher to be more successful with her students. Watching children acquire skills they would never have thought possible all because you figured out the right task analysis or were able to put new powerful reinforcers in place has to be one of the most significant achievements that anyone in the helping professions would aspire to accomplish.

Working as a behavior analyst is *not* for those who love a routine and must know exactly what will happen each day they go to work. Each new day will bring different, unconventional challenges to overcome— new people to persuade, dealing with frustrations over a behavior program that didn't work, and the anticipation of taking on a new case. The work is never boring and is quite unpredictable. It keeps you on your toes and keeps your mind busy. Thinking up new ways to train and how to best modify contingencies are a part of applying what you know about human behavior.

• •

Key Concepts:
Traits of behavior analysts, characteristics of job assignments, analytical thinking

EXERCISES:

1. Make a checklist of the traits, aptitudes, and skills needed to be a good behavior analyst.

2. Using your checklist, check off your own skills. Are there any areas in which you need to improve?
3. Make another list of the characteristics of the daily job of a behavior analyst.
4. Discuss any of those that appeal to you.

QUESTION #61.

How Do I Find a Behavior Analyst for a Child, Adolescent, or Adult?

If you are someone who might need a behavior analyst, finding one is made quite easy by the Behavior Analyst Certification Board. You can start by going to BACB.com, looking on the front page for "Find A Certificant," and clicking on that button. This takes you to the BACB Certificant Registry,[9] where you can begin your search. Your first choice is for either a general search or to search by certification number. You will probably want to use the general search if you are just looking for assistance and need to hire a behavior analyst.

Next, look down the page for "Certification Type" and select the category of behavior analyst that you need: RBT, BCaBA, BCBA, or BCBA-D (The BCBA-D is for a person with a PhD or EdD degree). Then to the right of this is a "Status" column, where you will want to select "Active."

After you have done this, look down the page at the various selection categories. You can select your country, and then to the right select the state, and below that, you can get more specific. If you need a behavior analyst, you will probably want to indicate your city and possibly your postal code if you want to find someone fairly close by. You can even narrow the range from 5 to 200 miles to see who is available. Don't forget to click the "I'm not a robot" box before you are done.

Depending on the size of your town or city, you may find anywhere from three to several hundred behavior analysts who can help you. If you click on a name, you will find their certification level, their status, and whether they are active or inactive. Finally, under "Contact," you will find the person's name, and if you click on that, you can send them an email. After filling out an information form, you can select the notification type, indicating the nature of your inquiry. If the person is willing to correspond with you, you should hear from them in a day or two.

Key Concepts:
BACB.com, find a certificant, certificant registry, status

EXERCISES:

1. Go to the BACB.com site and click on Certificant Registry. Follow the previous directions to see how many behavior analysts there are in your town.
2. If you need a behavior analyst for some reason, fill out the form, state the nature of your inquiry, click send, and the behavior analyst should respond to your inquiry.

QUESTION #62.

What Are Some of the Areas in Which Behavior Analysts Can Work?

As a profession, the vast majority of behavior analysts (73%) are currently providing services in the area of autism spectrum disorders.[10] The next largest percentage is in education at 7%, and after that it drops to clinical behavior analysis at 4%, intellectual and developmental disabilities at nearly 3%, and behavioral pediatrics at 1%. Fewer than 1% are working in health, corrections and delinquency, sports and fitness, brain injury rehab, parent training, business applications (organizational behavior management), and higher education.

The BACB has a whole set of videos that address these specialty areas,[11] and we strongly recommend you take a look at them to get some idea of what it would be like to work in the specialty areas, which include:

- behavioral pediatrics;
- education;
- organizational behavior management;
- sustainable practice;
- clinical behavior analysis;
- animal training, care, and welfare;
- health, fitness, and sports; and
- intervention in child maltreatment.

In addition, there is currently research going on in a wide variety of areas, including teaching piano skills, yoga, mixed martial arts, youth soccer, and increasing physical activity in PE classes. In the health area, there is research on children who have food refusal issues, and the goal is to increase their consumption of fruits and vegetables. In the community, there is work going on with seniors in nursing homes and at zoos to increase employee-guest interactions and improve animal welfare by teaching the animals to cooperate with their care and daily health maintenance. Really, the sky is the limit in this exciting field. Behavior analysis can be applied to any learned behavior (good or bad) with both animals and humans (of any age), and the opportunities are limitless.

* *

Key Concepts:
Specialty areas in applied behavior analysis

EXERCISES:

1. Go to BACB.com, click on Videos, and choose a specialty area that you would like to learn more about.
2. After watching the video, write or type some notes on what you learned about this specialty. If it looks like this is something you might be interested in, look just above the videos to a section called Fact Sheets. Right below that is *ABA Subspecialty Area Summary* (PDF), and there are one-page fact sheets with an overview and initial resources you can look into.
3. Go to any issue of the *Journal of Applied Behavior Analysis* and scan the table of contents. Find topics that you might be interested in and look at the references at the end of each article to find more articles that might be of interest to you.

QUESTION #63.
Once I Have My Degree, How Do I Find an Ethical Place to Work?

Whether you are an RBT, BCaBA, or BCBA, it is important to be selective in looking for your first job. Despite all of the great things we have said about being a behavior analyst, it would be dishonest to suggest that all is well in our profession. We receive concerns on a regular basis from consumers and behavior analysts alike about unethical practices of organizations that result in their leaving the company, sometimes with a strong distaste for behavior analysis. This is disappointing, to say the least. Our hope from the beginning was that this field would uphold the highest standards of ethical conduct. The first author served on the initial board that reviewed and promoted the first code of ethics for the BACB, and since then, he has been involved in writing a series of books on ethics to promote this cause. In the third edition of *Ethics for Behavior Analysts* (2016), we included a chapter titled "A Code of Ethics for Behavioral Organizations," the intention of which was to extend ethical values, policies, and procedures to businesses that employed behavior analysts. That concept has recently been included as part of the criteria for organizations to be qualified and recognized as a Behavioral Health Organization of Excellence (BHCOE).[12] The following are slightly reworded and edited from the BHCOE "Full Accreditation Checklist."

> *"It is important to be selective in looking for your first job."*

In looking for an ethical place to work, we recommend reviewing the following questions and bringing them up with the recruiting officer where you are applying for your first position.

Does your organization act honestly and responsibly to promote ethical practices of its behavior analysts and other employees?

Do you support your BACB employees, including RBTs, BCaBAs, and BCBAs, in compliance with the ethical and professional requirements of the BACB?

Does your organization have a policy such that it never directs employees to act in violation of those requirements and supports the resolution of any conflicts between company policy and those requirements?

Is this organization dedicated to ethical and fair competition, and does it agree not to improperly coordinate to sabotage, speak ill of, or undermine other ABA service organizations?

Does this organization ensure that employees will avoid dual relationships that might impair their ability to make objective and fair decisions?

Does this organization protect the privacy of its workers?

Does this organization not offer incentives or remuneration to current clients in exchange for recruitment of other clients (remuneration refers to cash, cash equivalents, or anything of value)?

Does the organization provide guidelines for employees regarding the exchange of gifts, money, or personal fundraising to avoid potential dual relationships and conflicts of interest?

Does the organization have a designated ethics officer and/or ethics committee to address ethical issues related to client programming and/or employees or client concerns?

Does the organization provide employees a confidential means to report suspected impropriety or misuse of organizational resources such as billing fraud?

Does the organization have a policy prohibiting retaliation against persons reporting improprieties?

How does the company handle Diversity-Equity-Inclusion (DEI), both in terms of providing training, but more importantly, by truly believing in and acting on this. In a large consulting firm, is every BCBA a white person? If so, diversity might not be a value. (While this could happen depending on factors such as the geographical area, you should ask about recruiting practices). Are there any consultants working for the company who identify as LGBTQ?

And if so, do they appear to be comfortable working for this company? How about equity? Is everyone treated the same with regard to salaries for a given position, or opportunities to advance? If you recognize religious holidays, will the company respect this?

It is important to note that RBTs and BCBAs are in great demand, and most likely, there will be several agencies from which you can choose when you are looking for your first job. You should hold to these high standards for ethical conduct so that you are treated with the proper respect as a new employee.

● ●

Key Concepts:
Behavioral Health Organization of Excellence, ethical practice, dual relationships, conflict of interest, remuneration, ethics officer, billing fraud, retaliation

EXERCISES:

1. Go to BHCOE.com and search for the Self-Evaluation Checklist to see the original version of these ethical requirements for organizations.
2. You may also want to look at their requirements for diversity, equity, and inclusion, since these are important factors in selecting your first employer.
3. To have a good understanding of what it takes to meet all the standards of the BHCOE, review the rest of the document.

NOTES

1. www.bacb.com/wp-content/uploads/2020/08/BCaBA-task-list-5th-ed-2008318.pdf
2. www.unr.edu/psychology/degrees/ba-behavior-analysis

3. www.abainternational.org/vcs/directory.aspx
4. www.bacb.com/university-pass-rates/.
5. www.bacb.com/wp-content/uploads/2021/06/BCBA-Pass-Rates-Combined-210601.pdf.
6. www.bacb.com/wp-content/uploads/2020/11/BCaBA-2022EligibilityRequirements_201119-2.pdf.
7. www.bacb.com/wp-content/uploads/2020/05/BCBA-Pass-Rates-Combined-201228.pdf.
8. BACB fourth edition coursework requirements p. 6, www.bacb.com/wp-content/uploads/2020/11/BCBAHandbook_201119.pdf.
9. www.bacb.com/services/o.php?page=101135.
10. www.bacb.com/wp-content/uploads/2021/01/200107-YearInReview_FINAL.png.
11. www.bacb.com/about-behavior-analysis/.
12. BHCOE.com.

REFERENCE

Bailey, J.S., & Burch, M.R. (2016). *Ethics for Behavior Analysts*, 3rd Edition. New York: Routledge, Inc.

Ethics in Behavior Analysis

DOI: 10.4324/9781003160915-12

QUESTION #64.

Is There a Code of Ethics Behavior Analysts Must Follow?

If you decide to go into the field of behavior analysis, you will find that we have a strict code of ethics that all certified individuals must follow. We actually have two codes, one for RBTs and one for BCBAs. One purpose of a code of ethics is to provide guidelines, which are basically rules for professionals to follow when providing behavior-analytic services to the public. These are to protect the public from harm that might come from the misapplication of procedures. Behavior analysis procedures are fairly powerful, and, if used inappropriately, a client could suffer physical, emotional, or psychological damage. Another purpose of a code is to protect the practitioner from false accusations of malpractice. However, as long as the RBT or BCBA follows the rules, they should be insulated from critique or criticism. A final purpose of our codes of ethics is to protect the profession. We have a vital need to present to the public a standard of professionalism, competence, and expertise that they can trust, and the initials BACB represent a brand of quality delivery of service. The code sets a standard that says you can put your loved one in our hands and know that we will deliver the highest quality of behavior-analytic service available.

> "We have a strict code of ethics that all certified individuals must follow."

The RBT Ethics Code (2.0)[1]

The 2022 code for RBTs[2] has 29 items, plus some additional items that pertain specifically to the RBT's responsibilities to the BACB. Here are some examples from that code:

1.01 RBTs are honest and work to support an environment that promotes truthful behavior in others. They do not lead others to engage in fraudulent, illegal, or unethical behavior. They follow the law and the requirements of their professional community (e.g., BACB, employer, supervisor).

1.07 RBTs work directly with their supervisor to ensure that they are culturally responsive in their work.

1.10 RBTs avoid multiple relationships with clients, coworkers, and supervisors.

2.01 RBTs do no harm and work to support the best interest of their clients.

2.07 RBTs take necessary actions to protect clients when they become aware that a client's legal rights are being violated or that there is risk of harm to a client.

2.08 RBTs protect the confidentiality and privacy of their clients, stakeholders, and others in the workplace . . .

The thrust of this ethics code is to emphasize that RBTs are honest and trustworthy, they work under the close supervision of a BCaBA or BCBA, and they protect clients and the rights that clients have in our society. If you become an RBT, you will be expected to know this code by heart and be able to apply these standards in your everyday practice of behavior analysis.

The Ethics Code for Behavior Analysts

The Ethics Code for Behavior Analysts is longer and more complex than the code for RBTs.[3] It begins with a set of core principles:

1. Benefit others;
2. Treat others with compassion, dignity, and respect;
3. Behave with integrity; and
4. Ensure their competence.

The aim of these statements is to give a broad view of the intent and purpose of the field to our consumers so they know what to expect from professional behavior analysts and to remind certificants of their obligations to their clients. In addition, there is a recommended ethical decision-making process that emphasizes the importance of considering the risk of potential harm to relevant individuals, gathering relevant documentation, developing possible actions that might be taken and selecting one that seems most likely to resolve the ethical problem, and evaluating the outcome of the decision.[4]

The code consists of six sections: 1) responsibility as a professional, 2) responsibility in practice, 3) responsibility to clients and stakeholder, 4) responsibility to supervisees and trainees, 5) responsibility in public statements, and 6) responsibility in research. Following are some examples of specific items in the code:

Responsibility as a Professional

This section deals with issues involving being truthful and accountable and maintaining competence. Behavior analysts are forbidden to discriminate or harass clients, other behavior analysts, or stakeholders; they are not allowed to have sexual relations with clients, trainees, or supervisees; and they are discouraged from entering into multiple relationships with clients or stakeholders.

There is an emphasis in the Codes for RBTs, BCaBAs, and BCBAs that advises behavior analysts to avoid any behavior related to discrimination or being biased. We can all benefit when we recognize the benefits of working with individuals with diverse needs/backgrounds (e.g., age, disabilities, ethnicity, gender expression/identity, immigration status, marital/relationship status, national origin, race, religion, sexual orientation, socioeconomic status). While the Code relates to how behavior analysts behave, it unfortunately does not cover the situation where a parent/client, member of the community, or a professional in another area discriminates against or treats someone badly. In this case, behavior analysts should do everything they can to provide a support system for their behavioral colleagues. Companies who employ behavior analysts should provide strong Diversity-Equity-Inclusion (DEI) education and they should have practices in place to protect all employees.

Responsibility in Practice

This item describes the way in which behavior analysts conduct themselves, including providing effective treatment in a timely fashion, protecting client confidentiality, involving clients in treatment decisions, and evaluating behavior-change interventions.

Responsibility to Clients and Stakeholders

Important topics in this section include the responsibility to clients and stakeholders, clearly stating the financial arrangements, consulting with other agencies, protecting confidentiality, and transitioning services.

Responsibility to Supervisees and Trainees

This section covers a behavior analyst's responsibility to supervisees and trainees, supervisor competence, and the volume of supervision, as well as how to correctly terminate supervision.

Responsibility in Public Statements

Since behavior analysts may be called on to speak in public or may find themselves on social media, there are some rules that must be followed here. These include the nature and content of public statements, advertising their services, and using testimonials from clients.

Responsibility in Research

Since a significant portion of behavior analysts are involved in basic and applied research, they must conform with certain laws and regulations, provide informed consent to their participants, and ensure the confidentiality of those participants. Finally, they must give appropriate credit to research assistants and co-authors, avoid plagiarism, and maintain their data for a certain period of time.

The *Ethics Code for Behavior Analysts* is 18 pages long and single spaced, and it has very small type. Although it is quite complex and requires a great deal of attention to detail by professional behavior analysts, this level of complexity is necessary when there is so much is at stake. Thou-

> *"The Ethics Code for Behavior Analysts is 18 pages long single spaced with very small type; it is quite complex and requires a great deal of attention to detail by professional behavior analysts."*

sands and thousands of vulnerable clients and their caregivers are usually under a great deal of stress, and they are looking for answers and quick improvements in their loved one's condition. The implementation of our behavior-analytic technology, primarily via RBTs who require close supervision, is akin to putting astronauts into space and bringing them back alive. There is an incredible amount of planning involved, and the implementation must be errorless or there will be a failure of the treatment endeavor. The ethics codes are a trusted guide to the careful, considerate handling of each individual client and are necessary to ensure their safety over an extensive therapeutic period usually lasting for several months and in some cases stretching into years.

• •

Key Concepts:
RBT Ethics Code, Ethics Code for Behavior Analysts, core principles, decision-making process, responsibilities of a behavior analyst to their clients and stakeholders

EXERCISES:

1. Go to BACB.com and search for the RBT Ethics Code. Review the code and see if you can find any items that pertain to a client receiving treatment by an RBT that you might know.
2. Go to BACB.com and search for the Ethics Code for Behavior Analysts. Review the core principles. Is there is anything you would add?

QUESTION #65.

What Is a Dual Relationship and Why Is This a Problem?

In most people's daily lives, they are involved in social dual or multiple relationships with friends, neighbors, and relatives, and they don't even realize it. This is often known as sharing or helping others, and this is what creates a supportive community. If you are going out of town, you may ask a friend or relative to take care of your cat or water your plants. In return, they may want you to help them move furniture or loan them your lawn mower. This is not considered a problem as long as both sides feel that there has been a fair and equitable exchange of services, but these are clear example of multiple relationships. Usually there is no harm to the parties involved unless the cat gets out of the house and runs away or the lawn mower comes back damaged.

In the professional world, a multiple or dual relationship (the terms are often used interchangeably) consists of a personal relationship and a professional relationship. This might happen if an RBT were assigned to a family where the client was a cousin of the RBT. The concern is that the RBT might not be able to remain objective or be effective in implementing the behavior program consistently (e.g., cutting the cousin/client some slack on meeting goals). Another example that came up recently involved the mother of the client asking the BCBA to go into business with her in making training materials. If this were to go through, it is clear that the BCBA would treat the client much differently due to the business relationship with the mom. In this case, the dual relationship for the behavior analyst (business partner/BCBA) could end up in a conflict of interest as well. A *conflict of interest* usually involves a situation where the aims of the two individuals are incompatible. For example, in the previous case, the mom may be interested in increasing her profit margin on the educational materials, while the BCBA is primarily interested in producing quality information at a lower cost so that many more clients could benefit. This conflict could boil over to the delivery of behavior-analytic services to the child client, who could receive lower-quality training as a result. Another example was the proposal by an agency that they would hire a clinical psychologist part time to test children, who would then be referred to the agency for behavior-analytic services.

There are many, many other examples of dual relationships that can cause problems, such as an agency hiring a parent of a client to work on staff or serve as a bus driver or CPA. Experience has shown that most often these multiple relationships do not work out; for example, the CPA/father cannot meet the agency's accounting needs and is fired, and he then withdraws his child from receiving behavioral services. Within an agency, BCBAs are discouraged from socializing with their supervisees and trainees, since this would constitute a dual relationship (supervisor/friend) and could easily affect the BCBA's ability to supervise the RBT.

Here is an example of a dual-relationship question that was submitted to the ABA Ethics Hotline.

Q. I am a BCBA/manager in a small town. My child has autism, and my insurance company will only cover our facility. One of my colleagues, a BCBA, has offered to take the case and provide mostly parent/caregiver training. Because we live in such a small town with no other options and we are both well aware of the potential effects of a dual relationship, would we be permitted to proceed? If we can't, my child will not be able to access treatment.

A. I'm sorry to hear about your circumstances. Despite this, this would still be considered a dual relationship, and we advise you to not pursue it. I would continue to fight your insurance company for a single-case agreement with another provider since you have a very valid request. There are two main concerns and one recommendation: first, you refer to this person as a colleague, so I assume you are both employed by the same company. As an employer, I would not permit this to happen, because in the case of a falling out, that could negatively affect your clients—one of you could quit or there could be negativity brought into the workplace. What if this person provides feedback about your parenting that you do not agree with? It can be a difficult conversation for one BCBA to provide feedback to another BCBA on the work they are doing with their own clients—let alone their own children.

Second, this proposed dual relationship also poses a lot of liability as an employer. You and your colleague most likely are able to practice because you are covered by their employee professional liability policy. If you felt that this BCBA abused your child or committed malpractice, the employer would be liable.

Last, my recommendation is that you may be able to access similar types of parent/caregiver training via telehealth with another provider. I truly hope this advice is helpful.

· ·

Key Concepts:
Dual relationship, multiple relationship, conflict of interest

EXERCISES:

1. Think about your interactions with friends, neighbors, and relatives over the past month and list any multiple relationships. Assuming they went well, as an exercise, think what you would do if you did not feel that the exchange was fair to you; for example, your neighbor asked for a ride to school, but a week later when you asked for help picking up a shipment from Sears, the person said she didn't have time.

2. Have you ever been involved in a business transaction where a conflict of interest developed? If so, what was it and how did you resolve it?

QUESTION #66.
Is It Ethical to Try to Change Someone Else's Behavior Without Their Permission?

In the professional setting, where we're talking about clients, you must follow the Guidelines for Behavior Analysts and obtain all necessary permissions (from the client or client representative) in order to work on behavioral issues. You must also follow all of the recommendations in the Guidelines about procedures, including taking a baseline, evaluating data, and modifying the program as needed.

But we assume this isn't what you're asking about. You're asking about your significant other who throws wet towels in the laundry hamper, so all of your clothes get wet and full of mildew before you wash them. Or maybe you're talking about your sister who calls far too often to complain, complain, complain about everyone in the family.

So, your question is, if you've got the skills, is it ethical to try to change the behavior of these people? You bet. You'll be using prompts; a ton of reinforcement for appropriate behavior; some extinction of inappropriate behavior; and in some cases, some "job aids." An example job aid for a person who forgets and throws wet towels in the laundry would be placing a sign near the laundry hamper saying, "No wet towels, please. THANKS!"

When you can use behavioral procedures to save relationships with the people you love, you're doing them a huge favor. You might initially get some resistance ("What is this . . . pick on Susan day?"), but if you keep your behavior analyst hat on, don't get emotional, and be consistent, it won't be long before you and your sister can laugh and enjoy each other on the phone.

• •

Key Concepts:
Ethics and changing behavior of others

EXERCISES:

1. List some of the behaviors of others around that you would like to change. Think of family members, friends, roommates, or people in the service industry, then list:
   a. Where you've gone wrong in handling these issues before. Have you actually been reinforcing and maintaining these behaviors?
   b. How you can handle the behavioral concerns differently using sound, systematic behavioral procedures.
2. Have you been in a situation where someone was trying to change your behavior using coercive methods? How did this make you feel? How did you respond?

QUESTION #67.

When You Are Introduced to Someone as a Behavior Analyst, What Do You Say When the Person Asks if You Are Going to Analyze Their Behavior?

If you're a behavior analyst and it hasn't happened to you yet, get ready, because it will happen. You'll be at a party having a jolly good time meeting new people. The food is great, and the conversation is lively. Then someone will find out that you're a behavior analyst, and they'll say, "Oh, you're a behavior analyst, so are you analyzing *my* behavior?" One response is, "Yes, I can't help myself, I'm really interested in people and what they do; you're doing great by the way."

Or you could say, "I'm just here to enjoy the music, the company, and the great food, like everyone else." But remember, we're behavior analysts, and we are trying to win friends and influence people. You can ignore the question, smile, and say, "Isn't this a great party?" and redirect the conversation, or you can offer nicely, "Do you know much about behavior analysis?" If they say no, you can tell them where you work and something about what you do (without breaking confidentiality, of course).

> *"When you find yourself in a social situation where someone knows what you do for a living, this is a chance for you to represent the field."*

Light-hearted jokes with people you know are acceptable as long as they are in good taste. The main thing to remember is when you find yourself in a social situation where someone knows what you do for a living, this is a chance for you to represent the field.

Key Concepts:
Behavior analysts in social situations

EXERCISES:

1. Groups that teach professionals how to speak in public have exercises designed to teach you to get your message across in a short period of time. This is referred to as an elevator speech. One exercise is to assume you are at a Chamber of Commerce meeting; you have one minute to stand up, say that you are a behavior analysis consultant, and tell what you do. Use a stopwatch. What would you say?
2. If you met a behavior analyst at an informal gathering, what questions would you ask them?
3. If you live near a university, check the website for the psychology department and see if they offer courses in behavior analysis. If they do, contact the instructor and see if you can conduct an interview to ask them what they enjoy about the profession.

QUESTION #68.

I Think My Cousin Has Autism. Can I Tell My Aunt That He Needs ABA?

Making a diagnosis of autism is serious business, so serious that it is not something that behavior analysts do. This is left up to physicians and clinical psychologists who have special training in assessment. More specifically, these medical professionals who are trained in ASD diagnostics include developmental pediatricians, pediatric neurologists, child psychologists, and child psychiatrists. The reason for this is that to diagnose this disorder, the professional must look at the child's developmental history, since there is no x-ray, MRI, or blood test for autism. Then, looking for early signs, the child's developmental milestones should be considered. Some of the signs they look for include delayed speech and language skills; obsessive interests; self-stimulatory behaviors; avoids eye contact; avoids physical contact; uses few or no gestures; talks in a flat, robot-like voice; and does not understand sarcasm or teasing.[5]

Your average person may notice some of these or other unusual behaviors, but it would be inappropriate and possibly damaging to tell someone that you think their child is autistic. Parents would be shocked and horrified to hear something like this, since it would mean their child has a possibly untreatable disorder. If parents heard this from a friend or neighbor, it could be even more devastating. They would be rightly worried that others were spreading rumors or gossiping about their family, which could cause no end of personal pain and emotional

> *"Your best bet is to keep your opinions to yourself and let the parents decide for themselves if they need to seek a diagnosis from a professional specially trained in this area."*

trauma. Your best bet is to keep your opinions to yourself and let the parents decide for themselves if they need to seek a diagnosis from a professional specially trained in this area.

* *

Key Concepts:
Medical professionals specializing in diagnosis of ASD

EXERCISES:

1. To learn more about the diagnosis of ASD, go to this CDC website: www.cdc.gov/ncbddd/autism/signs.html
2. For more in-depth information, here is a related book: *Diagnosing and Caring for the Child with Autism Spectrum Disorder: A Practical Guide for the Primary Care Provider* by Tina Lyama-Kurtycz, 2020, Springer Publishing Co.

QUESTION #69.

If I Have Questions About Ethics Related to Behavior Analysis Who Can I Turn to?

If you know a behavior analyst, the most straightforward way to get an answer is to ask them. Behavior analysts have received ethics training, and they have practical experience related to ethics questions. They should be able to give you an answer that will help you understand all the considerations that go into understanding ethical issues in our field. If you do not know someone, or if the question involves a behavior analyst who is working with your child, so it would be too awkward to ask, your next best bet is to go online to the one and only ABAEthicsHotline.com. This site is staffed 365 days per year, and you will almost always get an answer within 24 hours, including weekends and holidays. The site was set up by the first author and is independent from any organization. Questions are answered by a team of professionals with expertise in various aspects of ethics, from complex clinical issues to dual relationships to supervision and insurance and billing.

Here is a recent example:

Question #1

"I have a question that may seem odd about our code of ethics. It is readily understood that the code of ethics should be applied when working with clients and implementing behavior programs. I also understand that we should be representing the field of ABA by emulating the code during all professional activities. However, what about when we are not wearing our behavior analyst hat and in our personal lives? Should our code of ethics be an extension of our personal morals and values as behavior analysts? I am not referring to multiple relationships or illegal activity in your personal life, but for example, do no harm, being just, treating others with care and compassion and benefiting others. Should a behavior analyst choose behavior that falls in line with these core ethical principles when not providing service? I understand this is a loaded question and not a specific scenario question about an experience; however, I am extremely interested in knowing what your perspective on this is."

Answer

Yes, the values expressed in our code of ethics and in the nine core ethical principles[6] really should be universal values in our culture for not only all professionals but all citizens as well. It does not seem unreasonable to expect that those in service to others, including doctors, nurses, clinical and school psychologists, counselors, teachers, occupational and physical therapists, social workers, and abuse investigators, to name just a few, will adopt the core ethical principles as a way of life, not just 9 to 5. As a society, we presume that these exemplars will take care not to do harm to children, the elderly, sick, and infirm in their community through their words and deeds. We have good reason to be shocked when we hear of callous, malicious, or even deadly actions on their part. And yet there are regular headlines that reveal quite the opposite: "Doctors and Nurses Who Kill"[7] or "Travis Psychologist Sexually Assaulted Patients."[8] Clearly there is something wrong when those we trust with our very lives and deepest traumas engage in such cruel and inhumane conduct. Following their code of ethics 24/7 would change the world, but it means being constantly on guard against challenges and temptations that come up every day. Studying a code of ethics for a few weeks when a professional is in medical or graduate school is not enough for a whole career lasting decades.

And what about our average citizens? Would it be too much to ask them to "Be just" or work to "Benefit others"? Currently there is no training in ethics for the general population, but the nine core principles would not need any modification to suit them as well. Perhaps it is time to set a higher standard for everyone, starting with our education system. It should not be too hard to insert a few of the nine principles in kindergarten and then expand the training up through high school. Imagine what our world would look like if everyone followed these simple ethical principles: doing no harm, being just, treating others with care and compassion, and benefiting others. There would be no war, no poverty, no unequal justice; we could go on and on. Behavior analysts can start this trend by serving as ethical role models in their daily lives. Let's do it!

Here is one more example that will give you a sense of the various ways that ethics can be involved in in-home treatment.

Question #2

"I am a BCaBA who works with children with autism in their homes. I unexpectedly encountered the babysitter of one of my clients at a social function. The babysitter approached me and wanted to discuss the child. I told her I couldn't have this conversation due to ethical concerns. She then started a conversation with some of our mutual acquaintances about the child and I heard her describing my role with the client family. I politely redirected the conversation and later explained to her that this could make things awkward for me. She apologized. Now when we are both in the client's home, she will start discussions of our mutual friends. I smile and nod, say nothing, then restate that I have to focus on my client. How should I deal with this if it persists? What do I do if we are both at another social function? Does this count as a dual relationship? Do I need to quit the organizations where we have mutual acquaintances?"

Answer

This is a complex situation since it involves a third party over whom you have no direct influence. And the babysitter, since she is not board certified, is actually not covered by the ethics code. You, on the other hand, are required to under 2.03 to "take appropriate steps to protect the confidentiality of clients, stakeholders, supervisees, trainees, and research participants; prevent the accidental or inadvertent sharing of confidential information; and comply with applicable confidentiality requirements (e.g., laws, regulations, organization policies.)" Our clients have a *right* to confidentiality, and our code makes clear under 2.04 (d):

> Behavior analysts only share confidential information about clients, stakeholders, supervisees, trainees, or research participants: (1) when *informed consent* is obtained; (2) when attempting to protect the client or others from harm; (3) when attempting to resolve contractual issues; (4) when attempting to prevent a crime that is reasonably likely to cause physical, mental, or financial harm to another; or (5) when compelled to do so by law or court order. When behavior analysts are authorized to discuss confidential information with a *third party*, they only share information critical to the purpose of the communication.

The babysitter may be "concerned" with the matter of the child client, but that does not give you permission to discuss your work with her.

In this case, the additional steps would include speaking directly to the parents of the child client about the problem because they may not be aware of the issue or implications of confidentiality. Then, ask for their support in suppressing the babysitter's gossiping about their child. You could help them develop a confidentiality agreement that they would present to the babysitter and require a signature by her confirming her understanding.

We do not feel that you should feel compelled to quit the organizations where you and the babysitter have mutual acquaintances, and in our estimation, this situation does not constitute a dual relationship. Once the confidentiality-signing meeting occurs, you may wish to establish a professional relationship with the babysitter since what she does with the client when you are not present could very well affect your impact as a therapist.

* *

Key Concepts:
Core ethical principles, ABAEthicsHotline.com

EXERCISES:

1. If you are employing a behavior analyst to work with your child or a loved one and have a question about ethics, ask the behavior analyst to help you understand the situation.
2. If you don't feel comfortable asking your behavior analyst about the ethical situation, write to the ABAEthicsHotline.com for an answer.

QUESTION #70.
How Does One Report Unethical Conduct?

Behavior analysts have an obligation to inform clients on how to file a complaint; this is included in Section 3—Responsibility to Clients and Stakeholders under code 3.04 Service Agreement (BACB.com).

If you have employed or observed a behavior analyst, including an RBT, BCaBA, or BCBA, and have noticed unethical conduct, you should know that our Behavior Analyst Certification Board has a process for reporting this. It is called filing a Notice of Alleged Violation and is done by going to their website, BACB.com; looking at the top bar where it says "Ethics"; and then scrolling down to "Reporting to the Ethics Department." Here you will find details on reporting someone for violating our Code of Ethics, including graphic displays of the process that is used by the Ethics Department and specific instructions for doing so.

IMPORTANT INFORMATION ABOUT SUBMITTING NOTICES OF ALLEGED VIOLATION

When completing the appropriate online form, the notifier is asked to indicate the specific code violation, give a description of the code violation, and provide supporting documentation. If accepted, the notice and all supporting documentation is shared with the subject, who is given an opportunity to respond to the allegations and provide their own supporting documentation. See either the RBT Considerations for Reporting an Alleged Violation or the BCBA & BCaBA Considerations for Reporting an Alleged Violation, as well as the Code-Enforcement Procedures documents for more information about processes and timelines.

(BACB.com)

Before filing a notice, it is important that what you have observed actually be a violation of the code, so it is necessary to review the code itself. You can do this by again going to BACB.com, finding the top bar on the site and locating the "Ethics" tab, and scrolling down to the first item, which says, "Ethics Codes." Here you will find the ethics codes for RBTs, BCaBAs, and BCBAs. Before filing a notice, it is important to remember that you must have first-hand knowledge of the incident and some sort of documentation that it occurred. The board will not accept a notice based on second-hand information or hearsay, and it will not accept a notice that does not have documentation to accompany it.

Note that the process is different if you are a behavior analyst. In this case, you have an obligation to try to resolve the issue informally unless there is some risk to a client's health or welfare. If this is unsuccessful, then the normal process is followed, as described previously.

• •

Key Concepts:
Filing a Notice of Alleged Violation

EXERCISES:

1. Go to BACB.com and search for the Code of Ethics for Behavior Analysts if you have a question about something you have observed. Review the code to see if your question fits the description there.
2. Go to www.bacb.com/ethics-information/reporting-to-ethics-department/ and review the estimated timeline and processes that are involved once a notice is received at the BACB. How long does it take for the initial intake and review? What is the total processing time?

NOTES

1. This is the new RBT Ethics Code that went into effect in January 2022.
2. www.bacb.com/wp-content/uploads/2020/05/RBT-Ethics-Code_190227.pdf

3. www.bacb.com/wp-content/uploads/2020/11/Ethics-Code-for-Behavior-Analysts-210106.pdf
4. www.bacb.com/wp-content/uploads/2020/11/Ethics-Code-for-Behavior-Analysts-210106.pdf
5. www.cdc.gov/ncbddd/autism/signs.html
6. J.S. Bailey & M.R. Burch (2021). *The RBT® Ethics Code: Mastering the BACB Ethics Code for Registered Behavior Technicians*. New York: Routledge, Inc.
7. https://people.com/crime/doctors-and-nurses-who-kill-gallery-2/
8. www.airforcetimes.com/news/your-air-force/2018/12/11/travis-psychologist-sexually-assaulted-patients-who-were-recovering-from-sexual-trauma/

REFERENCE

Bailey, J.S., & Burch, M.R. (2021). *The RBT® Ethics Code: Mastering the BACB Ethics Code for Registered Behavior Technicians*. New York: Routledge, Inc.

Glossary of Terms

Accredited program: In behavior analysis, academic programs are accredited by the Association for Behavior Analysis International.

Alternative replacement behavior: (see also replacement behavior) A behavior that will replace one that is harmful, destructive, or dangerous; chosen to match the function of the original behavior.

Analysis: A method of determining the causal variables which produce or maintain a given behavior; often shorthand for functional analysis.

Analyze behavior: To observe a behavior and attempt to determine causal environmental variables.

Antecedent: An environmental event or behavior that *precedes* a specific behavior and sets the occasion for it to occur; may also be referred to as an S^D.

Attention-maintained behavior: A specific behavior that has been shown to be a function of attention provided by others.

Autism: A term from the Greek meaning "self." A disorder that appears as a strikingly abnormal social interactions and deficit communication and patterns of behavior, usually seen before the age of 3.

Aversive event: A consequence of behavior that punishing affects (reducing behavior).

BACB.com: The Behavior Analyst Certification Board, the organization that certifies RBTs, BCaBAs, and BCBAs.

Baseline: In research, this is the period where data are taken frequently until they appear stable. Only when data are stable can an intervention begin.

Behavior: Anything that a person says or does.

Behavioral economics: A subfield of behavior analysis in which responding is viewed as an interaction between price (behavior required) and consumption (reinforcers obtained).

Behavior analysis: An approach to behavior, which began with the publication of the *Journal of Applied Behavior Analysis* in 1968, that emphasizes determining causal variables for socially significant behaviors and developing ethically appropriate treatments that produce socially valid changes for the participants. Also known as *applied behavior analysis*.

Behaviorist: A person who is primarily interested in studying animal and human behavior.

Behavior modification: A term used in the 1960s to describe an approach to behavior that emphasized behavior change using consequences, often aversive consequences. The term is largely out of date and has been replaced with behavior analysis.

Behavior program: A systematic way of changing behavior by way of a written description of procedures using reinforcers to help the person reach their goal.

Best practice: A term borrowed from business management to describe the generally accepted *best way* of implementing certain procedures that is also ethical.

Billing fraud: In ABA, this may involve billing for more hours than actually worked; for example, a staff person marks on their hours sheet that they worked 20 hours when they actually only worked 15. Since these hours are reimbursed by the government or an insurance company, it is considered fraudulent and is punishable by termination, fines, and even jail time.

Board Certified Behavior Analyst (BCBA): A person who has been certified by the Behavior Analyst Certification Board as qualified to provide supervision of RBTs and behavioral programs and treatment.

Bribery: The offering of money or other incentives to persuade somebody to do something, especially something dishonest or illegal.

Challenging behaviors: Behaviors that put stress on parents, caregivers, and teachers (e.g., non-compliance, aggression, defiance, elopement).

Class of behavior: A group of behaviors that have the same or similar effect on the environment (e.g., a supervisor gives a supervisee feedback in person, and in another session, the feedback is written. The behavior change of the supervisee might be the same with both methods).

Consequences: Environmental changes that occur after a behavior.

Contingencies of reinforcement: A complex interrelationship of behavior and environment that specifies the stimulus, the response, and the reinforcing consequences that generate behavior.

Controlling variables: Those contingencies of reinforcement that have been demonstrated to reliably produce a certain behavior.

Critical thinking: The process of analyzing and evaluating facts and information to determine if the scientific evidence supports a certain proposition.

Data: Quantitative measures resulting from direct observation or other methods with regard to behavior and to independent variables.

Data-based: This is a reference to decisions that are based on objective data, as opposed to opinions, theories, anecdotes, or case studies.

Diagnosis, behavioral: A method of determining the controlling variables for a specific behavior by asking diagnostic questions and testing certain conditions to determining controlling variables.

Diagnostic questions: A series of questions that probe for possible controlling variables.

Differential reinforcement: Following only some selected behaviors with a preselected reinforcer; this is also called shaping or behavior shaping.

Discriminative stimulus: A stimulus that signals that a reinforcer is available.

Disease model of behavior: Also known as the medical model; a proposition that certain behaviors result from sickness or disease rather than from contingencies of reinforcement.

Downtrend: An observation of behavioral data that they are trending in a downward direction, usually toward zero occurrences. This is not desirable during baseline, as it can indicate a lack of stability of behavior.

Dual relationship: A situation where multiple roles exist between a professional and a client, such as an RBT providing treatment to a relative. Dual relationships are not allowed in ABA.

Environment: Objects, people, and events in the immediate surroundings that impinge on sense receptors and that can affect behavior.

Environmental design: The deliberate modification or placement of certain stimuli in the surroundings in order to produce some behavior change.

Escape and avoidance: An escape response is one that terminates an aversive event; an avoidance response prevents the aversive event from occurring. They often go together as a pair so that a person who learns an escape response often then learns to avoid as well.

Escape-maintained behavior: Behavior that occurs when an aversive situation is presented, such as a task requirement; the person then leaves the situation and escapes the task.

Establishing operation (EO): An environmental event that momentarily alters the effectiveness of some other event or consequence. This term has been replaced with the term motivating operation (MO).

Evidence-based treatment: This is a movement that began in the 1990s that stressed the need for scientific evidence to support the continued use of treatment. Behavior analysis has been evidence based since its inception in the mid 1960s.

Experimental Analysis of Behavior: This is the flagship journal of laboratory researchers in behavior analysis.

Experimental control: A method of showing with a good deal of certainty that a certain variable was in fact responsible for the behavior change. The reversal or ABAB experimental design does just this by repeatedly presenting and withdrawing some independent variable.

Extinction: A method of reducing a behavior by withholding a previously known reinforcer.

Facilitated communication: A now largely discredited method that purports to help people with speech problems spell out words and sentences. The practice is controversial, since a majority of controlled studies have shown that it is not the patient who is producing the words but the facilitator.

Feedback: A method of providing information on a person's performance. Feedback is generally considered a positive reinforcer but could be corrective as well.

"Free ride": Graduate programs that offer students free tuition and an assistantship to cover the bulk of their academic expenses.

Functional behavior analysis (FBA): An experimental method of determining what the controlling variables are for a given behavior. It involves presenting certain stimuli and consequences, usually in a random fashion over time, and attempting to discover the "causes" of a behavior in the sense of the maintaining variables for its occurrence and nonoccurrence.

Functional assessment: Generally, this includes informal and formal observations, including data collection and interviews, to determine the likely controlling variables of a behavior. Once a conclusion is reached, the likely "cause" can be tested in a controlled or natural setting to determine if the functional assessment was valid.

Function of behavior: The result or outcome of a behavior.

Generalize, generalization: A behavior trained in one setting may occur in a second setting where no training took place; we would say that the behavior generalized from one setting to another. Or a behavior is modified through behavioral procedures and then it is observed that a similar behavior now occurs as well; we would say that there has been a generalization of the behavior.

Good Behavior Game: A group contingency used in classroom settings to encourage students to cooperate toward academic goals.

Grandma's rule: When you eat your vegetables, you can have dessert. See also the Premack Principle.

Group contingency: Used with cohesive groups of individuals, a method of offering reinforcers to each one if the group as a whole meets certain objectives; alternatively, a contingency could be set so that if one individual meets certain goals, the whole group is reinforced.

History of reinforcement: A theory that the accumulated experiences of contingencies of reinforcement begin to predict future behavior.

Intermittent reinforcement: A reinforcer is only available some of the time; a common example is the lottery, where the odds of winning might range from 1:50 to 1:2 trillion.

Inter-observer reliability (IOA): A procedure in which two observers independently record behavior and then their data are compared to determine if they were consistent.

***Journal of Applied Behavior Analysis*:** The flagship journal in the field of ABA, started in 1968.

Learned behavior: Behavior that is acquired through the learning process rather than being reflexive.

Maintaining variables: Those stimuli and consequences that can be shown reliably to produce certain behaviors.

Mediator: The person who serves as the intervention agent in a given situation.

Mentor: A senior person in a company or organization who takes on new recruits and employees and teaches them the skills they need to succeed.

Manipulative behaviors: Behaviors that are maintained by their controlling effects on others, usually thought to be undesirable.

Motivation: A term used to describe the conditions which predictably produce certain behaviors; they generally include the presence of aversive stimuli and certain deprivation conditions such as thirst or hunger.

Motivating operation (MO): An environmental event that momentarily alters the effectiveness of some other event or consequence. See also establishing operation.

Noncompliant behavior: The lack of an appropriate response to a specific request.

Obsessive-compulsive disorder (OCD): The repetition of a particular set of behaviors where the individual appears to be "driven" to repeat a routine or engage in meticulous behaviors such as cleaning the environment or washing the hands. OCD is thought to be an anxiety disorder by psychiatrists but is treatable with cognitive-behavior therapy.

One-on-one treatment: A behavioral method invented by Ivar Lovaas that involves one therapist working for an extended period of time with one client in a behavior-shaping treatment model.

Operant behaviors: Learned behaviors that are controlled by environmental events.

Operant conditioning: A method of training that uses consequences to change behavior.

Oppositional defiant disorder: Usually children or adolescents who have been shaped by their parents to be disobedient and hostile; this includes extended periods of arguing, losing of temper, being angry and resentful of others, and spiteful and vindictive behaviors.

Performance improvement plan: In performance management, a proposal to implement a set of procedures to modify behaviors in a business, industry, or organizational setting. The proposal is usually based on an ABC analysis as well as a functional assessment of the pinpointed behaviors.

Performance management: The application of basic principles of behavior in business, industry, and organizational settings to improve human performance.

Personality: A consistent pattern of behaviors that occur in most settings regardless of the circumstances.

Placebo effect: A reported effect from an ineffective treatment thought to be the result of the subject or patient trying to please the experimenter.

Positive reinforcement: A consequence following a behavior that increases the likelihood of similar behavior in the future.

Punishment: A consequence following a behavior that decreases the likelihood of similar behaviors in the future.

Predictability: The notion that it is possible to determine in advance how a certain individual will behave under specific circumstances.

Premack Principle: Using high-probability behaviors as reinforcers for low-probability behaviors; see also Grandma's rule.

Pseudoscientific: Fake theories designed to make the public think there is a scientific basis for their statement.

Registered Behavior Technician: An RBT is a Registered Behavior Technician® who is a **paraprofessional in behavior analysis who practices under the close, ongoing supervision of a BCBA, BCaBA, or FL-CBA.**

Reinforcement: Consequences that follow behavior and increase the likelihood that a behavior will increase in probability.

Reinforcer survey: A method of asking questions of individuals to determine what consequences might serve as reinforcers for the person.

Replacement behavior: Usually a specially selected behavior that is taught to an individual to take the place of a behavior that is dangerous, counterproductive, or bothersome to others.

Respondent behaviors: Behaviors that are elicited by unconditioned stimuli.

Respondent conditioning: Pavlovian classical conditioning where food that elicits salivation is paired with some stimulus, and over time, presenting the stimulus alone produces the salivation.

Response cost: This can be a consequence of a behavior such as a parking fine or a description of some aspect of a task that makes it difficult for the person to master the skill (e.g., avoiding learning a new app because it takes hours and hours).

Reward: A colloquial term that is used to generally convey the concept of a consequence that is desirable, but there is no evidence that it changes behavior.

Schedule of reinforcement: A statement of the probability that a behavior will be reinforced.

Scope of practice: The list of tasks and procedures that behavior analysts are allowed to engage in under the terms of the Behavior Analyst Certification Board.

Self-management: Procedures used by an individual to change their behavior. These may range from leaving Post-It Notes to remind yourself to carry out a task to the systematic use of the Premack Principle to manage consequences.

Shaping: A procedure for changing behavior that starts with setting the criterion for reinforcement just a little higher than it was previously. Also see successive approximations.

Self-injurious behaviors (SIBs): Operant behaviors that produce tissue damage to a greater or lesser degree.

Single-case (or single-subject) design: A method of using each participant as his/her own control where, through repeated measurements, a baseline is established, and then various treatment conditions are implemented and then withdrawn.

Socially significant behaviors: Those behaviors that are important to the person because of the consequences that they bring, usually in the form of approval from others as opposed to trivial behaviors of little consequence.

Social reinforcement: Reinforcers delivered by other persons rather than the natural environment.

Social validation: A set of procedures established by Dr. Mont Wolf from the University of Kansas for determining if the targets of behavior change are supported by the consumer, if the procedures are acceptable, and if the resulting behavior change is acceptable.

Statistically significant effects: Usually effects that are so small that they need to be analyzed or "cooked" by statistical methods to determine if they could have occurred by chance; if not, they are deemed "significant" regardless of whether they made a socially or clinically important change for the person.

Stimulus: A measurable event that may have an effect on behavior; this can be either an antecedent or a consequence.

Stimulus control: The demonstration that when a certain stimulus occurs, a particular behavior usually occurs.

Successive approximations: When setting a goal, the therapist will first reinforce small steps toward that goal; then, over time, the steps become a little more difficult, and the standard for reinforcement is raised again, a.k.a. *shaping*.

Talk-therapy: A colloquial expression used to describe psychoanalysis, psychotherapy, and counseling where the major treatment comes from the patient discussing their problems with another person.

Time-out: A method of removing a person from a reinforcing environment (time-in) to one that is less reinforcing; commonly understood to be a punisher for its suppressive effects on behavior.

Theory of behavior: A systematic and comprehensive account of the relationship of behavior to the environment.

Thinking (from a behavioral perspective): According to Skinner, "thinking is behavior" that is covert but nonetheless responds to the same principles as overt behavior. Thinking is learned and can be useful in producing more effective overt behaviors.

Token economies: A motivational system where tokens are given contingent on certain behaviors and then exchanged for reinforcers at a later time for "backup" reinforcers.

Topography: The form of a behavior, what it looks like.

Tourette syndrome: A nervous-system disorder involving involuntary repetitive movements or unwanted sounds (e.g., blurting out words).

Train for generalization: A method of producing generalization rather than "hoping" for it that involves additional training in those settings where the behavior is desired.

Trigger: Colloquial term for a discriminative stimulus.

Verbal behavior: Behaviors that are maintained by the behavior of other individuals; specifically, the behavior of a speaker is maintained by the behavior of a listener.

Appendix

Behavioral Journals

American Journal of Mental Retardation
Analysis of Verbal Behavior
Animal Behavior
Australia & New Zealand Journal of Developmental Disabilities
Autism Research
Behavior Analysis Digest
Behavior Analysis in Practice
The Behavior Analyst
Behavior and Social Issues
Behavior Therapy
Behavior Research and Therapy
Behavior Therapy and Psychiatry
Behavior Modification
Behavior Therapist
Behavior Therapy
Behavioral Disorders
Behavioral Interventions
Behavioral Technology Today
Brazilian Journal of Behavior Analysis
Child and Family Behavior Therapy
Education and Treatment of Children
European Journal of Behavior Analysis

Focus on Autism and Other Developmental Disabilities
Journal of the Association for Severely Handicapped
Journal of Applied Behavior Analysis
Journal of Behavior Therapy and Experimental Psychiatry
Journal of Behavioral Education
Journal of Organizational Behavior Management
Journal of Positive Behavior Interventions
Journal of Precision Teaching
Journal of School Psychology
Journal of the Experimental Analysis of Behavior
Learning & Behavior
Mental Retardation
Mexican Journal of Behavior Analysis
Performance Improvement Journal
Performance Improvement Quarterly
Perspectives on Behavior Science
Psychology in the Schools
Research in Autism Spectrum Disorders
Research in Developmental Disabilities
School Psychology Review

Index

functional assessment 33
functional behavior analysis (FBA) 168
functional communication (FC) 123
functional definition 98
future of research 98–99

generalization, train for 132
generalizing results 11
goals of behavioral treatment 68
gold standard 22, 118
graduate programs 251–253, 255
group contingency 302
guidelines for responsible conduct 241, 275, 284

habit reversal 54
habits 9, 54–55, 115, 135
history of reinforcement 43, 47
HOAX 95
How to Think Like a Behavior Analyst iii,
 xx–xxiii, xxix–xxx, 45, 206
hyperactivity disorder 73
hyperbaric oxygen therapy 175

immediate reinforcement 69
intermittent reinforcement 43, 89
intermittent schedules 88, 89
interobserver agreement 69
inter-observer reliability checks (IOR) 303
interpersonal relationships 116
introspections 92
IQ (Intelligence Quotient) 162

job prospects 231
Journal of Applied Behavior Analysis
 (JABA) 19, 22, 67, 77

learned behavior 10, 49
Let Me Hear Your Voice xxviii, xxxi, 22, 23, 118

maintaining variable 10, 302, 303
mandated reporter xxv, xxvii
manipulation 115–116, 122–123
memory 8
mental disorders 149, 151
methodological behavior 84
Miracle Mineral Solution 174
motivating operation 164
motivation 162, 164

multielement design 170
multiple baseline 70

Notice of Alleged Violation 295, 296

obsessive compulsive disorder (OCD) 149,
 303
one-on-one training xxvi
operant 49, 66; behaviors 49, 51, 76, 77, 89,
 149, 303, 305; conditioning 50;
 learning 51
operant chamber *see* Skinner box
operationalism 83
oppositional behavior 37
oppositional disorder 25, 26
organizational behavior management (OBM)
 134
organizations, consultation 126
over-justification effect 192

parental applications
payment contingencies 154
pediatrics, behavioral 158
performance improvement plan (PIP) 125
performance management 126
permission xxiii, 6, 284, 293
personality 44, 47, 57, 58, 60
perspectives 57, 101, 131, 145, 152, 211,
 214, 291
PhD (Doctor of Philosophy) programs 255
pivotal response treatment (PRT) 194, 195
Ponzi schemes 173
prediction 33, 34
Premack Principle 122, 144, 190
principles xxix, 37, 38, 50, 76–77, 83–84,
 91, 102, 109–110, 113, 116, 122, 124,
 128, 131, 134, 136, 161, 212, 257, 276,
 291–292
pseudoscientific treatments 172
psychotherapist 156, 159
psychotherapy 156, 157, 159
punishment 53, 98, 99, 153; history 44

radical behaviorism 84
rationalism 83
RBT® (Registered Behavior Technician®)
 107, 225–228, 231, 235, 237, 238;
 supervisor 107

RBT® Ethics Code 275, 276
"Real life" applications 114–117
reinforcement: automatic 55; conditioned
   122; differential 122, 123
reinforcers survey 304
replacement behavior 53, 54, 55
research: behavioral 68; methods xxix, xxx,
   19, 67, 78, 230, 251; psychological 63
respondent behavior 49, 50, 77
respondent conditioning 46, 51
response cost procedures 123, 204, 304
responsible conduct 237
reversal designs 69
rewards, tangible 190

schedules of reinforcement 44; escalating
   154; intermittent 144
schizophrenia 10, 149
school settings xxviii
scientific skepticism 83
scope of practice 200
S^D (discriminative stimulus) 30, 31
self-esteem 143
self-injurious behavior (SIB) 15, 119, 167
self-injury 15
self-management 110, 112
self-report 159
self-talk 161
senior citizens 160, 231, 266, 303
sensory diet theory 170
sensory integration 167
shaping 10, 51, 52
skepticism xxx, 83, 96, 101, 173, 176
Skinner box 66
social: media 214; reinforcement 305; skills
   59, 60; validation 18, 69
socially appropriate behavior 37, 193
socially significant behavior 10, 11
Son-Rise Program 96
statistically significant 168
statistical research 66
stereotopy 55, 169
stimuli 92
stimulus: aversive 99; control 30;
   fading 115, 123; generalization 30

successive approximations 52
supervision 233

talk therapy 156
task analysis 36, 160
task list 109
theory of behavior 25, 26, 113, 305
think aloud 161
thinking 85, 161
thinking aid 112
thought field theory 96
time-out 10, 26
token economies 109, 192, 248, 306
top ten tasks of analysts 53, 108, 304
Tourette syndrome 150
training xxiii, xxvi, xxviii, 11, 19, 25–26,
   28–29, 58–60, 69, 88, 96, 100, 107,
   109, 122–125, 128–134, 136–137, 146,
   154, 157, 160, 191, 194, 200–201, 218,
   226–232, 237, 241–243, 247–250,
   257–258, 266, 269, 281–283, 288,
   290–292, 302–303, 306
treatments xx–xxi, xxv, xxviii, xxix, xxx,
   5, 9–12, 14–23, 25–26, 34–37, 50,
   67–70, 72–73, 76, 79, 84, 91, 96–97,
   100, 102, 116, 118–120, 136–138, 143,
   145, 148–151, 153, 158–159, 164, 168,
   172–176, 190, 194–196, 198–200, 206,
   216–217, 231, 257, 261, 266, 278–280,
   282, 292, 300–301, 303–305
trigger 73

verbal behavior 10, 30, 84–85, 157, 161,
   199, 306
verbal tics 150
verified course sequence (VCS) 249
visual analysis 112, 122

water intoxication 17
weighted vest 167
work behavior *see* performance
   management
work environment, ethical 268, 269

YouTube 207